BLOOD RELATIONS

CHARLOTTE MONTGOMERY

BLOOD

RELATIONS

ANIMALS, HUMANS, AND POLITICS

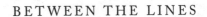

BETWEEN THE LINES

Blood Relations

First published in Canada by
Between the Lines
720 Bathurst Street, Suite #404
Toronto, Ontario   M5S 2R4

Canadian Cataloguing in Publication Data

Montgomery, Charlotte, 1950–
    Blood relations : animals, humans, and politics

Includes bibliographical references and index.
ISBN 1-896357-39-3

1. Animal rights movement – Canada. I. Title.

HV4768.M66 2000   179'.3   C00-931072-X

Cover and text design by David Vereschagin, Quadrat Communications
Printed in Canada

Between the Lines gratefully acknowledges assistance for its publishing activities from the Canada Council for the Arts, the Ontario Arts Council, and the Government of Canada through the Book Publishing Industry Development Program.

THE CANADA COUNCIL | LE CONSEIL DES ARTS
FOR THE ARTS | DU CANADA
SINCE 1957 | DEPUIS 1957

Canada

For Tom

CONTENTS

ACKNOWLEDGEMENTS

A great many people allowed me to impose on their time, intelligence, and files. For this I am grateful. Most were never quite clear about what I was doing but, to my good fortune, didn't let that stop them. None is at all responsible – or even necessarily in agreement – with the end product. Most I won't thank by name, because there are too many. Others have asked not to be named at all, but their help was valued.

Liz White and Stephanie Brown were more than generous with time and assistance. Lesli Bisgould, Troy Seidle, Ainslie Willock, Rob Laidlaw, Arryn Ketter, and Catherine Ens answered innumerable questions. Pat Milke and Denna Benn allowed me to tour their animal-care facilities and spent hours answering questions. Their efforts were appreciated. Thanks also to Len Goldberg, Kate Smallwood, and Dr. Jacques Caron. Alison Folkes and Gerry Weinberg were repeatedly available to answer niggling questions – with Alison Folkes's cheerful efficiency in particular saving me a lot of time and heading off a few errors. Nicholas Read helped considerably, and I benefited from reading his excellent *Vancouver Sun* columns.

I thank David Barbarash, Hilma Ruby, Darren Thurston, and Gary Yourofsky for their courtesy during times of considerable personal stress. It was more than I expected, and probably more than I would have done under the circumstances. Robyn Weiner revisited unpleasant memories with a candour I appreciated and offered useful comments. An anonymous correspondent also took time to provide thoughtful answers to questions and has my thanks.

Bob Hunsberger, Bruce Weber, and Mike Cooper answered questions about farming and showed me around for large chunks of the day. They will no doubt disagree with pretty much everything here, but I sincerely thank them anyway.

My journalist sister, Christina Montgomery, and her photographer husband, Ian Smith, made it possible for me to spend time in

Vancouver. Mary and Robert entertained me, while Max and Betty showed me around. Christina's insights were, as usual, designed to prove that brains are not evenly distributed in any family. Robert Montgomery Sr.'s suggestions and Mary Montgomery's encouragement I will take for granted, as always. Tom Walkom, my husband and hero, handed over air travel points for this project with all the eager enthusiasm of someone who was actually going to have those ski trips and beach holidays they would otherwise have provided. His professional advice on many drafts was offered with the sort of honesty you can only hope to get from your best friend, a reminder that being married to a great newspaper journalist is as practical as it is delightful. But not even he can be blamed for the views or any errors. They are all mine.

To Between the Lines, my thanks for having the odd conviction that ideas matter. May you be rewarded.

PREFACE

At the end of June 1997 I set off for an animal rights conference in Washington, D.C., telling myself (officially) that it would be journalistically useful. I was, after all, going there as a journalist. Mentally, ever since my first job at the *Niagara Falls Review* in the 1970s, I have gone everywhere as a journalist, trying hard to be unobtrusive.

One thing that has always appalled me about television, in comparison to print journalism, is how television just rolls in and makes events change and reorganize themselves around the cameras. So I went to Washington planning, as always, to be the quiet person at the back of the room. I was barely on the ground and heading off in a shuttle bus to the conference site with a little band of genuine animal people when the driver turned to one of them and goaded her, "You swat mosquitos, don't you?" He had aimed his challenge at a petite, southern woman who earlier, while we were waiting for the bus, had been sweetly telling me about her job as a nanny, her life at home with her mother, the boyfriend she hoped to marry some day, and how much time they both spent with their dogs. Now she struggled to explain her views, while the driver grinned. "Won't somebody help me with this?" she appealed to the rest of the bus. They did. I didn't.

What I did was think about whether the driver would have challenged a bus full of priests about whether they ever swore or lusted after women. What is it about the idea of people taking animals seriously that seems to bring out the aggression in so many humans? That day I was also a little embarrassed, because I had arrived wondering just how hard it would be to blend in at this conference. I figured, probably like the driver, that the people were likely to be a little much. But the only oddball at the conference – unless you count me, as a misfit of sorts – was a hairy guy in leather and tattoos who, it was said, had been dumped there by some motorcycle pals when he wasn't quite himself the night before. For two days I kept bumping into him. He would be sitting on floors at little discussion groups, smiling and applauding. The last I saw of him, he was lecturing another person about animals, something about how "they only want you to like them."

What I realized in Washington was that one of the reasons I knew so little about what to expect at the conference was that, in Canada, so little is written about people who devote themselves to animal issues, or about their concerns. The idea for this book came from that thought.

Because I knew so little, I didn't realize how many people were out there, spending extraordinary amounts of time, and showing so much passion, in working to change the world or even just to improve it. Clearly, no one book could cover all of the people or groups working on "animal issues" in Canada. I had to make choices about what I could and could not do. For someone involved in those issues, my choices might seem wrong or odd. I made them based, roughly, on what I thought other outsiders like myself might know least about and might find most interesting or useful to learn. Then I cut the results in half.

I decided that the fur trade, in most of its aspects – seal hunting being the most notable, perhaps – was something people might already know a little about. Research using animals, I guessed, we know virtually nothing about, even though it raises some of the most profound questions and heated opposition. The same, surprisingly, holds true for agriculture. As countless people have stressed to me, city people haven't got a clue about farming. Fine. The fact that agriculture is also the biggest user of animals in the country, and one of the most important, meant that it, like research, would get a lion's share of the book's space. Human treatment of wild animals, in or out of captivity, could fill an entire book on its own, and it deserves one.

What I could do was offer a representative sampling, a selection of people and issues that would give the gist of the animal movement. Think of it as somewhere to start. The activists who once rescued living turkey chicks from a garbage bag full of dead bodies are not here. Nor is Floyd the lonely monkey, who doesn't know humans are trying to help him, nor a special green parrot, both of whom I met during my research and will remember. Nor are the people who defend whales or give donkeys and greyhounds a home – or a lot of issues and people who, arguably, should be. I have tried to sample people and issues across the country and, with one exception, have focused on local or national groups rather than better-known international organizations. The exception is a Canadian contribution to the international scene, the International Fund for Animal Welfare, now one of the largest organizations, with representatives in ten countries. It had its origins in Fredericton, New Brunswick.

I ended up spending more time on the outlaw side of the animal movement than originally planned. My decision may appall some of the law-abiding activists who believe they struggle daily to stay free of the bad image associated with the "illegals." But I came to the conclusion that the illegal activities were not the outrageous, senseless actions of dangerous misfits, as sometimes described. Instead, they seemed to me to be an inevitable part of a political movement that has been greeted too often with scorn and exclusion.

I also concluded that people in the animal movement will face increasing obstacles. It seems to me that some of their most significant successes are more a result of their movement being underestimated by the people and industries affected than a result of a meeting of minds. Rather than more success and greater understanding, I would expect them to face critics who have become more sophisticated and more determined about dividing the movement's ranks, blocking its message, and convincing policy-makers to resist its ideas. Even though critics of the animal movement repeatedly told me that, in Canada, we sit down and talk things out, I did not sense much interest at all in their doing that. Instead, it seemed a way of pretending that the animal movement already has access to the country's policy-makers, which it hasn't in any significant way, while avoiding public discussion of the issues and ideas involved. If I am right about the future, then it will mean increasing confrontation, because one prediction I can offer with absolutely no qualms is that the animal people will never give up.

Pigs from Mars

Imagine that the big news today is that we are going to be able to put men and women on Mars. Actually, that is not such a faraway notion. But imagine that we are doing it now and that the plan is for residential development that will sustain human life, perhaps a little band of scientists, with a few modifications to the environment outside. That would be exciting. There would be lots of talk about it on television and in the press. There would be alien jokes and film clips from all the old (and new) movies about men from Mars or travel to other planets.

Serious people would agonize over this. They would ask whether humans would do better on the new planet than they have done so far on Earth. They would ask what would happen if that old men-from-Mars fantasy came true. What would we do if we found aliens living on Mars? We would have to work out an understanding of how humans should treat Martians. It would be a serious discussion, and perhaps many of us would feel good dealing with that spiritual side of ourselves. We would ask if we have the right to take over someone else's world, perhaps changing it to suit ourselves rather than them. We might even draw some lessons from the experience we have had with colonization right here on Earth. All of those simple but endearing ideas that breathe life into television shows like *Star Trek*, into nearly a century of science fiction, and into movies like *Contact* or *E.T. The Extra-Terrestrial* would enter the real world. Who wouldn't consider it an incredible opportunity to make contact with another species, to find out, finally, that we are not alone in the universe? Who wouldn't feel contempt for anyone so crass as to suggest that we needed, first of all, to make clear to these Martians that people from Earth run things, or to find out if Martians are edible?

Now change that picture to something much less fantastic. What if we already had the chance to make contact with non-humans, to communicate with other minds, to see if we are intelligent enough to escape our particular limits and find the common bond? After all, isn't that what most of the magic about meeting aliens from space amounts to? So the point is this – if a pig came from Mars, wouldn't we gaze respectfully into his or her eyes, past those long lashes, and maybe feel charmed by that enigmatic little smile? Let's not imagine it further: Pig from Mars Meets Prime Minister, Scientists Dispute Meaning of Grunts – though that is probably about how it would go. Some people might worship the pigs or just be happy that the Martians made such nice neighbours. Others might decide that what the pig from Mars proved was that humans were still tops, that it was safe to develop that planet, and that maybe there were big bucks to be made in taking this pig on the road.

The point is, the whole alien scenario becomes silly when the pig figures into it. That's because we all know about pigs, or think we do. They are something to eat, something smelly. They are an *it*, not a *he* or *she*, aren't they? But actually, for a lot of people, a pig is most definitely a he or a she and deserves a whole lot better than he or she gets. For these people, humans have some changing to do. Humans have to realize that non-humans also live on the planet and that, like us, these non-humans also have a claim to the Earth and to their lives on it. They are not here on sufferance or as raw materials until we need them for dinner or for an extra body organ or for a science experiment. They have *rights*, to use the language we are most familiar with, or perhaps *inherent rights*. Their value does not depend upon how useful they are to us.

It is not news that there are animal rights people. It's just that most of us don't know much about them. Nor do most of us know how animal rights people differ from people who are concerned about animal welfare. Protecting *animal welfare* means ensuring that animals are treated humanely, or as humanely as possible given whatever humans have decided it is essential to our interests to do with them. So humans can make a fur coat or a hamburger or test a product using animals, but when we do that we should not make it any worse for the animal involved than is necessary. The animal welfare world does not challenge the established social order. Although its ranks are fragmented, it does not usually argue against the accepted lot of animals in modern Western society, except to urge that whatever is done to them be done as kindly as possible.

People who support the concept of *animal rights* believe, basically, that animals – like humans – have lives to live that are valuable in themselves and that humans must accept this. This belief is not about being an animal lover, any more than believing in human rights means being a lover of humans. It means leaving the fur coat on the animal, eating something that isn't made from animals, and finding an alternative way to test products. Animal rights advocates reject many ordinary uses of animals no matter how they are carried out or how important humans might consider the use. Animals' inherent claims on their lives outrank human interests, they argue. Animal welfare advocates do not accept the existence of animal interests or independent animal lives that outweigh in moral importance or legitimacy the use humans regularly want to make of non-humans.

If we can think about animals as pigs from Mars – which is to say we need to empty our minds of all those entrenched ideas and come at the subject afresh – if nothing else it allows us to meet some intriguing people. We might not like them, and we might decide we don't agree with them. But we might also be surprised, especially about the issues they raise. At the least, it will fill us in on a world that we don't hear much about. If those aren't reasons enough, try this one: even if we don't like these people, they are part of a political movement that is increasingly making a difference in Canada. The other reason we should pay attention to this political movement is that a lot of people would rather we didn't. That's not as childish a reason as it sounds, or as fantastic. If the animal movement is as irrational and even ridiculous as some of its detractors suggest, why does it stir up so much reaction?

Certainly there is an outlaw side to the movement, but that side is smaller than some alarmists claim. It is deprived of support from most other animal groups, but it is also made up of people who make far more sense than anyone wants to admit, whatever your view of their tactics. Then there is the traditional, conservative side, which fills the familiar role of dealing with animals we no longer want as pets. These people, largely on the animal welfare side, are the only ones usually taken seriously when they raise issues about animals in public. In between is a whole array of individuals and groups – much more hard-working and serious than the stereotypes suggest – who have clear ideas about reforms needed in the interests of justice for animals. They are usually dismissed as animal rights radicals or extremists who don't like animals to be used for anything and who should therefore never be allowed a public platform or serious hearing. It is as if people with views against capital punishment were pronounced too entirely unstable and narrow to have a say on the subjects of parole or the choice of lethal injection over the electric chair as a means of execution. But perhaps the real problem with the animal movement is that it threatens lucrative interests, such as the research establishment or the agriculture business. Perhaps if we look into these matters we might also find there are things we don't like about how our society deals with animals, things we might like to see changed.

• • •

The century ended with a blossoming of genetic engineering and a vast explosion in the possibilities for biotechnology. The year 1999 closed with news of cloned sheep and human genes being injected into animals, with the prospect of using pig kidneys or other organs in humans, with the certainty that in this new century we would see things become practice that were just science fiction to past generations. We also closed out the century with few hard and fast laws on all of this and with scientists and others charging ahead – after all, billions of dollars are to be made in new products and drugs. While the prevailing rhetoric is about the vast new horizons for human life, the reality is that the animals essential to delivering on this vision are non-human. That reality makes this one of the most inconvenient times in half a century, at least, to raise questions about what we are doing with other species.

A number of books published at the end of the century tried to capture in words the combination of unease, stock-taking, and expectation that people had. In one of them, *The Biotech Century*, author Jeremy Rifkin concluded that all this strange new science had brought us face to face with some important questions. "How do we value the many creatures that travel with us here on Earth? How do we see our relationship to them?" he asked. "The answer to that question will determine the kind of science we practice and the kind of world we inhabit in the next age of history."[1]

In times of major change, we do tend to ask ourselves questions about what to make of that change and whether or not we approve of it. As Rifkin's book points out, humans prefer explanations of the natural world that match the ways in which we happen to be living.[2] Otherwise, our lives would seem wrong. So if the world is an unfair place, we can make sense of it by thinking that it is the law of the jungle, a dog-eat-dog world, survival of the fittest, the way the world works, just human nature. That certainly is convenient for people who would just as soon you didn't raise too much fuss about the unfairness.

In our relationships with other species, aside from the sales pitch to pour taxpayers' money into research, the public has not exactly been welcomed into the discussion about genetic engineering and the mixing of species of animals together, of cloning and growing organs in animals for human use. So far the discussion has been kept under the control of people who are already well down the path to doing some or all of those things, and the public has largely been left on the sidelines. To talk about social ethics and the value of other, non-human animals would just muck things up. It's a power play of sorts, a way of sidelining the concept of society's moral judgements at least until the basic directions have been set. Then we will be left with those numbing explanations – you can't stop science, it's progress. The need for a discussion of how animals are treated and who they are – compared to us – seems obvious at a moment when borders among species are being violated physically right and left. But a full-fledged discussion would not be very convenient for scientists or business or politicians.

Usually, people on the left of the Canadian political spectrum can be expected to barge into such an opening. There's nothing like the hint of being shut out to make leftists suspicious that the powerful are up to their usual tricks. Major social change without public involvement, like the denial of rights, is just the sort of issue that the left prides itself on challenging. But when it comes to animals, the political left, with a few exceptions, does not force these issues onto the public stage as matters of equality and social justice. Maybe that's because animals don't rate on their own, because they aren't human. They don't have minds like humans. It's really not even that they might have a different number of legs and different skins or that they are judged, rightly or wrongly, as being less intelligent than humans. After all, some people have fewer than two legs. Some humans live with much less than "normal" human intelligence. Some primates have been taught sign language and have passed IQ tests. Some creatures can communicate with humans. So it is not so much the smartness or the language as it is the difference in species. Obviously, you might say.

As animal movement activists are quick to say, there was a time when it was "obvious" that blacks were less intelligent, when women were "obviously" not up to voting, and when what happened to children was considered "obviously" their family's private business. In those cases, people finally began to ask why these assertions were so obvious. We shifted the onus to make it necessary to prove that the difference, whether skin colour or maturity or sex, was a valid reason to treat these people differently. Then, of course, we realized that difference in these cases was an artificial divide erected for reasons that were often less than noble. So if it just comes down to animals being a different species, being different in their minds, shouldn't we have to show why that difference is a valid reason to treat them as subordinate, expendable, and completely unlike humans?

The only time proof is called for, though, is when we *question* the assumption that animals are completely different from humans. If we talk about animals suffering, for example, in laboratory or intensive farm conditions, we are quite likely to be chided for anthropomorphism, for attributing human feelings to animals. Proof is not required for the assumption that humans – evolving and living on a shared planet in a common environment with other species that also eat and drink water and sleep – are unique in having feelings or ideas or thoughts. Why should animals have to laugh like humans or cry like humans to prove they are happy or amused or sad? And since we don't entirely understand even the human brain, let alone the brains of non-humans, science offers nothing definitive to back up those kind of unproven assumptions about animals.

The word animal, for much of the animal movement, means all sentient creatures, human and non-human. But to escape the endless use of the phrase non-human animal, books by animal activists often accept the use of the terms animal and human. Some, like U.S. writer Amy Blount Achor in her encyclopedic *Animal Rights – A Beginner's Guide*, note that this conventional language is to help the reader, not to accept any idea of superiority or us-and-them relationship.[3]

Canadian scientists do seem to consider it quite possible that other life forms have at least some feelings and mental or emotional responses similar to our own – as long as those life forms exist on other planets. In June 1999, when a coded system of symbols about the Earth and its inhabitants was being transmitted in an attempt to contact other life in the universe, there was great embarrassment over two mathematical errors made in the message. The astronomers were worried that the mistakes would cause extraterrestrials to judge Earthlings "a sloppy species," the way humans might judge other humans who made those kinds of mistakes.[4] It's just when we confine humans to thinking about other species on Earth that assumptions of similarities among life forms are considered insulting, unproven, or sentimental.

"Even the left that supposedly understands, they draw the line at animals," Lesli Bisgould told me.[5] She is a Toronto lawyer who specializes in law affecting animals, fighting thankless, non-lucrative battles to make humane societies do their duty, to protect wild animals, and to defend activists.

"It's not central to the concerns of the left," Toronto lawyer Clayton Ruby said of the lack of left support to animal rights.[6] Ruby is well known and deservedly respected as a left-liberal defender of human rights, civil liberties, and issues of social justice and the environment. He helped to defend activists convicted in a southwestern Ontario mink raid, and he went to court over the seal hunt. In the mid-1980s, he engaged as a lawyer in the heated battle for the soul of the Toronto Humane Society. Animal issues are connected to the environment, he said, and in fifty years matters will have changed enormously. But he does not consider animal issues as important as those involving humans, and he does not see animal rights as a political movement. "Animal rights people approach it from the moral," he said. "So it's personal. That makes it private."

That's as good an explanation as any, except that it's wrong. The push for animal rights is quite clearly a political movement, with political goals and political opponents, and has nothing private about it. We have only to consider the issues of research using animals to see how much the debate is connected to public policy and taxpayers' money, never mind social values.

Reputable members of the left championed a small downtown Toronto café owner who was going to be forced out by a corporate coffee-shop chain. Why shouldn't these same people fight for mice or apes in laboratories – for animals whose lives are reduced to the status of raw material for giant drug companies? Why protest the destruction of old-growth forests that humans cherish, but not the rights of any particular bear to live in that space? It comes down to a judgement about whether what all of us do as a human society can be unjust to animals, or whether injustice only happens to humans. If we can be unjust to animals, it must be because they have some claim to something better. If they do, then what are we prepared to do about it?

People who try to put these issues on the political agenda are often ridiculed or treated as fanatics. For example, Canadian author and long-time fur-industry defender Alan Herscovici asked in one essay "why some people feel so passionate a need to dictate what the rest of us should eat, wear, think or do."

> Animal advocates may consider themselves more ethically evolved than most of us. The sensitivity and compassion of animal rights doesn't embrace Inuit hunters or Newfoundland fishermen, however, except in the most paternalistic sense: "They should do something else." Nor does it take much account of those suffering from AIDS and other diseases which medical researchers are working to cure. Ironically, animal rights is often described by its advocates as an extension of the civil rights or feminist movements. "Speaking for the animals," however, offers some definite advantages over these models for the leadership: the oppressed cannot question their policies. Human supporters have little say either, since many large animal rights groups don't bother with voting memberships or elected boards.... So long as they can pose as idealistic crusaders, contributions will flow into the animal rights coffers."[7]

At least Herscovici was assuming that, however villainous the animal advocates were, they were also crafty. The assumption of silliness is as common as that of malevolence. Animal rights activist Karen Davis – a woman with a postgraduate degree and published writings to her credit – expressed the frustration she and others felt with battling these assumptions. In a 1994 speech Davis, president of United Poultry Concerns, a U.S. national organization dedicated to getting domestic fowl some compassion and respect, said she was tired of what she called the "rhetoric of apology" in the animal rights movement, of activists apologizing for the animals (including birds and fish) they championed and for their feelings about them. "As human beings, we do not know what it feels like to have wings or to take flight from within own bodies or to live naturally within the sea," Davis said. "Our species represents a smidgeon of the world's experience, yet we patronize everything outside our domain."[8]

It's the same with comparing animals to human infants or people with mental impairments, she said, as if "all of the other creatures on earth have a mental life and range of experiences that are comparable to diminished human capacity and the sensations of newborn babies."

David Selby, director of the International Institute for Global Education at the Ontario Institute for Studies in Education in Toronto, came from England, where animal issues have been debated for much longer. He has had a taste of what can happen when you raise those issues in Canada. In England, individual teachers might discuss controversial topics such as fox hunting or the gassing of badgers. When Selby began his work there, the idea was to develop practical suggestions for lessons that could form part of an overall curriculum, a workbook for humane education. EARTHKIND: A Teachers' Handbook on Humane Education, explained, for example, that classes might talk about how many animals go into the making of a fur coat. Teachers might get students to restrict themselves to a small piece of floor space for a while, then talk later about how animals might feel in intensive farms. In Canada, after a teaching magazine published a feature based on the book, the reaction in complaints to the editors was intense. "The fury it caused!" Selby remarked. "It was pretty sensational. I was under the heat."[9]

Certainly one book central to the animal movement everywhere is *Animal Liberation*, published in 1975 by the now world-famous Australian philosopher Peter Singer. His description of what he called "the tyranny of human over non-human animals" and its comparison with slavery have become classic and inspired a whole generation of animal activists. Singer posed valid questions. "If possessing a higher degree of intelligence does not entitle one human to use another for his or her own ends," he asked, "how can it entitle humans to exploit non-humans for the same purpose?" He argued that by portraying animal advocates as sentimental animal-lovers, critics excluded the whole issue of the treatment of non-humans from serious political discussion. Any danger of being overly sentimental about animals, he said, was far less serious than the opposite danger of animals being treated as lumps of clay. His is probably the book most read by animal activists – it has sold some four hundred thousand copies in nine languages.[10]

Singer also co-edited *The Great Ape Project: Equality beyond Humanity* in 1993, its essays arguing that great apes are entitled to certain basic rights, including life, liberty, and freedom from torture.[11] According to Singer, that idea is opposed in part because humans have a hard time believing that we are not utterly unique. Supporters of greater legal and moral status for apes proposed to the New Zealand government that its animal welfare laws be amended to provide for that status. The parliamentary committee reviewing the laws balked, saying that such a move would change the purpose of the current laws from protecting the welfare of animals to accepting the notion of rights. It would mean that individuals could step in and demand protection for these animals, as they might do with children.

Despite the qualms of the committee, the New Zealand Parliament decided that, given the cognitive and emotional capacity of great apes, it would go ahead with the changes. In October 1999 it enacted a provision in its laws to protect great apes against such uses as teaching, testing, or research unless those uses were in the animal's best interests. The amendment was a world first, celebrated by animal groups in many countries.

The New Zealand proposal about great apes represented a move from theory into practice. Political philosophers describe how society moves from a consensus on what is right and wrong to making laws when it is clear that leaving the decision to the individual causes serious harm to the well-being of others. Affirmative action and sexual harassment laws, for example, have come to regulate behavioural choices that were once left to the individual. Laws are used to protect humans from the behaviour of others. But for animals there have traditionally been only basic laws about cruelty. For those who ridicule the campaign on behalf of apes – it was dismissed as easy for a country with no real great ape population either wild or captive – it is sobering to consider that if the justification for the move was that apes share traits with humans, such as self-awareness, intelligence, or social systems, it is entirely possible that in future other species might be acknowledged as sharing traits with humans. And there are other interesting signs of change. Two giants of the U.S. educational establishment, the Harvard and Georgetown law schools, decided in 1999 to institute courses on law involving animals and rights. Across the United States, some thirty lawyers were working full-time on such cases.

While it might seem that laws against cruelty to animals are enough, there has been a growing conviction that much animal suffering comes from so-called normal practices that are still quite legal. U.S. academic Bernard E. Rollin connects the development of this view in the United States to revelations about research using animals and, in Britain, to the publication in the 1960s of Ruth Harrison's book *Animal Machines*, an original study of the industrialization of agriculture and what that meant for animals.[12]

To give animals greater legal standing or rights protection in law means acknowledging that they are living beings and not simply property. Most people already do accept this distinction in an instinctive way. You can toss your shoe into the oven, if you want, but put your pet into the microwave and you can end up in court. Still, there are things done legally to animals used for food or animals used in research that people cannot do legally to their dogs or cats. Farmers or scientists can perform castration without anesthetic, for example, or deliberately inflict a disease or amputate a healthy limb. The law protects human interests in research or agriculture.

For that reason, Gary Francione, a U.S. lawyer, professor, and author, describes animal cruelty laws as selfish. They only *seem* to be about kindness, he says in his book *Animals, Property and the Law*. The laws are built around defining and prohibiting *unnecessary* suffering. If animals are used in some way to generate wealth, as happens in research or agriculture, that use is regarded as legitimate and the animal suffering that goes with it is deemed necessary. Only when there is no socially accepted economic benefit to animal suffering is it considered unnecessary and therefore wrong.[13] As a result, parts of the animal movement deem it important to establish the legal framework of animals as having more status than property and to protect this status with the notion of rights.

One of the key ideas upon which the animal movement builds its case is the obvious: animals can suffer. This ability to suffer gives animals the right to compassion and to a recognition of their status as more than property. The nineteenth-century British philosopher Jeremy Bentham is usually quoted to help make this point. Bentham argued that, in comparing humans and non-humans, "The question is not, can they *reason?* not, can they *talk?* but, can they *suffer?*"[14]

These philosophical debates form the backdrop to issues involving animals – to arguments about fur-farming or intensive agriculture or animal experiments or circuses. The philosophy stakes the claim of non-humans to justice. The issues that activists raise join philosophy to contemporary politics. And the political dimension challenges how human activities and laws dictate what life will be like for animals. When the animal movement moves from theory to reality, the response is often that animal activists are entitled to their opinions but that they should not try to foist those opinions on others. Yet these are serious issues with ethical dimensions that are a legitimate part of debates over public policy.

The debates can become intricate, but the issues are plain: chickens with their beaks sliced off; chickens scalded to death; millions of animals packed dying or badly hurt in the backs of trucks; sows trapped in stalls so small they can't walk; squalid zoos where animals go mad; cruelty laws randomly applied; animal laboratories where secrecy rules and law doesn't. These are not scandals. Scandals would mean a system broken down and in acknowledged need of fixing. This *is* the system. The animal movement wants to improve it, or replace it altogether. That movement appears in action at its most angry in the outlaw fringe, a secretive side that is small in numbers and large in legend.

CHAPTER ONE

The Outlaws

In early May 1994, in the middle of a seemingly normal day in Scotts Valley, California, David Barbarash drove straight into a roadblock of police cars. Officers leaned out from behind the cars, guns drawn. A voice amplified by a bullhorn ordered Barbarash out of the car. "With your left arm, open the door. Get on your knees. Put your arms over your head."

"It must have been a dozen cars," Barbarash recalled, a trace of awe crossing his face even several years later. "FBI and immigration and Scotts Valley police. It was kind of surreal."

It was the takedown of an officially dangerous man, a Canadian who had entered the United States illegally and was wanted by police forces across Canada. The loot was twenty-nine cats. The crime scene, damaged to the tune of about $100,000, was a University of Alberta laboratory complex where the cats were being readied for use in medical research. Some five years after that event David Barbarash and his co-accused partner, Darren Thurston, were still enmeshed in the courts.

• • •

In the spring of 1999, Barbarash, thirty-five, and Thurston, twenty-nine, were sitting in an almost empty Vancouver courtroom. Their convictions from the University of Alberta lab raid were well behind them, and they were in the midst of a preliminary hearing into new charges, which they flatly denied: for Barbarash, twenty-two charges of sending letters booby-trapped with razor blades to various hunting guides and outfitters; for Thurston, twenty-three charges. The court had imposed a publication ban on the proceedings. In the courtroom the slight, spectacled, dark-haired Barbarash took notes, conferred quietly with his lawyer, and talked to Thurston, his friend.

The hearing would conclude, after about a month, that the two would indeed be sent to trial. They faced the prospect of going back to jail if convicted. If not, the seizures of their belongings would at least have given the RCMP some excellent files on animal rights and samples of legal publications that report on and explain the intricacies of illegal animal actions. That kind of material is legally accessible in Canada, but it takes time to compile.

With their past convictions and jail time served, these two young men had become Canada's most notorious animal activists. They had been in and out of the courts for years. They had been wiretapped and followed by local and national police forces, with the Canadian Security Intelligence Service (CSIS) somewhere in the shadows. By the summer of 1999, the scrutiny of the two had cost the state hundreds of thousands of dollars at least, and the meter was still running.

The animal movement's outlaw side, the side of breaking the law, is its bogeyman. It carries the spectre of fanatics. It is a side that is used to thwart serious consideration of issues involving animals and humans. The threat of this side is invoked when voices are raised against hunting or when demands come for information about what is being done to animals in laboratories. There are nuts out there, the argument goes, animal extremists and terrorists. To respond to complaints or demands for information, to accept that there is actually something wrong being done with animals, will only encourage those nuts. To persist in examining the merits of activists' arguments is to raise eyebrows and perhaps suspicions. For as long as this kneejerk, fear-mongering dismissal of questions about the treatment of animals prevails, the political agenda will have little room for issues dealing with animals. It is an attitude that deliberately chills discussion and poisons the atmosphere for activists who are trying to build a public constituency for their cause. Even the larger animal movement in Canada, made up of thousands of law-abiding activists, would mostly rather not talk about the "illegals" unless it is to condemn them.

Animal rights enthusiasts are not all ashamed of the law-breakers, but they tend to balk at being connected to them, even in conversation. Most seem convinced that illegal activities give all of them a bad name and close doors. Whether that is true is debatable. What is not debatable is that two widely held assumptions burden the world of activism over animals in Canada and a lot of other Western countries, and these assumptions limit the movement's public constituency. One is that if anything really wrong or cruel is being done to animals, the police or a humane society or someone somewhere will do something about it. The other is that the animal movement, aside from its long-established and conservative side, is peopled by oddballs or zealots with little respect for humans or property. Neither assumption is true – cruelties to animals get defined away as legal every day, and people involved with animal politics are more commonly compassionate than mentally unstable or weird. But both notions – about the people and about the existence of adequate protection for animals – underlie the dismissive and even derisive treatment of the movement and the issues.

For one thing, there are not that many people in Canada who will deliberately break the law in the name of animals. Very little evidence exists that many people will venture very far across the legal limits in pursuit of animal rights issues in Canada with any sort of regularity. By mid-1999, not a high point for the outlaw side of the movement by any means, insiders estimated the number of Canadian activists willing to take serious illegal action at twenty people maximum. In other years the number has been higher, according to one convicted animal liberationist.

Those who do work at breaking the law are not all that willing to talk about it, for the obvious reason that they would be giving themselves away. So you have to conduct anonymous interviews or talk to people who have already pleaded guilty and are willing to discuss it.

When you venture into this outlaw territory you also quickly run into dilemmas. You can lose your certainty. Just as you would accept without question the need to break down the door of a house to save someone from a fire, you would probably find it acceptable to do the same to save a dog or a cat from a burning building. Why not, after all? Some animal activists who heap scorn on the outlaw fringe easily agree that they would be willing to walk through an unlocked door to remove a dog or a cat or a monkey who was clearly in pain from a medical research project that was not going to produce any lifesaving breakthrough. It's not so hard to find the hypothetical case in which you just might be willing to agree on taking action, even if it were illegal. *Technically* illegal, you would tell yourself. You could dream up a far-fetched scenario, the circumstances in which you might agree. What if it turned out not to be so far-fetched?

Go a little further. What if you knew that the animal with the apparatus screwed into his head, an animal taken out of a laboratory, would simply be replaced tomorrow with another animal, or ordered back into his misery? If you thought that the experiment was too cruel to be justified by its intended outcomes, you might demand that the authorities put a stop to the practice – which would not be so easy to do, but let's leave that for now. If the authorities didn't put a stop to it, you might not see anything wrong with smashing the cage, or stealing the animals, or maybe just leaving a nasty note on the scene or on the researcher's door or car window, just to tell him or her it really must stop. Maybe you would settle for an angry protest outside the research facility and then not feel guilty, maybe even secretly pleased, if the institute got a few broken windows or had to shut up for the day.

What if you knew someone was neglecting a cat or letting his kids torment her and nothing happened when you called a humane society? Would you steal her? Would you mind if someone else did? Or if dogs that used to be someone's pets were being kept in cages, unloved and lonely for years in an isolated university building where they were being used in experiment after experiment to refine drugs – not drugs that would cure cancer, just new versions of drugs or new uses for old ones to keep them on the market? If you knew where the door was, and you knew when no one would be there, and it wasn't locked, would you open it? If you knew that twenty-nine cats were about to be used in painful experiments and you knew where you could find good homes for them, would you condemn someone for sneaking in and taking them out? Would you help? Well, if you haven't become disgusted with all this, if you don't reject these scenarios outright as criminal behaviour that can't be defended, then you would be called an extremist in Canada.

Let's begin by meeting a few outlaws of the animal movement in the flesh. We'll start gently, with someone not even counted in the estimates of activists who regularly break the law, those twenty or so. We'll call this one Sandra, because she hasn't yet been caught and what she does is illegal. When I spoke to her she was living in a major Canadian city, in a good neighbourhood, in a pretty, well-kept home, and she paid her bills with her own hard-earned money. Sandra, a middle-aged woman, was stealing animals. She called it "rescue," and that sounded like a fair description when she detailed the circumstances of animals she had stolen over the years. Her descent into a life of crime came when she met someone who was stealing cats. She went along, half curious and half sympathetic. It seemed not so bad, really. Soon she was out on her own, stealing as successfully as you please, working out her own practical rules of operation, her underground reputation spreading.

"My first save," Sandra told me, laughing at the memory, "the set-up was five creeps in a house . . . a dog they kicked around and never fed. A little old lady across the street had been feeding it. She called. She said, 'You have to be careful dear, they have guns.'"

Sandra's first visit was advance work, to scout the situation. As it turns out, that is the very step that Animal Liberation Front primers recommend. The household in question partied all night and slept all day, which ruled out a night raid, which is usually considered the safest approach. So Sandra made her move by day. She later remembered thinking, "Okay, I'll grab him and he'll be happy to come with me." She rolled her eyes at her naiveté. "The dog dug in his heels. It was like moving a piano across a football field. I was choking him so he'd shut up. He was barking. I kept thinking, 'I'm going to get my head blown away.'"

Finally the dog began to run and the two of them made it to the car. The neighbour later reported that, less than a minute afterward, the dog's outraged owners came tumbling out of the house, yelling and swearing. It cost Sandra close to $2,000 to treat the dog's hip problems before he went to a new home.

"Then I did it again," Sandra said happily. "Normal, sensible people would think, 'Well, I'm never going to do that again.' But the criminal mind thinks, 'I got away with it. I'm going to do it again.' So I say I have a criminal mind, but I put mine to a good purpose."

When she talked to me, hundreds of animals later, she was blaming authorities for her actions, saying that calls to those who should have acted were fruitless, either because of the perceived limits of the law or what seemed to have been indifference. "I have had inquiries made by police forces," she said. "But it's hard to prove that a dog's stolen and not that it just got loose. It could be serious, but what judge would come down hard on a middle-aged lady, especially when they've heard the story? I'll worry about that when it happens. I can't turn away. I can't say it's too risky."

There are dozens of Sandras out there, some of whom will break the law only once or twice in their lives to help an animal they believe needs rescue. Others are repeat offenders who plan their actions carefully and with a clear conscience. They are the soft side of the illegal world, focused solely on individual cases of animals in distress, and they are so respectably mainstream that they are neither suspected in their communities nor even counted among the ranks of the illegals by more ideological liberationists.

David Barbarash and Darren Thurston are more likely than Sandra to scandalize law-abiding citizens. They would probably say the citizens are scandalized by the wrong things. The two Canadians were understandably wary of inquiring strangers. Involved in ongoing court battles, they had no illusions about their prospects, despite their not-guilty pleas.

Of the two, Barbarash has been willing to be interviewed by mainstream media, despite his suspicions and a far from flattering clipping file. He would take an interviewer carefully through the explanations of why he has done what he has done. He would explain the differences among groups: some condoned actions that might harm humans, while others, like the Animal Liberation Front, in whose name he had operated, did not. If he recognized that few people might be willing to believe in this difference of principles among outlaws, if he grasped that the media were often more interested in the vicarious thrill of listening to an officially dangerous person than to the philosophy, it did not show. In a way that was incongruous for someone whose life had been lived partly underground, Barbarash wore his heart on his sleeve. His clippings described him as a hardliner, an extremist, and sometimes a terrorist. But, to me, it was mostly his sense of vulnerability that was startling. This was a man who could end up spending many of the best years of his life in jail, who had crept out in the night to break laws, who was now working as a courier because it was one of the few jobs he could get. He was angry but not bitter. It was hard not to wonder what would become of this almost wistful believer with so few hard edges.

In April 1999, more than a decade after his first brush with the law over animal rights activities in Toronto, Barbarash sat through the preliminary hearing in Vancouver with almost no public attention. The court's publication ban meant the media stayed away, and it also means I can't repeat any details of the proceedings. But what did occur in the courtroom suggested that the trial, when it eventually took place, would be sensational. At the very least, the trial of Barbarash and Thurston could provide an engrossing case study in how the country's police and security systems operate.

The Vancouver Sun newspaper reported on March 30, 1998, on some of the contents of a police search warrant, which said that more than nine thousand of Thurston's and Barbarash's phone calls, faxes, and e-mails had been intercepted during a three-year police investigation into parcel bombs and letters containing razor blades.[1] The RCMP had searched downtown Vancouver storage lockers, where they found cardboard slips and razor blades that they marked with ultraviolet ink, the news report said. Then police had set up a hidden camera to watch the lockers. When the letters were later received in the mail by people in the hunting business, among others, they carried the same sort of invisible ink markings, the search warrant said. This led to the charges against the two men of mailing material with the intent to do bodily harm. In the preliminary hearing the defendants' lawyers challenged the police evidence, but that challenge, like the evidence, is covered by the publication ban and cannot be repeated here. (Barbarash and Thurston had not been charged with sending parcel bombs. The parcel bombs, sent in the summer of 1995, went to different people than did the razor blade letters, which were received in January 1996 by twenty-two guides and outfitters. The parcel bombs were a separate, unsolved case.)

On November 18, 1998, Barbarash sat for hours on a wooden chair in the mall outside the Vancouver Public Library, patiently and politely answering questions and tracing his progress from a teenager interested in Toronto's anarchist, punk-rock scene to anti-nuclear protest and then the environmental and animal rights movements. He explained, as he has repeatedly in interviews, that he was from a normal suburban background, an ordinary school. In the late 1980s he got a job at the Toronto Humane Society, during a period in its history that would become the stuff of legend, to research the source of dogs used in scientific experiments in laboratories at the University of Toronto. After hours he and four friends decided to break windows at a Kentucky Fried Chicken outlet and write anti-meat and Animal Liberation Front messages on the walls. A few weeks later, driving a Humane Society vehicle, they made a rash return visit to the same restaurant. This time the police were waiting, and Barbarash and his friends ended up in jail for ten days awaiting trial. Then they were put out on probation and made to perform community service (working with a youth outreach group to produce a video on safe sex).

The young vandals, jokingly called the Kentucky Fried Five, were clearly not seen as threats to society. There had been suggestions that they might be implicated in a series of similar protest activities still on the books, but nothing came of that. When they appeared to plead guilty in court, Judge Ted Wren noted that they were "motivated by humane and moral considerations."[2] All of this minor law-breaking might have been good training for a future liberationist – it did give him practice in working in a group, Barbarash said – but the cost was high.[3] He had become known to police. Publicity about the vandalism, with its image of out-of-control hooligans, came at a time when a pitched battle was being fought between activist and conservative factions at the Toronto Humane Society, and allegations of misuse of funds were flying. His ill-fated direct action did not help.

The Society dropped him "like a hot potato," Barbarash recalled. "Of course, it was terrible timing." When his probation ended, Barbarash headed west.

In Edmonton, Thurston followed a similar route to his animal activism. He moved from punk-rock music into anti-racist and animal rights protest. Like Barbarash, he became notorious among the police and CSIS sections that had the job of tracking people officially deemed extremist. But even more than Barbarash, he was practically unknown to the Canadian public. Unlike Barbarash, he did not give interviews to the mainstream media. There was no reason, he explained, to expect his message to get through.[4] News reports tended to carry a grim mug shot that made him seem frightening. The most memorable bit of media coverage was in *The Vancouver Sun* during the time when charges were laid against him. He was, the *Sun* told its readers on March 30, 1998, known as the Mad Bomber in his high-school days. The report of the nickname, Thurston later told me, was simply not true. The report did not even get the name of his old high school right, he complained. But yes, as it said, he did once belong to Skinheads Against Racism. He managed a pained smile. "They love to mention that."

Up close, Thurston was a wiry, intense man with a quick wit and a gentle manner that seemed at odds with the newspaper image. Like Barbarash, he spoke with a passion that softened the impression made. During our interview his face lit up when he talked about lab cats stolen years earlier – the cats remained at large, in new homes.

He said he didn't know where they were now, but he still had a photograph of one of them. And to him, that was worth two and a half years in jail. Thurston's animal rights group, the Citizens Organized for Animal Liberation (COAL), was one that he formed himself, when he found existing organizations too timid. With that group he set in motion relentless rounds of anti-fur demonstrations every weekend in Edmonton throughout 1985 and 1986. He was invited to speak at high schools and at rallies on anti-racism during a time when there was a little bubble of activity by white supremacists. But then he started comparing the results of his legal protest activity with what he had read of the actions of the Animal Liberation Front (ALF). Legal protest just didn't seem to have accomplished enough. So, carefully and methodically, he set about organizing a raid on the University of Alberta laboratory facilities, with a painstaking preparation that would do a scholar proud.

In part the raid was intended to show that university labs could still be raided. There hadn't been such an attack since 1989, he said, not since an outburst of activity in the 1980s had taught universities to tighten their security and be on guard. In part it was to show other activists – law-abiding and otherwise – as well as the public what was inside. He had easily traced the kinds of research being done in the university through its own library. From research journals and other university publications he learned that scientists were conducting what he considered invasive, painful experiments on cats, with little or no pain relief. He arranged with Dr. David Neil, the university's chief veterinarian, for a tour of the laboratories for his animal rights group. Neil, an outspoken British-born scientist and something of a maverick in his own circles, remembered thinking when Thurston was jailed, "There is a young fellow who has done this to himself – misguided, yes. But driven by what he believes. He does this desperate act because everything else he'd ever done had been useless."[5]

"I was quite impressed with how much they showed us," Thurston said of his university tour. "Neil struck me as a very smart man."

Most police and anti-terrorist agencies interested in animal rights activities have by now read the interview, headlined "Doing Time with the Animal Liberation Front," in which Thurston described the June 1, 1992, raid on the university. He gave the interview to the U.S. direct-action magazine *No Compromise* while he was in jail, and it is his best, most graphic outline of how these things work.

Thurston's disciplined approach also stood in stark contrast to some of the more impetuous actions that took other liberationists to jail. He watched the chosen target, the animal facility, for whole days and nights, checking when the staff arrived and left, learning the routine of the university security. He found road and aerial maps at local libraries. He and his colleagues picked a quiet, dark night with no moon for their raid and visited the night before in a practice run. Then they came back with tools – crowbar, hammer, electric drill, radio scanners, cardboard cat carriers, spray paint – loaded into a duffle bag and a backpack. There was a security system – a card entry and an alarm – but many of the windows could easily have been broken, he said. Many of the doors could have been drilled or forced. But, "mysteriously," a door leading into the cat kennel room was unlocked. (Some staff at the university remain convinced the raiders had inside help.)

The only hitch came when the raiders put the cats into bags to take them away, and the first cat, alarmed, promptly shredded the fabric. That meant using the backup plan, the cat carriers. But using the bulky carriers also meant that only two cats at a time could be carried away across a long field to a waiting vehicle. That part of the job was the most time-consuming, bringing the total time inside the facility to nearly three hours. Inside the lab the raiders opened cabinets, dumping their contents on the floor. They smashed equipment and splashed red paint around. They carried off some research documents and drenched others with acid. They sprayed a delivery truck outside the lab with slogans, as well as the inside walls. Thurston's *No Compromise* interview offered helpful tips – that red paint mixed with a bit of thinner is easy to splash from two-litre soft-drink bottles to leave slogans and imitation blood, that coveralls and balaclavas and cheap throwaway shoes are useful protective clothing.

"They wreaked a considerable amount of vandalism," Neil told reporters in the aftermath. "That's an act of terrorism, it's not an act of rescuing. It's calculated to try to strike fear into the research community so that they will move away from the use of animals."[6] Although the university had recently opened improved facilities on its main campus, the Alberta Society for the Prevention of Cruelty to Animals had criticized the institution in the past for poor conditions and pointed out that laws were needed to protect research animals.

Even years later, as he waited to find out if he was going back to court on other, unrelated charges, Thurston sounded satisfied with the raid he had planned. The fatal flaw, he noted, came later. It wasn't in his part of the job.

A young woman had taken on the chore of renting a motel room for Thurston and the others. The room was to be used as a safely anonymous place for assembling information and pictures for the media, so the public would see what the university was doing to cats. The group sent a press release to the Edmonton media, saying the cats were to be used in "useless and painful experiments," and an accompanying film showed cats cradled by persons in balaclavas. However, the woman renting the motel room used her own name on the register, and, unknown to the others, she was on police files. When police made the rounds to motels during their investigation, they noticed her name and went straight to her. She was, Thurston said, "too young and too scared," and when the police came, she talked.

On June 19, 1992, at about 5:30 p.m., Thurston walked out of an Edmonton shoe store, where he worked as manager. He had just crossed the parking lot to a bus stop when a police car zoomed up to him. Two officers leapt out, guns drawn. He was arrested, handcuffed, and taken to the police station's holding tank. He would be charged with break and enter, theft, and mischief from the university raid. Later he would be charged with arson and mischief for the burning and vandalizing of trucks at a local fish shop. On October 12, 1993, more than fifteen months later, all of them spent in custody, Thurston pleaded guilty to charges that had been boiled down to break and enter to commit theft, from the university raid, and arson, from the fish-truck fire. He was sentenced to time served, but he was barely out of jail when he learned there would be an appeal of the sentence. In

March of the following year the court agreed to send him back to jail for a sentence of two years less a day. In January 1995 he was released on probation under partial house arrest. It meant four months of being at his family home from 6 p.m. to 6 a.m., with random calls and visits from parole workers. He had spent almost two years in jail.

He remembered the Edmonton jail, where he served some of this time, as an awful place. It had no library. Exercise was a twice-a-week outing on the roof. The clientele ranged from minor offenders to murderers. After the first, worst few months, letters of support began pouring in for the man who for some time held the record as the North American animal liberationist with the longest jail sentence. Sometimes fifteen letters would arrive in a day, and he would spend time answering them. He managed to arrange three open visits – two with his girlfriend and one with his mother – at the jail. That meant face-to-face meetings across a table, without glass partitions. He was transferred to jail in Calgary, where there was a library – and more yelling and fighting among prisoners. By March 1994 the idea of returning to jail for another two-year sentence was a depressing, if unsurprising, development. But, Thurston said, he had learned you could survive jail by keeping your head down, minding your own business, and enduring.

Not long after Thurston was heading back to jail for a second round, Barbarash was being seized in California and returned to Edmonton to stand trial on charges for his role in the University of Alberta lab raid. His thumbprint had been found on a bit of sticky tape left in the motel room, where he had helped to prepare information about the lab for the media.

The day in California when Barbarash drove into the massive police roadblock, he was in the midst of moving his belongings from the home of a friend, animal activist Jonathan Paul. Paul had himself just spent months in jail for refusing to testify against another liberationist, Rod Coronado, who was later to replace Thurston as the North American liberationist with the longest jail term. That meant that Paul's house was not the safest place to have chosen as a hangout, Barbarash admitted ruefully. A Canada-wide warrant had been issued for his arrest just days after Thurston was picked up in 1992 but, because he was already in the United States, Barbarash said, he chose not to go back. He had already been deported once from the United States years before. By comparison, that was a tame event. That first time he had sneaked across the border into Montana after being refused entry because of a marijuana conviction. He was quickly spotted by police at a bus stop and spent ten days in an immigration detention facility before being shipped home. It was, Barbarash recalled in a whimsical aside, "a Wackenhut facility. Really, an excellent facility. I was impressed." He remembered the name of the company because Wackenhut was his former employer during a brief security career.

"I really didn't have any defence," Barbarash said of his 1994 arrest. "I wasn't supposed to be in the country." He was detained for about three weeks before being escorted to an airplane for a flight home to Vancouver, where the police were waiting. He had "a few hours of freedom" on the flight home. "I drank all the beer I could. I didn't know what to expect." Barbarash knew that Thurston had spent a long time in jail. Perhaps the same future was in store for him.

From Vancouver he was taken to Edmonton, where he pleaded guilty to accessory after the fact in break and enter, theft, and mischief. From his arrest in California to his release, he spent four months in detention.

Then he was back in Vancouver and working for Bear Watch, a B.C. group that had worked since 1988 to protect bears and their habitat from trophy hunting, poaching, and death as nuisance animals. The year and a half he spent staffing the organization's Vancouver office and conducting an anti-hunting campaign may have been Barbarash's happiest time in years. He liked his life and his work. Thurston was also happily occupied doing computer work for Bear Watch, a task well suited to the computer whiz. While Thurston worked on records and computer programs, Barbarash ran an anti-hunt direct-action campaign — legal efforts to scare the bears before hunters could kill them. It is a venerable anti-hunt tactic in Britain and among North American whale, bear, and seal defenders. There was no shortage of volunteer help for Barbarash, including one fearless woman in her seventies.

Bear Watch had no problem with his criminal record, Barbarash said, until a Vancouver *Province* reporter wrote about "terrorists" at Bear Watch. However, the other local paper, *The Vancouver Sun*, said that Bear Watch got rid of the two activists when it learned of their backgrounds. In a March 30, 1998, report, it quoted Bear Watch spokesman and researcher Eric Donnelly as saying that the headlines Barbarash made by chasing licensed hunters and guide outfitters in the field involved actions not sanctioned by the organization. He was, Donnelly said, "a little out of control. We didn't like what they were doing. That's why they're no longer with Bear Watch."

"Bear Watch was *formed* for direct action," Barbarash said. "I felt really betrayed." He admitted that he didn't help things along with an impulsive decision to pose, in a balaclava, for a photograph to go with a media report about hunt disruptions. It did contribute to "that terrorist thing," and he regretted the fallout for Bear Watch. But the idea was to make hunters think they might face nuts in the bush, to discourage them from coming. A charge was laid against Barbarash at one point for interfering with a legal hunt, but that was dropped on a technicality. He wasn't the only Bear Watcher charged.

According to Donnelly, the balaclava photo was the final straw, and Barbarash was fired for hurting the organization's image. Moreover, Bear Watch dropped the whole aggressive witnessing program that put supporters in the field to discourage hunters. Not only the public but also some other groups that were willing to side with Bear Watch had been put off by "the in-your-face stuff," Donnelly said. Now the organization confines itself to lobbying and activities that are more publicly acceptable. Thurston, Donnelly said, "wasn't doing his job" and was fired.[7]

By July 1995 the RCMP in British Columbia were already investigating a series of attacks claimed by a group, little known until then, which identified itself as the Earth Liberation Army in a letter to local newspapers.[8] One of the province's largest outfitting companies, which charged $2,000 to Americans and Europeans aiming to hunt black bears, had suffered property damages, including slashed tires, a damaged hovercraft, burned cabins, and poisoned hunting dogs. These actions, police stressed, were altogether different than the actions of legitimate groups using legitimate means to protest. It made Bear Watchers feel even more pressured about their hunt campaign. It was left to a seventy-five-year-old hunt protester, Ruth Masters of Courtenay on Vancouver Island, to defend direct action to reporters. She had run into trouble with police just weeks earlier for blowing whistles and throwing rocks to scare a bear when she thought she saw a hunter taking aim. Masters, who said she lost control on that occasion, explained that she could understand the desperate frustration of those who resort to vandalism for the cause. Sport hunting, she said, was "as sick as you can get."

The fall 1996 *Bear Watch Journal* carried an article by Barbarash celebrating the spring anti-hunt campaign conducted in Campbell River on north Vancouver Island. (Thurston did the layout and design for the *Journal*.) Two dozen activists had monitored the hunt and there were signs that foreign hunters had been put off by their presence. One angry outfitter had been filmed smashing the windshield of a car belonging to a Bear Watcher. But that same issue also revealed signs of the growing discomfort over direct action. The *Journal* reported that the B.C. Wildlife Federation had apologized after comparing Bear Watch to "terrorist groups who . . . send razor blades in the mail" and hurt people. The *Journal* scoffed at the accusations, but Bear Watch had gone to some lengths to get an apology rather than ignore them.

But Barbarash's and Thurston's troubles were really only starting when they were dropped by Bear Watch. That attempt to move back into the world of legal animal activism was a failure. Just as they had in 1992 after the University of Alberta raid, the police were soon keeping the two under surveillance, and Barbarash and Thurston were being pulled into an enormous investigation that would take over their lives. This time, they both insisted repeatedly, they were innocent.

In the spring and summer of 1995, four pipe bombs were mailed to four different people, including Toronto Holocaust-denier Ernst

Zundel in Toronto, white supremacist Charles Scott in Chilliwack, B.C., John Thompson, executive director of the Mackenzie Institute, a Toronto think tank that studies terrorism and revolution and keeps tabs on animal rights activists, and Terry Mitenko of Alta Genetics Inc., a Calgary genetic research company. At the time Thurston was out of jail but reporting daily to Edmonton parole officers. By July that parole condition was eased to weekly reports. Police opened attempted murder investigations into the pipe bombs. Then, in January 1996, dozens of people in the fur and hunter guiding and outfitting businesses received a series of threatening letters spiked with razor blades supposedly dipped in deadly substances. In press releases sent to B.C. media, a group called the Justice Department claimed responsibility for the letters.

One of the packages went to the *Times Colonist* in Victoria. It arrived on January 9, 1996, and included a sealed envelope containing a short, razor-sharp knife blade placed to cut anyone opening it. A sample of the message sent to outfitters said, in part: "Dear animal killing scum! Hope we sliced your finger wide open and that you now die from the rat poison we smeared on the razor blade. Murdering scum that kill defenseless animals in the thousands every year across B.C. for fun and profit do not deserve to live." A second note, a press release, said sixty-five such letters had been sent in hopes that all recipients would die.

The Vancouver Sun had received a communiqué in July 1995 about the parcel bombs. The message, signed by the Militant Direct Action Task Force, said the Calgary company Alta Genetics was trying to control other species with its research into breeding technology.[9]

The pipe bomb sent to the Calgary cattle-breeding business was the only one that exploded, and it harmed no one. The bomb sent to Zundel was detonated safely after the controversial Zundel, a frequent target of anti-racist groups, became suspicious and called in the police. The bomb sent to Scott in Chilliwack did not explode.[10] The one that arrived at the Mackenzie Institute in downtown Toronto was detonated by police after it was unwrapped.[11] The Militant Direct Action Task Force sent messages about the bombs to the Montreal

Gazette as well as to *The Vancouver Sun*, saying the targets were chosen for their "racism" or support for "right-wing hatred" or, in the Calgary case, for the genetic "tampering" of its research.[12]

At the Mackenzie Institute, the postal carrier had jammed the slightly too big parcel into the little postal box in the building's main floor, executive director Thompson said. The Institute's secretary had to tug the package out when she went to retrieve the mail. When it was opened, they found a pipe filled with nails resting on a bed of tissue. A battery connection had jiggled loose, which apparently kept the bomb from exploding. Although it was a bare-bones version of a bomb, it could have killed someone if it had gone off, Thompson said. For him, the motive behind the parcel bomb remained a mystery. The practical outcome – aside from new security cameras installed in the lobby and a certain discretion about the office's location – was the terror that gripped other tenants in the building. It meant that Thompson had to spend a lot of time talking to them about how it would be wrong to give in to terrorists by hounding the Institute out of the building.

The Institute had issued several reports on animal rights activities – reports widely circulated and thoroughly resented by animal activists, most of whom were doing nothing illegal but might find their names included. Barbarash and Thurston were among those named in the reports. Thompson said he didn't know who sent the bomb, but that he would like to see the guilty person jailed. He also wanted to see animal rights actions taken more seriously, because he believed they would escalate.

According to Barbarash, when police across the country began to investigate first the pipe bombs and then the razor blade letter campaign in early 1996, it was only logical that his and Thurston's names would come up. "I don't regret anything I've done – well, maybe that [balaclava] photo," he said. "I haven't perpetrated any evil or done anything I consider morally wrong. I understand why I'm a suspect. I can understand why I'm charged. I can even say the RCMP is doing their job. It seems almost logical that they would focus on the two most visible activists in Canada."

Despite that concession, he said none of the material the police seized on March 20, 1997, when they suddenly appeared at his door in Vancouver with a search warrant, could possibly prove him guilty of the latest charges. He didn't do the deeds, he said. The evidence presented to the court in April 1999 remained circumscribed, but in our earlier, November 1998, interview, Barbarash talked about the unexpected police raids with search warrants. He said he had concluded that the police moved in suddenly after the cops realized that he and Thurston had discovered electronic surveillance devices placed in their rooms and in a vehicle. The surveillance had been going on since 1996, he said, with thousands of hours of intercepted communications. He had long grown accustomed to the idea that the police were following him. Sometimes they were easy to spot and, because of a rash of ALF activities in the province, he knew that police were making inquiries of some of his friends.

"If anything happens in B.C. or Canada, they always check out Barbarash," he said. "So, to see people follow me on the street is nothing much."

But he did experience one major shock. When the police came equipped with a warrant to take away files and belongings from his apartment and from his girlfriend Rebecca Rubin's apartment, and when simultaneous raids were made in Edmonton on Thurston's apartment, Thurston's mother's home, and some storage lockers, Barbarash and Thurston discovered that the investigations might involve charges of attempted murder or of sending the razor blade letters. (Rubin, a university geography student whose goal was to find work with wildlife in Africa, was charged jointly with Barbarash for possession of an explosive substance.)

"The thing with letter bombs is a postal employee could get injured or a secretary," Barbarash said. "I would almost say it's a cowardly action, although I don't think I would cry if Ernst Zundel dropped dead of a heart attack."

The raid "scooped up a lot of my life," he said. For six months he was devastated. "My life was turned upside down. I was obsessed with my stuff." But when the letters and music CDs and files began to be

returned, after a court challenge to the warrant, he found the posses-
sions no longer seemed so precious.

On March 27, 1998, the police charged Barbarash with mailing the
razor blade letters and with possession of a prohibited weapon, a stun
gun. Shortly after that, Thurston turned himself in to be charged as
well with mailing the letters. Over a year later, with the charges
against him based only on the razor blade letters and not on the pipe
bombs, Barbarash almost felt more frustrated for *not* having been
charged with attempted murder and blamed for the bombs. Although
he did not send the parcel bombs, he said, at least if he had been
charged the suspicion and insinuation would have been dealt with.
The charges changed his life and all his personal relationships.
"When people see me, they see something else. I'm always going to be
known now as the guy who's been charged with this stuff. . . . Once
you've been convicted, all the rest seems fair game." He repeatedly
insisted that the police were abusing their authority and the notion of
national security.

Even in November 1998, on a cold and rainy day in Vancouver as
he contemplated a seemingly endless stretch of court proceedings
ahead and forecast that, after thousands and thousands of dollars had
been spent on investigating him, the police would never allow him to
be found not guilty, Barbarash did not waver in his defence of animal
liberation actions.

"They claim that we're violent. How do you do violence to an
inanimate object?" he said. "They say we're destroying businesses and
families. I guess it all depends on how you look at it. But from my
point of view, a farmer that is systematically killing thousands of mink
every year doesn't have anything to complain about. How does loss of
all that life compare to the loss of income of one family?

"It's as if humans can have all the power and you justify them doing
whatever they want because they're human. It's an obscene mentality.
I don't think that's a gap that will ever be bridged. . . . The only hope is
that these people die off and let the new generation take over."

By spring the following year Barbarash was cheerier. The preliminary hearings had at least got things moving along. He seemed

buoyed by what he said seemed to be problems with the evidence. He appeared on a cbc Newsworld television show to explain that his life as an alf activist had ended with his 1994 arrest. Now, he said, "My future is to support them in any way possible."[13] He explained the reason for the alf's use of economic sabotage: protesting and writing letters did not change things, because it is not passion but economics that matters to the people who use animals for profit.

"People do see us as fanatics'" he told *Big Life* host Daniel Richler. "They see us as terrorists. I mean, my God, we're breaking laws. We're destroying property. . . . [But] we're here to save lives. We're here to protect the Earth."

• • •

By July 1999, when David Barbarash became the above-ground spokesperson for the clandestine Animal Liberation Front, based in Courtenay, B.C., the alf had clearly registered on police radar screens. In April 1992 an analyst with the Canadian Security Intelligence Service had blamed about forty acts of vandalism, arson, and break and enter on the alf, calling it the most radical of hundreds of groups across the country involved in animal protection.[14] G. Davidson (Tim) Smith of csis warned that the actions of animal rights militants could raise basic concerns about the economic livelihood of some Canadians. He warned that the atmosphere of animal rights had a certain chic, that it offered "an exciting outlet for the trendy types bored with their tame lifestyle." But, he wrote, it also offered an avenue for extremists with a more sinister agenda, because "many of the supporters of the alf in Canada are known to have extreme left-wing or anarchist views."

In a later commentary published by csis in the winter of 1998, Smith dropped his slightly patronizing tone about animal rights extremists, perhaps because he had concluded that "extremist activity has been more prevalent in Canada of late than in the usa or the uk."[15] Smith, now a counterterrorism specialist with csis, noted that the alf had made it onto the fbi's list of domestic terrorists in 1987 after a multimillion-dollar arson at a California laboratory (it was eventually dropped from the list because it was deemed too amorphous to be included). Scotland Yard had made "eco-terrorists" a security priority in 1995. CSIS was also busying itself by then with the activities of what it loosely catalogued as environmental extremists in Canada. By the time it filed its 1997-98 annual report to the federal government, the intelligence service was listing animal rights along with the environment, anti-racism, and Quebec separation as issues that produced extremists willing to use violence to reach their political goals. According to the report, files had been opened on the animal activists.[16]

For Darren Thurston, life after jail became even more complicated when the police began to investigate the pipe bombs and razor blade letters. An October 10, 1997, visit to England would become a bizarre odyssey. He was invited to England to testify as a witness in a trial involving animal activists there. Excited about his first trip overseas and delighted that it would be at someone else's expense, he landed at Heathrow airport and explained his reasons for coming to Customs officials. They searched him and his belongings, he said, and told him they would have to make some telephone calls. When they returned the officials told him that Scotland Yard said there were outstanding firearms charges against him at home and that he would not be admitted to the country, despite the court's request for his presence. There were no such firearms charges, Thurston said. After his conviction for arson, he had been prohibited from owning firearms for five years. As a result, police had seized a rifle and handgun that he owned legally. He had also owned two inert hand grenades since he was a kid, he said. Those souvenirs had been mentioned as real weapons in several news reports. In any case, he sat in a holding room at Heathrow for several hours before being escorted to a plane, where the other passengers were careful to keep their distance. He flew to the Toronto airport, where he slept for several hours, and then back to Vancouver.

On a January 28, 1998, visit to California to visit his fiancée Gina Lynn, an editor for *No Compromise*, Thurston walked out of a grocery store and into a circle of police cars, police dogs, and drawn weapons. He was ordered onto his knees, seized and shackled, and driven by police to an immigration office in downtown Los Angeles, where he was transferred to another facility for a two-week stay. He was to be deported, Thurston said, as "a threat to national security." But a judge did not find the bare Immigration Department demand for his deportation sufficient and allowed him to make a voluntary departure a week later. The departure was dramatic, with yet another police escort to another plane with wary fellow passengers already on board. But there was no problem in his entry into Canada through Vancouver.

"That's my life and it's not going to go away," he said of his record. "I can tell it's not going to change. . . . I don't *want* to be the dangerous man with a 'caution violence' to police. I've seen that on my record when it was printed out."

Life is not easy when you are accused of sending razor blade letters or suspected of sending parcel bombs in an attempt to commit murder. For one thing, friends or fans of the people who received the bombs might be irritated enough to take it out on you, guilty or not. Thurston said that, since his arrest in 1992, he had not been involved in any illegal ALF activity. He stressed that he had never advocated or taken part in any violent activity, in anything that would harm life. But, despite his not-guilty plea, he said he wouldn't be astonished to be sent to jail for the offences. "They've gone to a lot of work for this investigation, so I wouldn't be surprised if they pulled something out of the hat."

Given the surveillance that he knew the police had undertaken, Thurston said he assumed all his telephone calls and communications were being monitored. That meant every contact with his fiancée would be overheard by others. Lynn had been forced to leave Canada and return to the United States because of a conviction on a trespass charge associated with an animal rights protest. She could not return, and he could not legally visit the United States. It was, he acknowledged, the most stressful time of his life. He dealt with the difficult years by burying himself in work, particularly with computers. He hoped to develop his own computer business, because employers might not want to hire him. He liked to immerse himself in research, to design Web sites.

If he could roll back the years, would he do anything differently? "I'd just do what I did – better," said Thurston. "I'm not sorry that I did it. There's twenty-nine cats that are out there. That's worth the two and a half years I had to spend in jail."

Gina Lynn also spent three weeks in jail in the fall of 1999 after refusing to co-operate with a U.S. grand jury. The jury was investigating threatening letters sent in 1995 and 1996 to Anheuser-Busch and its chairman warning them to release whales held in the company's Sea World parks. Based apparently on comments made in secret testimony by a witness who suggested the young California animal rights activist might be the kind to make threats, the grand jury wanted Lynn's fingerprints and a writing sample. Lynn denied having anything to do with the letters, and her refusal landed her in jail for contempt of court. She went on a hunger strike and was abruptly released.

Thurston's profile with police was so high that he well knew that it would be ill-advised to attempt any more illegal activity. He had come to see his role as doing anything he could, legally, to help the ALF. But there was really no one ALF, no liberation organization that you could join, no central membership or rules or executive. There was, though, an ALF credo, a common set of guidelines readily available on the Internet, through the Animal Liberation Frontline Information Service. And you could order its publications from the quite legal North American ALF Supporters Group that operated out of a Toronto-area postal box office and took merchandise orders by e-mail.

The publications make ALF goals and recommendations quite clear. One handbook states:

> The Animal Liberation Front carries out direct action against animal abuse in the form of rescuing animals and causing financial loss to animal exploiters, usually through damage and destruction of property. Their short-term aim is to save as many animals as possible and directly disrupt the practice of animal abuse. Their long-term aim is to end all animal suffering by forcing animal abuse companies out of business. It is a nonviolent campaign, activists taking all

precautions not to harm any animal (human or otherwise). Because ALF actions are against the law, activists work anonymously, either in small groups or individually and do not have any centralized organization or coordination.

If you are vegetarian – or vegan, which means using no animal products at all – and you carry out an action according to the guidelines, you can consider yourself part of the ALF. The system is designed for maximum involvement and maximum security.

After years of experience with illegal activities that did not always succeed, and with the twenty-four years of experience of British liberationists to guide them, North American ALF activists had put together some practical ideas about how to go about breaking the law. A small library of reprints of material from the United Kingdom and United States had become available. It included primers that warned readers to use caution if a fur farm had been raided before, to carry some emergency cash and no identification, and, above all else – repeated over and over again on each bit of written advice or tip sheet – was the admonition not to speak to police, not ever, not about anything. Breaking the solidarity that protects everyone was not to be tolerated.

In practice, this is an unforgiving attitude to take to your own side. But the theory is probably sound. The illegal side of the animal rights movement needs support from others who protest and campaign legally. They need donations when they are in jail and outside voices to explain why illegalities have occurred – things the illegals can't do without being arrested. They believe they are the ones who force a largely hostile audience of industry or government to give a hearing, however grudging and limited it might be, to the issues raised by legal activists. Illegal action, with its economic costs, creates a situation that must be dealt with, and it raises public awareness. The work provides an opening for the legal groups as the less bad alternatives. The illegals argue that without them what little tolerance legal groups get would quickly disappear. The respectability that comes with helping police, so the argument goes, is really an illusion.

One advice booklet based on the experiences of ALF activists in the south of England explains the need for silence as part of the battle: "Those people who snitch cannot really believe in what they are doing, otherwise they would have the confidence and peace of mind to recognize that in a direct action campaign, some arrests are inevitable and although they are unlucky enough to be arrested at that particular time, the struggle will go on. Their role once arrested is to say or do nothing to impair the struggle."[17] In North America the same message was delivered in *Underground*, the publication of the North American Animal Liberation Front Supporters Group. Since 1994 activists in general had been feeling under increased scrutiny from police, including the 1997 raid on Barbarash and Thurston by the RCMP and interviews by police as part of investigations into various illegal actions.

For a long time now the FBI and CSIS have considered animal activists worth tracking. CSIS documents warned that the activists could endanger livelihoods and that the ALF members were extreme left-wingers – the kind of people often unfairly targeted for surveillance in the past. Two activists, Barbarash and Thurston, became the objects of long, expensive investigations that seem to have been based as much on assessments of their politics as on their records. Most of us have no way of knowing who these closely scrutinized people are, or if the attention is valid. Barring a sensational trial or major crime – on those occasions when charges result from the police attention – there is little public notice of what is going on in this murky world.

In Canada most of us are comfortable with the assumption that, if we have a valid issue to put before the public, we can influence public policy. It is an assumption that makes it easy to accept that activists who break the law are social misfits who have rejected other legal avenues for making their case. But in reality these are often compassionate, well-informed people who have come to believe there is no other way. Their choice of action should raise uncomfortable questions about society and the political process.

The recent history of the extreme side of the animal movement certainly helps to put other parts of the movement in perspective. The great majority of activists – who never break the law, who lobby, demonstrate, and plead for a hearing on issues with such meagre success – come to seem much less radical. The targets for illegal action might even seem to be logical rather than innocent victims, regardless of whether or not you agree with the action itself.

The small but important outlaw fringe is, after all, the outer limit of the animal movement. Another extreme, not small in numbers but on the opposite edge in philosophical terms, is the animal welfare world, which is quite distinct from animal rights. The animal welfare world would seem to be the place to test the other mythology burdening the animal movement: that if something cruel or wrong is being done to animals, there will be action. Its adherents are the people who, using the law and generous public donations, should be the ones to do something about the issues. In a very different way from the illegals, this world can be equally shocking.

CHAPTER TWO

Polite Company

The Grey-Bruce Humane Society annual general meeting was tense from the very start. President Ross Trask had barely called sixty-some members to order when he was challenged over whether the gathering was even legitimate because it came on the evening of March 31, 1999. Society bylaws said it was supposed to happen *prior* to March 31. Just to get under way Trask had to appeal to the Society's lawyer to back up his insistence that this meeting in a high-school cafeteria in Chesley, Ont., a little town south of Georgian Bay, was in order.

At that point a lawyer seemed to have been perpetually at Trask's side, at a cost to the Society of thousands of scarce charity dollars. Grey-Bruce had been fighting lawsuits brought by some of its own members since 1996 – battles that pitted against each other competing ideas of what a humane society should do and stand for. An appeal of the last court fight still loomed, and this evening's business was overshadowed by the necessity of cleaning up after the latest legal action. Verbal potshots were still being traded in letters to the editor in the local newspapers. Still present were members considered to be troublesome activists by the Society's tight executive. Soon after the challenge to the meeting's legitimacy was squashed, another member was on her feet to demand answers from Trask.

"Is it your intent, will you take in strays and unwanted animals after you build the shelter?" Michelle Wang asked.

"I can't state anything specific at this time," a grim-faced Trask replied carefully.

An animal shelter built with public donations that won't promise to help homeless animals: this is the other side of the animal universe from the Animal Liberation Front. The illegals and their supporters might debate what sort of actions are okay, whether to do property damage, whether threats to humans are beyond the pale, or whether firebombs are too risky. By contrast, simply insisting on offering a place to sleep and a bowl of food to stray dogs or injured wildlife or promoting vegetarianism can mark you as a radical and outsider here, in the conservative world of animal welfare advocates.

At this end of the animal world medical experiments on animals are not necessarily considered a bad thing, nor are most routine farm practices. As animal welfare organizations and their advocates take pains to point out, they are most definitely not animal rights supporters by any definition of the term. Their ranks comfortably include farmers, hunters, trappers, researchers, and all sorts of people who make their living using animals. This is a part of the animal world in which an associate of the Mackenzie Institute, the Toronto research organization obsessed with "terrorists," can happily run the country's largest Humane Society.

The differences between the animal rights and animal welfare worlds of this universe are basic. Humane societies or societies for the prevention of cruelty to animals – usually interchangeable names – are the pillars of the animal welfare community. They are the animal groups best known to the public and generally the animal groups most accepted in polite, official company. Their members are not treated as nuts or extremists by politicians or police. Membership in their organizations is not considered grounds for surveillance. Their public image is wholesome and reputable and, because of that, they get public donations and sometimes contracts with local authorities to provide animal control and/or animal shelters. They are part of the established order, and their spokespersons can usually expect to be taken seriously and treated with respect.

Animal welfare agencies usually devote themselves to campaigns to convince people to spay or neuter their pets. They take in the abandoned or unwanted pets and adopt out the healthy and sociable among them. In some places they decide which animals will be killed or sold to research labs. In most places, agencies officially authorized as a Humane Society or an outlet of a Society for the Prevention of Cruelty to Animals (SPCA) investigate animal cruelty cases either alone or with the police. Sometimes they hammer out policy statements condemning cruelty in rodeos or circuses or opposing some forms of hunting or exotic animals being kept as pets. But policy is usually targeted at specific cases – against bunnies as prizes at Easter or horse-drawn wagon rides in downtown traffic – rather than at the routine treatment of animals in normal daily life.

Ardent animal activists are not found in these ranks. Rather, by treating those who call for greater change as extremists and by providing a non-challenging animal organization for business or government to consult or support, the animal welfare movement acts as a kind of foil. Intentionally or not, it seems more commonly to head off calls for reform than to pave the way for real improvement in animals' lives, although welfare advocates might argue that they are softening up social attitudes and making small strides so that some day animals will be better and more respectfully treated. This is like the paradox of the best of food banks or wage subsidy programs. They offer immediate relief to limited numbers and take the edge off demands for a change in welfare rates or employer practices that might mean lasting help for many more.

This pattern was set in place more than a century ago. When the Society for the Prevention of Cruelty to Animals formed in England in 1824, it had aristocratic patrons and even royal ones by 1835, when it added an R before the SPCA. It was an elite group, the high-born concerned about the morals of the lower classes. Its message of kindness to what were considered soulless creatures was intended to encourage kindness to humans. By the 1870s vivisection, or the dissection or painful treatment of living animals, was a key research tool in Britain. An anti-vivisection movement grew up that was less establishment and included more women. Its targets were not the lower classes but the educated – medical and research communities. These anti-vivisectionists split the animal welfare community into radical and conservative bents.

The same reverence for the status quo, and much the same battles, were transferred to Canada. In British Columbia, where the provincial Society for the Prevention of Cruelty to Animals is more than one hundred years old, the Vancouver branch dissolved in 1910 into bickering over having women on its executive. That dispute was solved with a ban on women officers lasting until 1915. By 1928 women held all executive positions and a men's advisory board was created. The local press responded by moving its coverage of the branch from news to society pages. In the 1920s the Victoria branch fought over opposition to vivisection. Branch president R.W. Hunter, who supported using animals in some research, worried about public reaction and loss of donations should his branch be linked to this "lunatic fringe" of research critics. The abolitionists were forced out.[1]

But in the animal welfare world, like elsewhere, battles against people who challenge the established order are never won forever. For one thing, the opposition members are often serious people who drift towards more significant change when they become convinced it is the only way to accomplish their goals. A former animal shelter worker, for example, talked to me about being overtaken by rage at the end of the day at the sight of yet another person dropping off yet another pet that had become inconvenient. The next day at the shelter would start, as they all did, on the same cycle. Decisions would be made about which of the resident animals would be killed and bodies loaded into an incinerator. More unwanted pets would be accepted without censure. In public the shelter would talk about heart-warming success stories in placing animals and say nothing about the dead ones. For that worker it became obvious that the attitude of humans towards animals must change.

In most Canadian animal welfare organizations, the term *animal rights* would never be spoken with real approval. Yet many of the organizations include workers with well-developed ideas for change, people who would find much common ground in any animal rights circle, except perhaps in tactics. And the animal welfare world is not without its shining moments – those examples to would-be reformers of what is possible in working with the relative affluence and status of the local Humane Society.

The tumultuous history of the Toronto Humane Society captures several of those moments. The Society began with the goal of serious change and the support of respectable people, like humane societies in other provinces. A letter published in 1886 in the Toronto daily *The World* asked why there was no society to prevent cruelty. It was written in simple compassion for a weary old work horse seen on city streets. The letter prompted an anonymous two-dollar donation that kicked off a fund. In 1887 the Toronto Humane Society, a humane and children's movement, was set up with the purpose of protecting both children and animals from being cruelly treated. Like the British RSPCA, the Toronto Humane Society was aiming at human betterment along with protection for animals. But it did set for itself a goal that meant interfering in a mainstay of business activity, the conditions for working horses, and in the treatment of children, a family realm considered quite out of bounds at the time. One of its first priorities was to establish hundreds of drinking fountains for the thousands of work horses in the city. This was not a tame project for do-gooders. In those days, as it did briefly a century later, the Toronto Humane Society must have seemed a beacon to ambitious social activists.[2]

The Grey-Bruce Humane Society offers a current picture of the world of animal welfare agencies, if a rawer, blunter version than most. For if the Toronto Humane Society in the late 1980s provides an example of a recent attempt to make significant change, Grey-Bruce provides a taste of the more widespread reaction to the influence of animal rights supporters. Toronto might stand as a failed dream to activists. To others, it was a lesson. While the Toronto media lavished headlines on the doomed apprehended coup of animal rights activists at one of the continent's biggest animal welfare agencies, the Grey-Bruce story is a largely unheralded example of another sort of coup. Increasingly a backlash has sidelined the activists who want humane societies to advocate more vegetarianism or oppose handing pets over to research laboratories. Now the activists of the animal welfare world tend to be hunters, trappers, farmers, or others who want to keep humane societies under their control and limit or roll back even the range of animals to be helped or the interpretations of cruelty cases in need of investigation.

That is why the Grey-Bruce meeting in small-town southwestern Ontario on a fine spring evening in March 1999 was illuminating. It was also the context in which a banal-sounding question about taking in stray dogs amounted to fighting words. The Society had a tidy bequest of more than $70,000 to aid in building its first animal shelter since its establishment as a registered charity in January 1991 and its affiliation with the Ontario Society for the Prevention of Cruelty to Animals (OSPCA) as a Humane Society in 1992. There had been talk of spending $300,000 in total. But despite its declaration in the incorporation documents that gave Grey-Bruce its government sanction as a charity – that it would operate a shelter for "all stray and unwanted animals, birds and fish" – there was now no promise that stray cats and dogs would be given any care or help. The charter was being reworked in murky language to suggest that only animals seized by the Society in cruelty investigations or handed over by owners would be accepted.

Even the details and records of how many animals were regularly seized in these cruelty investigations and how much their care in foster homes already cost were treated as secret from the members. Did it even make sense to build a shelter without strays? Who would know?

As the Grey-Bruce annual meeting in Chesley ground its way through three hours, Lore Weinberg wanted to know if the Society would give help to injured wildlife, to creatures like snapping turtles or raccoons hurt by cars. Some men laughed outright. Trask, the president, gritted his teeth and insisted that provincial Natural Resources officers would do the job, that it would be illegal for the Humane Society to take it on. An exasperated voice spoke from the floor to help him out. When wildlife is hurt, someone usually happens along and will either kill it or help it, the member said. And that's the way to do it, "not to get carried away . . . God gave us this world to use. There's animals that are pets and there are animals that are wild. Let's leave it at that." Applause followed.

Weinberg and her husband Gerry, a retired lawyer, were the members who had been battling the Society in the courts at their own expense. They had demanded in court that Trask, a hunter and the owner of a dog compound where dogs were trained by running down live foxes and coyotes, be removed from the presidency. They argued that he was in a conflict of interest and could not possibly do the job fairly. His activities involved practices condemned by the OSPCA. The Weinbergs made the same case against vice-president Peter Van Aalst, a trapper and former member of a local trapping council. The OSPCA has a policy opposing trapping wildlife. With these men at its head, the Grey-Bruce Humane Society stood no chance of working towards OSPCA goals in these areas, Toronto lawyer Lesli Bisgould argued in court for the Weinbergs. Having a dog-compound owner and a hunter and trapper as president and vice-president, she said, would be a sign to the public that such activities were approved.[3]

Trask was blunt with the court. His Humane Society would deal with domestic animals, and anything else was simply the provincial office's "wish list." His vice-president Van Aalst agreed, telling the court that the OSPCA had "no jurisdiction over trapping and hunting." Grey-Bruce lawyer David Lovell argued that the Society's executive officers could not be in conflict of any kind if they were dealing only with domestic animals. That other humane societies around the province dealt with wildlife, as did the central OSPCA, was not up for discussion, nor was the contention that the provincial Ministry of Natural Resources would come to the aid, for example, of a wild animal injured by a car.

(Even hungry bears wandering into backyards had been seen as a local problem in the berry-scarce summer of 1998 in Ontario. The provincial government offered only to loan traps to Timmins police and provide an officer with a tranquilizer gun, and it refused to take back the job of managing the bears. By Labour Day 1998 police in Thunder Bay had shot several bears, as had police in Sault Ste. Marie. In Timmins, they had five bear calls one day in the space of a few hours. Some communities were hiring trappers and others were making deals with local fur councils. What would provincial officials say to a call to help an injured raccoon?)

The Grey-Bruce Society, a recognized charity that receives donations and issues receipts for valuable income tax deductions, could be a case study in the diffident, almost bemused way the official world deals with issues relating to animals. The Society had been warned by provincial charity officials that it had better amend its letters patent setting out the activities it was supposed to be engaged in to bring them into line with what the Society was actually doing. Grey-Bruce had been using charitable funds, left to it specifically for a shelter, to finance its activities – cruelty investigations and placing seized animals in foster homes. It had no shelter and no firm plans to open one. Its letters patent said it would operate a shelter. After a court fight launched by the Weinbergs, the Society was ordered on August 6, 1997, to file a plan with the courts by June 30, 2001, a full four years later, to acquire and operate a shelter. Until then the bequest money was to be kept unspent. The letters patent were to be amended by the end of ninety days, and a delay beyond that would have to be shown not to be the Humane Society's fault. The charge that the president and vice-president were in a conflict of interest was rejected, as was the argument that affiliates had to abide by OSPCA policies on animals.

That the Public Guardian and Trustee, a provincial government office that polices charities, showed no interest in cracking down on the Society piqued the judge's interest during the court proceedings. It was public money being spent here, noted Madam Justice Nancy Mossip, and nothing had been done on the letters patent despite warnings for almost a year. "Why don't you care?" Judge Mossip demanded sternly of the Public Guardian's nervous-looking lawyer, Scott Vining, who replied that there didn't seem to be anything but a technical problem to overcome and that didn't merit the expense of an investigation. He did, however, want to argue that someone should pay the Public Guardian's legal costs for being there.

"The expense of an investigation outweighs your concern?" the judge asked with a laugh. She listened to his argument about costs and laughed again, saying, "I apprenticed in the wrong field. You guys get paid before you even walk out of court."

Indeed, a number of things about how Grey-Bruce operated might have interested anyone curious about the spending of tax-deductible donations. The Society's minutes, at least those that exist and are intact, show, for example, that the board of directors decided in October 1997 to halt work on the letters patent and get rid of its lawyer. They show an ongoing refusal to provide all board members, who are responsible for making decisions about what the Society does, with the names of the people who provided foster homes for seized animals, services for which expenses are paid. Sometimes there were promises, never kept, that the names would be given later and sometimes there were warnings that such a list might fall into the "wrong hands." At one point the minutes suggest that some board members or their relatives were fostering animals. At another, a letter from the Public Guardian's office in the fall of 1998 reminded the Society of a proffered bequest of more than $20,000. An estate lawyer had informed the Society in writing about the generous gift in January 1998, but had received no reply and could not disperse the money.

Concerns about how the Grey-Bruce Society operated were expressed to both the OSPCA and the Public Guardian's office in writing by Society secretary Alison Folkes when she resigned on January 30, 1999. She said she was fed up with being denied correspondence. She was convinced that the Society's mode of operation was not what it should be, in both common sense and legal terms, and she was worried about casual record-keeping or none at all for such things as funds from donation boxes. She was also tired of being treated like a meddlesome outsider. An energetic, capable women with years of experience as an assistant to demanding academics at McMaster University in Hamilton, Ont., she wanted to find less frustrating and more useful ways to volunteer her time. She spent hours of her own time on finding homes for stray animals. But she left the Society on good terms, saying she hoped the education kits she had assembled for schools would be used.[4]

In a way, even Grey-Bruce Humane Society members were outsiders. At the March 1999 annual meeting, members were told they would have to write in later and pay a fee of four dollars if they wanted to see the eight-page financial report for the year. That didn't make it easy to ask questions, certainly. On the blackboard the executive disclosed three totals: income, $113,254; expenses, $73,730; excess, $39,524. How much was spent on animals? By the president's reckoning, and attributing items like the full cost of telephones to that category, it totalled $14,640. Just what the rest of the expenses paid for in the total of $73,730 was not entirely clear, even if you had a copy of the financial statement. As for the cruelty investigations, the Society's one specific activity, taciturn agent Arnold Oliver admitted to about three hundred genuine calls from the public for the year. He said 122 animals had been removed from owners, but mentioned little else. He warned that all cases were "strictly confidential."

One Humane Society member, Frank Green, had worked as an animal-control officer for a dozen municipalities in the area and had offered his services as an unpaid volunteer to investigate calls from the public. Humane societies use many of these volunteers, although most do not have such relevant experience. Green got no response to his offer of help. Once, he told me, he and a provincial police officer had found two dogs being kept squashed together in a small, two-foot-square wooden box on a hot summer day and had called a Grey-Bruce agent to the owner's home. The agent found nothing wrong with the situation. Another time, Green said, he called the Society about a cat in need of veterinary care after it was badly scalded by liquid manure. He was told not to waste the Society's time, because "We don't do cats." Cats, like groundhogs, are considered pests in some rural areas, he said.[5]

"You'll see there's not much openness to change," he said. "Hunters control the society . . . . They don't do what they should as a humane society, that's my view. Grey-Bruce is kind of its own world. It could be a separate province. They don't like outsiders."

In the end, the Grey-Bruce Society elected a predominantly traditional board that night, including one past president, Doreen Ford, who would replace Trask. Soon after taking office, Ford declared her support of hunting to a local reporter.

Weinberg, who with his wife operated a private cat shelter in Meaford, said he pursued the Society in court because he believed the issues involved were significant for the state of animal welfare. He said he couldn't accept that a humane society could have the ability to control investigations into cruelty and then limit what they would investigate, as well as fail to get a simple shelter up and running. But a couple of years later, as he continued to work on an appeal, he found he was sometimes running out of steam. He had lived in the area for twenty years, but he wasn't seen as local. The community around him saw the business of taking the Humane Society to court as both odd and personal. "I'm going to be regarded as the biggest weirdo in Grey county," he said.[6]

As Weinberg tried without luck to find financial help for his appeal, he lamented the failure of the OSPCA to bring the Grey-Bruce Humane Society to heel or join his court action. The OSPCA was, after all, the most important force for animal welfare in the country's largest province. But by the early summer of 1999 it was struggling to get a grip on a provincial situation that threatened to spin out of control and overturn its policy-setting authority for local outlets. While animal rights activists had seemed easy to denounce or drum out at other times, activists from the opposite side of the political spectrum were handled delicately.

The OSPCA's twenty-five Humane Society branches had taken to acting like separate organizations, setting their own policies, sometimes hiding funds from head office and running up a tab of about $1 million owed to the provincial office in Newmarket, OSPCA chief executive officer Victoria Earle told me.[7] If the branches, which were actually part of the OSPCA, were carrying on this way, how could any control be brought to bear over the organization's much more independent thirty-five affiliate humane societies? The auditors were warning that the OSPCA's insurance policy and perhaps even its charitable status might be called into question, Earle said. Then came the court ruling over Grey-Bruce that suggested affiliates could disregard OSPCA policy. To make it even worse, the Society's fight in the tourist and farm area just two hours' drive north of Toronto was getting unwanted media attention.

So the OSPCA put a plan in place. Uniform policies would be set with input from the branches and affiliates; perhaps a moratorium would be imposed on any new branches or affiliates; branches would no longer have boards of directors but simply advisory committees. The public would know what humane societies were about when they gave their money or time or respect to them. Everyone would have the same notion about what cruelty investigations to undertake. These were the real prizes in OSPCA status: the sole authority to police animal cruelty cases and the public donations and often juicy municipal contracts that came with the respectable Humane Society label.

At least this policy conformity was the stated goal. Earle also made it clear that she was not out to be some big brother, laying down the law, confronting everyone and kicking out anyone who didn't come to heel. She believed she hadn't the legal authority, and she certainly lacked the taste for that approach. She would be trying for agreements. Perhaps there could be differences among different-size organizations, between rural and urban, she conceded. It might sound overly cautious, Earle said, but she had come to the OSPCA in March 1996 to find an organization rife with bad blood and a history of hard feelings. It's easy to criticize, she said, to propose that the Grey-Bruces of the group be kicked out, but these were volunteers and they wouldn't accept just being bossed around by paid OSPCA staff from out of town. All of that seemed to mean that the trend to making the local Humane Society even less active on the animal welfare front was not going to be reversed anytime soon in Ontario. (To be fair to Earle, there really was a bitter history that the SPCA in Ontario had to overcome, to which we'll return.)

By early 2000 the internal struggle had spilled into the open at a Toronto Board of Health meeting. A visibly angry Earle warned the city to think twice about continuing its contract with the Toronto Humane Society, the OSPCA's biggest and most influential affiliate. Outside the February 21 meeting, Earle described relations with the THS headed by Jack Slibar as "quite impossible." The THS had waged a back-room campaign to have the government strip the Society of its power to appoint inspectors, she told me. Slibar, who was not at the meeting, said he was "flabbergasted" by her comments to the board, which he put down to "institutional rivalry." He said he had advised the province to "modernize" the law so that a "neutral" body – not the OSPCA – trains and controls inspectors. The problem, according to him, was that the OSPCA could intimidate its membership and, as both advocate and enforcer, was in a position of conflict. The sentiment echoed the attitude of Grey-Bruce.

In Owen Sound the battle had often spilled into the public forum of letters to the editor of the local newspaper. One of them warned that the provincial OSPCA itself could be due for a real change of philosophy at the rate things were going. (OSPCA directors come from affiliates and branches throughout the province.)

"Across Ontario, pro-hunting and trapping communities have sought membership on local Humane Society boards with the objective of securing a seat on the OSPCA governing board of directors," S.M. Moss of Owen Sound wrote in a letter published in the local *Sun Times.*

> Why would sport hunters and trappers want to belong to the OSPCA? Because in its animal welfare position statement, OSPCA specifically condemns the hunting and trapping of animals for sport or by any person other than for their own consumption, opposes the farming or trapping of fur bearing animals, condemns the hunting of animals with dogs and the allowing of free running, non-tethered hounds or dogs to harass animals and . . . it condemns the use of

captive wildlife or species other than those being trained, during such training. . . . Clearly, a political battle is being waged locally which has little to do with animal welfare, or with a shelter for homeless, injured or abandoned animals. It has much to do with the preservation of power.[8]

Deanna Trask, daughter of then Human Society president Ross Trask, took animal activists to task in an April 24, 1999, letter. She quoted the Bible, from Genesis 1:25-26, to show how God gave man dominion over animals, and she asked, "What do they think animals were put on this good green earth for?" She talked about the "thrill of the hunt" and how proud she was that her father had stood up for his beliefs. Read further, C.D. White shot back in a letter to the editor on April 30. In Genesis 1:29, mankind is told to eat seeds and fruits. Besides, "Dominion can mean to rule, as in stewardship and protection, and not the right to destroy, as in hunting and killing."

As Weinberg struggled with his appeal plans, OSPCA's Victoria Earle waited for Grey-Bruce to prove that it would live up to its duty to all animals and to ensure that it followed up on cruelty cases. She expressed her frustration at the time and money being spent on such battles, saying she had been "building an organization from the ground up" since she had come to the job from a background in regional government. History dictated that she take a conciliatory approach, she said. She had already made a personal appearance at a Grey-Bruce board meeting to assert the head office's views. (By July 1999, with Grey-Bruce having failed to meet the court's June 7 deadline for changing its letter patent, Weinberg was back in court. The Public Guardian and Trustee's office said it was not to blame for the charity under its jurisdiction missing a legal deadline and that the Grey-Bruce Society, in a "quite extraordinary" delay in complying with a court order, had simply "done nothing" on the matter for two months.[9] Judge Mossip seemed unperturbed by the failure to obey her, asking Weinberg in one court appearance, as if he were the source of the problem, what it would take "for you to find joy in working with the humane society?")[10]

The Ontario SPCA is not unique in its problems. In Alberta some critics say the SPCA is too close to the agriculture industry, that it has not been critical enough of the Calgary Stampede. In British Columbia the SPCA has an outspoken critic in Judy Stone, president and founding director of Animal Advocates Society of B.C., a rescue and advocacy charity. Her organization, like many that operate across the country, takes animals that humane societies would otherwise put to death for reasons of age, health, behaviour, or simply lack of room and sticks with them until they can be placed in new homes. Stone, a retired roofing contractor, has countless stories about neglected, ailing, or abused dogs that, she said, the local SPCA shelter would not help even when notified. Groups like hers exist, she told me, because organizations that everyone thinks are protecting animals are not doing so, usually because they won't spend the money.[11] For individual humane societies, reviews are varied. Some, like the Winnipeg Humane Society, are singled out for praise even by activists who have little good to say about mainstream welfare groups.

If the Grey-Bruce battle in Ontario illustrates a lack of interest or concern by the authorities, it is part of a pattern that goes back decades for the entire province. When the OSPCA Act was amended in 1955, the provincial agency gained the power to enforce federal and provincial animal protection laws through humane societies, which it would charter. Existing humane societies became affiliates with separate boards of directors, and for a while all new societies operated as branches under the direct control of the central OSPCA.

For more than twenty-five years, from 1962 to 1989, Tom Hughes was OSPCA president. His was a stormy tenure for the most part, with affiliates and branches complaining about money from local donations being scooped up by head office, with member societies dropping out and new ones battling to become affiliates. Critics complained that while some shelters barely had enough money to feed animals in their care, the head office had gone to the expense of buying a farm north of Toronto and was even making plans for an animal art gallery and a library. There was controversy over the quality and quantity of cruelty investigations and the training of agents. There was anger at a sudden switch of policy – all the way from opposing legislation that would require shelters to turn animals over to research facilities to supporting the law, despite the collection of public donations aimed specifically at fighting the government move. Some people complained that Hughes himself had tested a pistol on seal pups and allowed dogs to be shot. In 1982 a report on the OSPCA prepared for the provincial solicitor general made a series of recommendations that would impose some order. Little happened.

Hughes, a colourful, outspoken animal welfare advocate with a tendency to personalize struggles, has stated that animal rights supporters make up no more than 10 per cent of the movement, and that the idea of rights is nothing more than a lazy media catchphrase. After forty-five years in the animal movement, he has concluded that pets now have a pretty good life and that it is farm animals that need attention. His criticisms have, not surprisingly, drawn fire from provincial farm defenders.[12]

In a June 1987 report to their colleagues four OSPCA board members argued that Hughes was running the Society as "an autocratic fiefdom," that he was out of the office half of the time yet refused to let staff make decisions, although they were blamed for any problems. Hughes's daughter, Debi Davis, was said to be invoking her father's authority in dealings with the staff, although she was only an accounting clerk. In September 1987 the executive committee narrowly passed a vote of no confidence in Hughes (in a 13-14 split), and the president agreed to resign and depart the board by 1989.[13] Still, throughout 1988 people complained about Hughes keeping opponents off the board by refusing to approve new societies.[14] A group in Alliston had been operating as a regular humane society and shelter for a year with town approval, despite Hughes's refusal to grant them status. The president argued that too many of the more independent affiliates failed for money reasons and that new outlets should be centrally controlled branches. In December a Barrie court upheld his refusal to recognize Alliston.

• • •

Earlier, in 1986, Hughes had leaped into a battle surrounding the Toronto Humane Society. In April 1987 he stripped the country's largest Humane Society of its affiliate status, saying its radical style could hamper the provincial organization and tarnish its image. One critic who worked at the Toronto Humane Society during the turmoil said that the Toronto Society had laid thirty charges in cruelty investigations in one year compared to the three or four laid by other OSPCA agents in the rest of the province, raising questions about the OSPCA's image. At the time the OSPCA boasted that its net worth was more than $2 million and the real value probably in excess of $7 million, based on increased property values.[15]

The battle in the 1980s for the Toronto Humane Society – not just the country's largest humane society but one of the biggest in North America – was flamboyant and fabulous, full of melodrama, inflammatory rhetoric, and genuine conflict. In other countries it would make an engaging fictionalized movie. In Canada it would merit a historic roadside plaque if it were any other sort of battle. It revealed the tantalizing possibility that activists from the animal rights side of the movement see in the agencies of the conservative animal welfare world – the classic lure of working from within. In the end it offered a real-life example of what serious animal activists might want to accomplish and what can happen when it seems they have a chance to make good on their goals.

The battle has deservedly become a legend, both for what it says to a new generation of activists and for the enduring lessons it taught opponents of animal rights groups across the country. It was a pivotal battle in another way, because the so-called troublemakers who were driven out today fill key positions in national animal organizations. It even provided a legal living, if only briefly, to David Barbarash, who went on to lead police lists of animal rights activists in Canada and to become the public voice in North America for the underground Animal Liberation Front.

For a brief, thrilling, and utterly unrealistic time, the Toronto Humane Society seemed the place to be for animal activists. With the affluence and position of the Society as a springboard, they were going to do great things for animals. They were going to move the most respectable animal welfare organization into social activism. Today that sense of excitement and optimism of the mid-1980s seems like a distant dream. One former Toronto Humane Society board member (and its former wildlife co-ordinator) called it a "Camelot stage," a time when the Society was one of the best on the continent.[16] It was certainly one of the largest – with some $13 million in assets at the time. Ironically, the whole period that the conservatives of the Toronto Humane Society considered a time of never-to-be-repeated troubles was set in play by the Society itself. There had been a feeling that things were not going as well as they could, that this was an organization that could do more and should have a cautious injection of new blood.

The 1970s had been a bustling time, with noisy big annual meetings and policy debates about giving up animals to medical research, lobbying against leghold traps for wildlife and in favour of local bylaws to regulate pet stores. It was also a time when cobras were still on sale to snake fanciers in Toronto. But by the 1980s, things had soured. Long before the radicals arrived, there were complaints internally that the Society was not taking a strong enough stand on local slaughterhouse conditions, that it should be laying charges over animals suffering what one news headline aptly described as "agony before death."[17] There were complaints about the Society's lack of support for efforts to oppose the sale of live animals in downtown Kensington Market. One anonymous campaigner wrote to the directors in July 1982 to express disappointment that not one Society representative turned out to an investigative visit to the market, with its grim, caged animals, kept dirty and thirsty and prodded like so many melons by customers. Angry market shop owners had screamed obscenities and threatened to douse the investigator with boiling water and smash a news photographer's camera.

The early 1980s brought a steady undercurrent of complaint and, periodically, unflattering news coverage about the Toronto Humane Society's treatment of animals. Inside the Society's downtown Toronto office the mood was one of cynicism.

In September 1983 Society directors and the chief staff veterinarian were trading open hostilities in prominent stories in the Toronto
papers. Five directors wanted the City of Toronto to step in, as a key
funder and customer, because of mismanagement and, more troubling, what they considered poor care of animals. Reports of tension
appeared concerning the apparent resignation of acting general manager Michael O'Sullivan, who, according to confused news reports,
had either quit or was fired but kept coming to work. (O'Sullivan,
later president and executive director of the Humane Society of
Canada, said he was fired.) The directors complained that the last of
$200,000 left to the Society by Glenn Gould was going to be used to
buy one of his pianos, that four former employees were suing for
wrongful dismissal, and that jobs and contracts were going without
tender to board friends and family. They said animals were getting
sick from lack of staff to care for them and being returned to the shelter for treatment (43 per cent came back in June compared to a usual
18 to 25 per cent). The Toronto papers carried almost daily news
reports of the conflicts.

The chief veterinarian, Dr. Angelo Filiplic, blamed the board's no-
kill policy, as well as staff shortages, for the problems. He told the
press that by keeping suffering animals alive "against nature's way,"
the Society was being heartless. "We should actually be charged with
cruelty to animals," he said. The vet wanted the board to leave such
matters to professionals like himself. They should forget efforts such
as the foster care program, which sent pregnant and newborn strays to
outside foster homes for special care rather than simply killing them
off. The allegations and counterallegations were not the stuff to
inspire public confidence. The OSPCA's Hughes weighed in on that
argument, saying that the Toronto no-kill policy and foster care were
unrealistic, based on emotion, and the cause of an increase in disease
rates. The business of keeping animals alive was not a popular one at
the Humane Society in those years, it seemed.[18]

An internal March 1, 1984, managerial memo noted that there
were no hard and fast rules about which animals were to die. Many
young dogs and cats were killed because they were judged not to be

able to withstand the diseases and conditions of life in a shelter. It seemed the Society saw the buyers rather than the animals as its clients. The memo explained, "The Society attempts to adopt a good quality animal to the members of the public. . . . If very young or, for that matter, very old animals were put up for adoption, the reputation of the Society could be jeopardized as these animals would create many problems for the new owners."

At one point the board decided to put up a sign in the shelter saying that no animal was ever killed off because of lack of cage space. Actually, the board had been passing resolutions all that year that healthy animals would not be killed – unless there was a shortage of cage space. The killing policy was important on a practical level – it always had the potential to cause controversy. For example, Holly Flegg, a woman whose organization tried to rescue doomed cats when their time was up at the Humane Society, fought bitterly with the board over her thwarted attempts to rescue cats and kittens. One day she drove into the city from the suburbs in a snowstorm for a mother-kitten family she was promised would be held. When she got to the Humane Society she was told the animals must die because "they might at some future date become ill."[19]

At other times, Flegg complained to the board, some of her rescued kittens had been judged ill and were scheduled to die but turned out to be perfectly healthy. Adult cats doomed because of ear mites were treatable, and other cats or kittens released to her as healthy were deformed. One former employee told of dark jokes about a veterinarian known as Dr. Death who ordered baby squirrels in the shelter's wildlife area killed rather than care for them over the winter. Wildlife, said another former staffer, was usually killed off.

Caring for wild animals is a messy, difficult job at best and, it seems, the Toronto Humane Society in that period handled that business badly. Barry Kent MacKay, a writer, naturalist, and wildlife artist – and former wildlife co-ordinator for the Society – said he was once appalled as a board member to find a dead bird unnoticed in a cage, stuck by its intestines to paper towelling from a wound that had not been noticed.[20] He convinced a veterinarian friend, Richard Evans, the medical director of an Illinois wildlife centre, to make an after-hours visit to assess the Society's handling of wild animals. Evans' report to the board, dated September 18, 1984, was scathing. It talked of substandard medical care, of untreated, ailing birds, and of a lack of interest in treating common birds or young wild animals. He considered the let-them-die approach to be old-fashioned and a betrayal of the Society's stated goal of helping all species who could not help themselves.

In April 1983, former Society president and veteran animal activist Stephanie Brown joined other former officers in signing a letter to members of the Society. They charged that the organization was failing to treat the animals of low-income people or to carry on educational work and that it was attempting to keep out newcomers by trying to scrap a time limit on how long directors could serve. Brown, who served as president from 1974 to 1978, was later threatened with legal repercussions by a Humane Society lawyer if she did not stop making such accusations.[21]

By the end of 1983 the City of Toronto had decided to take over the Society for a year because of what appeared to be endless internal conflicts and charges of inadequate managing. By 1984 the city had decided that it would in future take care of the street control of animals with its own staff and equipment, the dog-catcher function. The Humane Society would do the sheltering and adoption. This move would halve the city's annual payments to the Society, to about $600,000.

What the Society needed, clearly, was something to boost morale, improve its image, and generally inject a little buzz. That's where Vicky Miller came in – and when all hell broke loose. Miller was a co-founder of ARK II, a high-profile Toronto animal rights group considered radical: "a fanatical animal rights group with links to the radical Animal Liberation Front," declared *The Toronto Sun*.[22] Miller had drawn public attention when she led an effective campaign against a U.S. animal show that was supposed to come to Canada, recalled MacKay, the board member chosen to approach her with an invitation to join the board. ARK II had had little success in getting the

Humane Society or other groups to join forces on issues, so Miller, deciding to try a little fighting from within, accepted the invitation.[23]

At the time she thought of the Toronto Humane Society as a body that rounded up animals and executed them. On one of the first occasions in which she was quoted in press after coming on board she complained that the Society was a "slaughterhouse" in which animals were killed or left to die in cages. Miller had star appeal in the younger, more aggressive animal world. An appealing, charismatic woman, she had proved herself in a genuinely gruelling thirty-day hunger strike in the fall of 1984 over the treatment of a yellow baboon at the University of Western Ontario in London. She and three other strikers staged their protest in a mobile home parked outside the downtown Toronto offices of the Heart and Stroke Foundation, the charity funding the research. She collapsed a month later, twenty-five pounds lighter, and had to call off the strike. It had failed to win the release of the animal, but at least had garnered some attention for the issue of animal research and for the sad little baboon who had been restrained for months on end, motionless and alone, in a chair in a windowless room. Vancouver activist Peter Hamilton of Lifeforce, a veteran of the animal movement who had been involved in high-profile lab investigations with activists in the United States and believed in the power of the law, tried to take the researchers to court.

The yellow primate had tubes in her stomach as part of a cholesterol study.[24] One news report described her as shedding hair, limp, with sores on her bottom, trembling at the approach of a visitor to the six-by-eight-foot room.[25] The charity said the baboon was not in distress. The university said that, given the loss of twenty-six thousand people in the province each year to heart attacks and strokes, "The ends justify the means."

Miller returned from her hunger strike to applause from the Toronto Humane Society board of directors. This was a woman whose efforts had brought full-page, sympathetic treatment of the doomed baboon, a woman who had suffered for what she believed in. She was hard to resist. They knew but didn't seem to care that unknown intruders had broken into Western's laboratory the summer before to photograph the baboon. Within months another break-in occurred, with theft of cats and a monkey, from the same university. The action sent shock waves through the research community. Later, in November 1986, *The Toronto Sun* published a photograph of Miller beside one of an unknown liberationist, face covered, holding a cat from the university raid. Both were wearing similar cable-knit sweaters. There was dark talk of radicals abroad in the animal welfare world. But before all that, the board decided to invite Miller to become its president.

A board committee including MacKay and other activists was put to work on recommendations for the Society's future goals. A preliminary report in March 1986 set teeth on edge. The document, "New Directions," proposed that the Society target the sources of cruelty to animals, not just clean up after them. The fashion-fur industry, medical research, and product-testing and wildlife issues were all considered prime areas for reform. Moreover, the committee urged the rich Toronto Society to see itself as having a national and perhaps international role as a leader in the animal world.

To reach its goals the Toronto Humane Society, according to this blueprint, would try just about every legal avenue, from lobbying to boycotts to protest and legal action. It would make serious fundraising efforts to put its work beyond the mercies of the revenue from a contract with the city for sheltering animals or random donations. This was an ambitious, forthright plan that would take the staid Society into the wars. But it was also, for all the fuss it caused, a rather orthodox plan to bring permanent change in many areas the board had been discussing in past years. What the new plan did suggest was that the Toronto Humane Society would go all out to make things change. Instead of periodically complaining about research using animals or garments made of fur, the Society would assign paid staff and give them time and a budget to lobby for changes in public policy on these issues. That was as radical as the attitude the Society had taken in its origins – and rarely since.[26] Above all, it would mean spending some of the Society's wealth rather than continuing, as before, to protect investments.

The first project launched, with funding from five Ontario member groups, including the Toronto Humane Society, was the formation of a coalition aimed at ending the seizure of animals from pounds and their use in research, teaching, or testing. The coalition would investigate the trade in these animals as well as the issue of stolen pets being used in research. At the time most of the dogs and cats used in Ontario research facilities were coming from pounds. This was one of the first projects to unite the animal movement in Ontario.

Things were now ticking down to trouble. Miller soon felt mounting frustration with the Society and her inability as president to make change. She told board member Robert Hambley that she wanted a few new animal people on the board. He refused, Miller said. "It was clear I was just intended to be a puppet sort of thing." So Miller and her supporters hatched a proxy plan, the notion of using the rules against the establishment to put activists on the board. In the June 1986 annual general meeting, Miller came armed with nine hundred proxy votes. When the smoke cleared, nine of sixteen places on the board of directors went to activists. And when it became clear that they had been thwarted and that others had won, the official slate of candidates and their supporters "just stormed out," Miller said. "Nobody actually said anything. It was a weird night."

Newspapers that summer regularly called the board election a "coup" and made a great fuss over the transformation of the Toronto Humane Society into one of the most powerful animal rights groups on the continent. With an operating budget of $2.5 million, even a 10 per cent limit on charities' use of money for lobbying meant there was a lot of cash to pour into the fight for key issues.

But the thwarted board members were not silent. Former director Adelaide Campbell wrote in August to ask the Public Guardian and Trustee's office to investigate the Society, arguing that money for services to animals was going instead to support international animal rights causes. The Public Guardian asked for financial reports and information on the coalition against pound seizure. In November 1986, Hambley urged Attorney General Ian Scott to act. The board, he said, had been seized through "electoral impropriety" – although he himself would later copy the proxy approach. He noted that the OSPCA was reviewing the Society's "fitness" to handle cruelty cases, that the City of Toronto was reconsidering its contract.

"A climate of fear has been deliberately created," he wrote to Scott. "Nobody knows who animal rights terrorists are, but they do exist. The clique running the Society is from ARK II, described by press reports as 'cult-like' in the eyes of the public. What individual can risk to be seen in the way of millions of dollars? Specifically there have been threats of violence. Managers fear for their jobs."[27]

Meanwhile, board meetings had become "crazed," Miller said. "We were way past rational. There was no discussion going on." She had plunged ahead, establishing new programs on the issues identified in the "New Directions" document. Eager young staffers were hired, thrilled at the idea of being on the cutting edge. But Miller was suffering from an illness, and the stress continued to mount. A *Toronto Sun* reporter followed her everywhere, she said, popping up with questions in underground parking garages in a way that she would have called stalking if the pursuer hadn't been a journalist. The angry board members were talking about misuse of money, and Miller began to wonder if she was being set up for a jail term. Later she would remember how mean she thought they were to each other. One board member, a discreet gay man, was sent roses at his office with a card bearing a man's name. Another board member was sent dog feces.

The new year, 1987, opened with Toronto city council wondering if money it had paid for an animal shelter was being used in inappropriate ways. By then Barbarash, hired by the Society to probe the source of animals used in university research, had been charged with vandalism at the Kentucky Fried Chicken outlet. He was driving a Society vehicle when he was arrested. By May 1987 the Society was in court facing an attempt by the Public Guardian and Trustee to put it into trusteeship and to stop funds for the campaign against using animals from pounds in research on the grounds that it was an unacceptable level of political activity for a charity. Hambley had begun another court bid to overturn the June elections. Eventually the elections were overturned, the old board reinstated, and new elections ordered.

Miller, the former ballet teacher who had gone from veterinarian technician to animal rights activist, had begun to lose her voice. First random syllables would fail as she spoke. Finally, for four years, her voice was stilled by her undiagnosed ailment. Before that happened, in 1988, she left the Toronto Humane Society and the experiment of working from within. She went home to her farm to recover and, later, to write a children's book, *Tribe of Star Bear*. She more or less disappeared from view, but she kept a heroine's status for many people in the animal movement. She didn't sell out, and she didn't flinch.

"I had a great regard for her," said Catherine Ens, who regularly travelled by bus from St. Catharines just to sit on the Toronto board, where the action was. "I would say that more than anybody else I ever met, she really put animal rights on the map in Canada."

Not long before Miller left, Holly Penfound arrived at the Society as co-ordinator of volunteers and then became program director. It proved to be an exhilarating experience.[28] The group worked weekends, at home, on their own time, and their lobbying and education programs hit what Penfound understood were hot issues – the fur industry, seal hunting, agriculture. But despite the excitement, everyone also felt the executive turmoil, as well as the increasing disapproval of what they were doing. To top it off, there was labour strife. The Camelot phase was almost dead.

Stephen Best, a veteran of the opposition to the seal hunt, had been brought onto the Society board by Miller in 1986 and quickly moved into a new position as executive director. But he was soon fired in a falling out with Miller. Kathleen Hunter, a co-founder of ARK II, replaced him. Her management in the time of troubles is not remembered kindly by the radicals.

In late May 1990 the board prepared to fill five vacant seats, a normal exercise. But feelings ran high. A vicious little newsletter of unknown origin was waiting on everyone's desk one morning, attacking staff members and spreading personal gossip. Staff access to the offices on weekends was cut off. Some thought voice mail was being intercepted. There were video cameras in the hallways and warnings that staff should not fraternize with board members. Anonymous literature named publicity director Liz White, wildlife co-ordinator MacKay, Penfound, and research co-ordinator Tita Zierer as friends of independent candidates for the board elections, people who favoured a no-kill shelter and a move into broader issues.[29] On May 30, 1990, the independents were defeated at a raucous annual general meeting. (In accounts of these times all meetings are described as raucous.) The meeting was chaired by treasurer Robert Hambley, who came equipped with hundreds of proxy votes from absent members. The old sense of order had returned to the board.

The Society's feisty program staff knew they were in trouble during the lead-up to the board elections, Penfound said. Programs were already under fire. The next day they were called one by one to Hunter's office, where the end was pronounced. After twenty years as a volunteer, four years as a director, and four years on staff, MacKay found out his position could no longer be afforded and he was laid off. White and Zierer heard the same verdict. Penfound, a non-union manager, was fired. All of them were told to leave the premises immediately. Defeated board candidates, crying foul, said the four were responsible for almost all of the legislative gains made over the past several years. Hambley called the losing candidates "crybabies" and blamed the moves on a deficit. Three other staffers quit immediately in protest. Catherine Ens, an admirer of the fired workers, said she had been given no hint that a decision was to be made on staff when she left the board meeting early. She herself soon quit the board. She said she had to fend off demands to sign statements that she had not leaked information to the public about the Society. For people like Ens, the promise of the place was clearly gone.

Penfound, former Society investigator Rob Laidlaw, and MacKay moved on to Zoocheck Canada, now a hard-nosed, crusading organization at work across the country on issues involving zoos and wild animals. White, a former nurse who got involved with animal issues in 1987 when Clayton Ruby convinced her to take on the communications job at the Society, went on with several others to found Animal Alliance of Canada. A woman with an impish air and deadly political instincts, White soon became one of the best-known names in

Canada's animal movement, and the Alliance would become the best-known group aside from local humane societies. It took on a full and aggressive array of programs – from the use of animals in research to pets and wildlife. Humane Society anti-fur campaign co-ordinator Ainslee Willock quit and organized the Canadian Alliance for Fur-bearing Animals. The Humane Society programs that had caused so much controversy largely left with all these workers. "This is the legacy. They weren't squashed," Ens said. "They've made a name for themselves in animal rights in Canada."

Though gone, the radicals were not forgotten. When MacKay, who went on to write a column for *The Toronto Star*, called members of the board to ask questions about a policy a year or so after his departure, he received a stiff legal warning from THS solicitor Howard Levitt, who told him, "We are extremely suspect as to your motives and your real purpose in gathering this information. If you use it for any purpose other than simply objectively writing a column, we intend to report your activities to your superiors at the Toronto Star." Levitt asked MacKay not to deal with the Toronto Humane Society in any of his columns.[30]

MacKay saw this response as a case of paranoia, and it reminded him of the attitude of the Mackenzie Institute's reports on animal activists. A January 1993 advisory on the animal rights movement from the Institute declared that "hard left/anarchist" animal rights activists had a self-hatred that they were projecting onto society and that had led them to support causes that might damage or warp "western values, customs, traditions or symbols."[31]

To activists who had followed the battle, the presence of Jack Slibar in the Society's office seemed to say everything about what had become of the organization. Slibar took over as chief operating officer in January 1997 after serving five years as a lobbyist. He was also a research associate of the Mackenzie Institute. Former executive director Kathleen Hunter, last vestige of the so-called radical period, was quietly ushered out, and chairman Dr. Howard Seiden pronounced it the end of an era. As Metro Toronto worked on integrating its parts into one megacity in 1997, Slibar began a long, hard pitch to take over all animal services in the city, with government buildings and assets to go to the Society. By late February 2000, the city still had not decided if it would strip $100,000 from dental programs for the poor to give the Toronto Humane Society an increase it was demanding to its $726,000 contract. Nor had it decided if it should give the Society a bigger role in animal services or if it even wanted to buy all the services that the Society was providing.

When I spoke with him, Slibar remained proud of his association with the Mackenzie Institute, which according to him needed no defence as a quality think tank. Any criticism of it, he said, probably came from activists not happy that the Toronto Humane Society was still operating and effective.[32] He said he could make no comment on the radical phase of the Society, which was before his time, except to say that in the aftermath he had to work hard to re-establish its credibility with government. The respect of the business community had become evident in the partnerships the Society was developing with pet store chains and food stores. The Society's priority under his leadership was to focus on front-line services – cruelty cases, pet identification, more traditional issues. Public policy, Slibar said, is the art of compromise.

Still, the purge of the radicals did not bring an end to the Society's controversial image. Toronto city councillor Pam McConnell quit the board in February 1996, complaining that requests for financial information were being "stonewalled" and her questions on other issues met with hostility. She had asked for information about a lawsuit against Penfound, then working as an assistant to another councillor. Lawyer Howard Levitt promptly sent her warning letters amid accusations that McConnell had threatened the Society. The city solicitor in turn chided Levitt for appearing to be trying to intimidate McConnell.

By early 1996 the Society was being twitted in the press for going to court to keep secret its $726,000 contract for shelter services despite a municipal freedom of information ruling to disclose it. In its defence, the THS provided a letter from John Thompson of the Mackenzie Institute warning of a real threat to humane societies from terrorists. Calls were being made for the city to tender the shelter services. But there were friends out there too. The Kitchener-Waterloo Humane Society took time to send its written endorsement of the Toronto Society to Toronto city council and to suggest, "Animal rights fringe groups, some of the same ones interested in taking over the OSPCA, are critical of the THS."

The controversy within the Toronto Humane Society did finally die down, but so too had something else. Like the 1997 meeting before it, the Toronto Society's 1998 annual general meeting took about half an hour. Held on July 24, 1998, in the middle of a hot working day, it was attended by only 21 of more than 814 eligible voting members, and there were no questions or even comments from the floor. The only sign of life came when the silent bodies responded to chairman Howard Seiden's cheerful invitation to help themselves to coffee and cookies. "Not like the old days," said one older man as he walked out.

"It's not like the old days," echoed a woman wearing a Humane Society staff shirt. "Is that good or bad?" she was asked. She shrugged, expressionless.

• • •

The Kitchener-Waterloo Humane Society was one of the few animal agencies voicing concern that the OSPCA was under any real threat of takeover from animal rights activists. But it was a society with its own views on many issues. When Grey-Bruce was taken to court by the Weinbergs in 1998 and 1999, Kitchener-Waterloo was invoked again and again as an example of a Society that did not follow OSPCA policies. On its Internet Web site and in brochures, the Society explained in detail its policy statements, including: support for the use of dogs in hunting; support for hunting wildlife, whales, and seals and for trapping; approval of beak-trimming of fowl and other surgical alterations to farm animals; approval of dog-training compounds using wild animals as quarry; and acceptance of the use of animals in rodeos, circuses, and other entertainments. The OSPCA opposed all of these practices either outright or with explicit restrictions.

Like the Toronto Humane Society, Kitchener-Waterloo had its own internal upheaval, which also came in the mid-1980s. But when the dust settled – with board members replaced and new elections held – the Society was left in the hands of firm opponents of animal rights. General manager Jim Cosgrove explained in a Society newsletter that animal rights supporters were people with a hidden agenda of vegetarianism and the abolition of any use of animals, people who see farmers and animal users as "depraved monsters." The newsletter disparaged the "movie stars, self-made wildlife experts and outright charlatans" of the animal rights movement. Animal welfare people, by contrast, were concerned about the well-being of animals and the right of people to use them humanely and wisely.

Like the Toronto Humane Society, the Kitchener-Waterloo Society was burdened throughout the 1990s by accusations that it was too ready to kill the animals it took in, though it repeatedly denied those charges. At one point a local veterinarian embarrassed the Society at a city council committee meeting with a graphic attack on its use of lethal injections into cats' hearts as a means of euthanasia. It was, said the vet, agonizing and unnecessary, a form of euthanasia not approved by the Ontario Veterinary Medical Association. The Society responded angrily that it had stopped the practice just days before, but defended the approach as less costly because it did not require a veterinarian to do it. At the time the Society was running up hefty surpluses and the public response to the controversy was not welcomed by city councillors.

As in Toronto, a controversy also developed about how the Kitchener-Waterloo Society was spending money. The Kitchener-Waterloo controversy of the 1990s focused for a time on the purchase of a farm as a long-term investment and large animal shelter.[33] Some critics attacked the decision to make such a long-term land investment – especially given that two Society managers rented houses on the property. In 1997, for example, only $28,581 would be spent on veterinary care for some twelve thousand animals handled by the shelter, more than three hundred and sixty of them picked up with injuries. It was, repeatedly, a debate about priorities and purposes. By June 1999, though, OSPCA chief executive officer Earle was describing the Kitchener-Waterloo Society as being in "a time of change."[34] A new president and new manager were being put in place, she said, and there had been an improvement in the Society's compliance with provincial policy.

When Toronto Humane Society director Ens went home to St. Catharines, she served on the board of the Lincoln County Humane Society there. She even made a run for the presidency in 1989, in an election of executive and directors that bogged down in accusations and counteraccusations and calls even from politicians for an investigation. Once again, the conflict ended with activists departing and the winners taking steps to ensure that their opponents would never again get so far, citing Toronto as the bogeyman.

Ens headed into the March 1989 Lincoln election expecting trouble.[35] She and others had complained in advance that prospective new members who supported her or other activist candidates for the board could not obtain membership cards. Photocopied forms they used as an alternative were rejected on the night of the election, preventing them from voting. She was defeated by an exotic animal collector in what was described as the worst rift in the Society's seventy-two years. None of the animal rights activists was elected, and six activist board members were defeated. The crowd was so tightly packed into the Society quarters that the meeting briefly considered adjourning until a larger hall could be booked.[36] The outgoing president, lawyer Dianne Grenier, said the rush for memberships in the weeks before the vote was overwhelming and acknowledged that the problems might have helped determine the outcome of the vote. One scrutineer of the voting wrote to the provincial solicitor general denouncing the proceeding as a fraud. Ontario Conservative Party leader Andy Brandt also wrote asking for an investigation. Neither the province nor the office of the Public Guardian and Trustee intervened.

New Lincoln Humane Society president Ashley Shannon invoked the need to prevent a Toronto-style takeover by animal rights activists when, not long after the elections, his board changed the rules. The new bylaws led one municipal politician to quit, expressing shock at the sight of the board rejecting applications for membership in the Society. Each application had been voted upon individually by the board. As well, anyone wanting to run for the board had to serve at least one year on a committee – only the board made appointments to committees – and candidates could be disallowed if they served on the executive of what was considered a competing organization. The board would determine what constituted a competing organization.

Shannon told reporters for the *St. Catharines Standard* that activists posed a big threat to humane societies. He referred to activists as people who were willing to break the law, who thought animals had the same rights as people, and who were so irresponsible that they were willing to distress people with upsetting allegations about mistreatment of animals. Shannon's neighbours were more interested in his private pursuits than his presidency. At one point Shannon had some thirty-eight animals (counting birds, monkeys, bears, tigers, cougars, and dogs) living in his backyard, and some of his monkeys had made repeated escapes. It was, he explained, a life-long hobby to own exotic animals and not a business, although he gave away some of the creatures to zoos. (The OSPCA disapproves of the sale of exotic animals.)

Ens, who helped to establish the Niagara-Brock Action for Animals group and was also president of the Animal Assistance Society, dismissed Shannon's views of activists and said she was tired of hearing of them spoken of as terrorists. If a humane society does nothing to champion causes and is nothing but a dog pound, she asked, why bother having a board of directors?

Safe from activists it might have been, but the Lincoln Humane Society was not safe from controversy after that election. By 1990 it was under fire for suddenly deciding to sell its nearly new shelter, to which the city had contributed $125,000.[37] By 1996 the Society was back on the front pages over complaints about how many animals it killed and its refusal to neuter or spay the ones it adopted out.[38] In 1998 it was the Society's use of carbon dioxide for killing animals that put it back on page one. It was one of the few societies in Ontario still using the process, and news of that practice brought a flood of outraged calls to the local radio show. The procedure involved trapping an animal in a wooden box, pumping the box full of carbon dioxide, and waiting a minute or two for the animal to suffocate. An injection of barbiturates or sedatives was the faster, less distressing choice of most societies by then.

"When you're fighting with the Humane Society, you're not really doing anything for animals. How much time do you want to spend on it?" Ens said to explain why she gave up on those mainstream groups after her experiences in Toronto and St. Catharines. "Thousands of young people won't give money or effort to humane societies because they don't seem to do anything."

After twenty years as an animal advocate (a term she said she often chose over animal rights activist to avoid the negative public image), Ens was not willing to fight from within that establishment any longer. She had arrived at her activism abruptly – a vegetarian boyfriend at university and the sight of a truck full of chickens with their wings sticking out, flapping in wrong ways, and "all of a sudden it became quite clear." It seemed a better use of her time, she said, to work with a group keen on making a difference rather than to join a humane society.

· · ·

Michael O'Sullivan of the Humane Society of Canada, a charity separate from the SPCA or Ontario Humane Society, said he has no time for the internal politics of the animal movement. The Humane Society of Canada – established for public education and the conservation and protection of animals and the environment – is one of the more affluent Canadian animal organizations. It attracted about $900,000 in donations from mail campaigns in 1998, with a special focus on preventing cruelty. Rather than providing shelters for animals, O'Sullivan said, its projects included a data base on cruelty cases for prosecutors, rewards for helping to convict abusers, eco-tours, and disaster relief for animals. All social movements have in-fighting, O'Sullivan said, and wrangling only discourages public support. A veteran of almost thirty years in the animal movement, O'Sullivan defends humane societies against criticism. In an interview he dealt with the issue of the illegal activists with his signature bluntness – they're "stupid." The notion of animal rights, he said, makes a great discussion but little sense in a world where even humans may lack rights.[39]

ARK II continues its radical, action-oriented existence in Toronto. It demonstrates and shows horrifying videos of animal abuse and prides itself on being the first to have put a genuinely naked person out in the winter for the "I'd Rather Go Naked" anti-fur campaign. It attracts people who don't mind being considered radical, who are prepared to be unpaid volunteers and who feel a need for direct action, said Danielle Divincenzo, one of ARK II's directors.[40] As a teenager, she was briefly involved with the Toronto Humane Society when its newsletter promoted vegetarianism and she was trying to figure out what she could eat now that she was one. The Humane Society was different then, she said. That was the 1980s. By the end of the 1990s her group was fielding inquiries about animal rights often referred to it by the Toronto Humane Society.

About 150 humane societies from across the country belong to an umbrella group, the Canadian Federation of Humane Societies (CFHS), which says it represents more than four hundred thousand Canadians. The CFHS is the animal organization that is most accepted in official circles in the country. It is invited to join in when the federal government is bringing together animal welfare and animal user groups to discuss issues ranging from transport to genetic engineering. It has membership on the Canadian Council on Animal Care, which oversees research laboratories, and it is included in the writing of voluntary national codes of conduct for the agricultural industry. Its critics call it a fig leaf. Executive director Frances Rodenburg has heard all the criticisms, and she has some of her own. Read back through the minutes of CFHS meetings since the start in 1957, she said, and you will see the same issues, over and over and over. "We always have this interminable debate about what our position should be on issues."[41]

CFHS members must reach a consensus for policy decisions, and the difference between rural and urban societies is marked. Rural societies don't want to be seen as radical lest they lose supporters. Even writing the menu can be a problem when the members gather annually. Vegetarianism is "political," Rodenburg said. "It's a moral judgement. It was a political question if the vegetable option was above or below the meat option."

But despite all the criticisms and the accusations of being used as a foil, Rodenburg said she considers it worthwhile for the Federation at least to be at the table with industry and government. In more than fifteen years with the CFHS, Rodenburg said she had seen public concern rise and fall over animal issues. The falls usually coincided with bad economic times, when the mood towards everything becomes less generous. In 1998 she considered it a period of "backlash from industry about animal welfare and animal rights." Rodenburg herself is respected by activists who have worked with her on issues, but the CFHS as an organization is more often panned for its status quo positions than praised. In its favour, it has been praised for producing a tough video about circus animals and for its help to Nova Scotian activists on that issue.

Retired Brig.-Gen. Chris Snider of Ottawa, a former vice-president of the OSPCA and later chairman, left the CFHS board after concluding that it was being crippled by its internal divisions.[42] When the Federation wanted to run a campaign on the seal hunt, the Maritime affiliates objected. When it was rodeos, the Alberta members refused. An article on vegetarianism for the CFHS publication brought complaints from British Columbia. The animal movement is huge, he said, but "horribly fragmented. All of the people in it are very enthusiastic and they all want to do things their way."

Stephanie Brown went on to work with CFHS after serving as Toronto Humane Society president in the 1970s because she wanted to come to grips with larger issues. For a time she was president. But she became frustrated. The CFHS rejected a paper she wrote on poultry because it talked about vegetarianism – "a red flag with some member societies," she said. Efforts to convince the organization to join an international coalition fighting for better conditions for animals on farms were rebuffed. Even the CFHS video on animals in circuses took painful efforts to produce because of the wide variety of members' views to be accommodated.[43] "They're moving further and further to the right," Brown said. "The CFHS is seen as respectable and it does dick all."

The way Stephen Huddart sees it, what the CFHS does is a very Canadian job. The conservatism is a virtue rather than a flaw. Huddart, the director of education and community relations for the B.C. Society for the Prevention of Cruelty to Animals, said the idea is to get people talking and find middle ground. It is the same job his organization tries to do provincially, he said, because it is a middle-of-the-road group with greater access to funds and openings into the establishment than is available to more radical organizations. According to Huddart, the more radical groups or those that focus, say, on animals used for food specifically, all have their place in the overall movement.[44]

The Calgary Humane Society is also a middle-of-the-road organization that sees its job as co-operating with people, educating and, when necessary, pursuing court cases. But it is a job made easier by animal rights groups, said executive director Cathy Thomas.[45] "We need to have animal rights people out there and we need animal welfare people," she said. "You need animal rights [people] to be the conscience and the animal welfare to get it done. The gains with livestock in the past five years have been because of fear of animal rights, no question. Animal rights doing their extreme thing opens the door for us."

The Winnipeg Humane Society is praised even by activists who would have no time for other welfare groups. The reason is largely Vicki Burns, a former social worker who looks and sounds like the epitome of a respectable woman – not an image to discount in a province in which one animal rights activist has heard himself described as a "limp-wristed lettuce eater" on a radio show.[46] Burns argued for better conditions for sows raised indoors in intensive farming operations, for example, at a time when the hog industry was expanding enormously.

"One of our roles is to get people to open their eyes and ask if this is the way we want society to go," Burns said. "It's time to start balancing ethical questions with scientific research. We don't always need research to support the idea that sows shouldn't be crated. There's a need for those of us who are not scientists to be able to say these things and not be considered flaky wing nuts. I don't have to apologize."

The issue of vivisection, which inflamed the original animal movement in Britain more than a century ago – transformed it from an elite group whose highest concern was humans into one that included a more radical side – was just that sort of demand to balance scientific goals against ethics. Today the animal issue that is the hardest sell of them all is the use of animals in research. Today the activists, both illegal and legal, are often quite highly educated or people of comfortable backgrounds. But the targets, now as before, remain the scientists, the miracle workers of a secular age who are not used to being attacked and who, until recently, found even questioning to be a bit much. This is a segment of society that used to be able to argue, quite straight-faced, that science was morally neutral, that it was just fact. We are less impressionable today and more likely to reply that, after all, people are deciding what to research, which makes it a very human and morally charged field.

It is historically and sociologically appropriate that the establishment sector of the animal movement, the animal welfare groups, is not at the barricades over this issue. Barricades are not their style, especially not when the targets are scientists. They are more comfortable with demands for action when the issue is, as in days of old, the link between cruelty to animals and to humans. That theme has been pursued by societies for the prevention of cruelty to animals in their quest for tougher laws. Research does show connections between assorted criminals and abuse of animals. It is a good way to sell a message to a public that might care more about humans at risk than about animals. But it also shows that conservative animal advocates have not moved far from the century-old notion of dealing with cruelty to elevate human morals.

Indeed, the essence of animal welfare isn't really so much the protection of animals as it is a concern for human society. It is about how to protect some humans from other humans with bad attitudes, as evidenced by their treatment of animals. It is about channelling human feelings of compassion for animals in safe and useful ways and about how to keep society humming along without the twinges of conscience or the opposition that the blatant human abuse of animals might generate. In short, animal welfare advocates generally want the status quo, with better manners. With a few exceptions, whenever animal welfare organizations get carried beyond the status quo towards calls for serious change in the human treatment of animals simply for the sake of the animals, the members pushing in that direction end up being labelled as extremists and are either pushed out or sidelined.

As well, it is socially safer to disapprove of serial killers or child molesters who used to pull the wings off flies or torment the family dog than to disapprove of scientists. Scientists are respectable people in the age of high technology. They are going to help us live lives far longer than we have any real reason to expect. They promise to tailor animal organs for us to overcome the reluctance of dying humans to hand over their bodies. They are what everyone wants their kids to grow up to be – people who can do math, wear white coats, get good jobs, and command respect.

The opposition to the use of animals in research follows the divide between the animal welfare and animal rights parts of the movement today, just as it followed the conservative and radical divisions in England in the 1870s.[47] If we are to understand the role of the law-abiding animal advocates who are struggling to be heard and fiercely determined to make a difference somewhere between the conservative and the illegal ends of the movement, the issue of animals in research is a perfect place to begin.

CHAPTER THREE

Research
Keeping Humans Alive

At the University of Alberta campus in Edmonton on a cold, grey November day, Pat Milke was handed the chore of showing me around.[1] As the assistant director of operations for the Health Science Laboratory Animal Services, she undoubtedly had more pressing work to do, but still she was thorough and deliberate in the tour. She listened attentively to questions and ensured that she made the points she figured ought to be made. For the mice, rats, ducks, dogs, primates, and whatever other animals are among the sixty thousand coming through here each year, death is usually the way out, she stressed. Researchers want to look at the tissue, blood, or body parts and draw some conclusions. Even for those animals who might survive the project, the university policy is generally not to adopt them out afterward because there is no way of knowing they wouldn't be going to something worse or to someone who couldn't care for their particular needs.

Clearly, then, the staff at this university lab need to know how to kill, and this is a place where killing is taught. They use anesthetized animals for the lessons, because the first few times are probably not going to work. There are definitely things to learn – like to use carbon dioxide only on adult rodents because it won't kill the babies. They will revive later. There is a guillotine for decapitation, or staff can break necks – cervical dislocation is the proper name for it. The reptiles – iguanas and snakes – are killed with barbiturates to make sure they are dead before they go into the incinerator. (If you lop the head off a snake or a turtle with their slow metabolisms, the horrifying thing is that they can go on being alive for quite some time.) Some staff find it harder to kill certain kinds of animals. It's a personal thing. Some find it hard to kill a research animal they have gotten to know, so they might swap animals. Milke herself breaks necks. It's the way she learned to do the job, and she feels a little squeamish about the guillotine. She sweats when she does it, she said, and she is afraid the animals will sense something is up.

This is the world of medical research, one of the oldest targets of animal welfare and animal rights activists, a world that for over a century has split the movement into conservative and radical factions. The welfare side works hard to ensure cages are bigger and more comfortable, that toys or exercise are available, that distress and boredom as well as pain are taken into consideration, that tests on animals are done only when alternative methods are said to be not available. For the more radical animal rights advocates, research using animals is institutionalized proof of human society's attitude towards non-humans.

With agriculture, it can be argued that until the moment of death animals can be kept comfortable and relatively content, that their deaths can be arranged to be painless and without terror. Things might not work that way in reality, but at least it is theoretically possible and officially the way things are supposed to go. In medical research it is officially acceptable to inflict pain without relief and cause continuous stress and impose, on animals' whole lives, lonely and uncomfortable conditions. That it is done in rooms with gleaming equipment, performed by people wearing white smocks and taking elaborate notes, only makes it seem worse. Can you argue that it is essential? If you accept that keeping humans alive is always a goal for which animal lives should be forfeit, perhaps. But wouldn't you have to show that you had first tried to do the research in some other way? Canadian researchers are asked if there are already in existence other, scientifically acceptable ways of doing what they want to do, without animals. But no one is under any obligation to develop those other methods, or to prove them acceptable. Unless there is some premium on developing alternatives – perhaps through a ban on animal use, for example – there is no motivating monetary reward for inventing them.

Sometimes the goals of research – the justification for using animals – are trivial: to find out if humans would be better off if they ate less, or to prove a new cosmetic product is safe for the market, for example. Sometimes the goals are arguably more valuable: to move a step closer to using animal organs to keep humans alive, for instance. In either case, research using animals is living testimony to the overriding belief that humans are more valuable than any other species on Earth. That belief means in turn that humans are entitled to use any of the other species not only in their attempts to stay alive, even beyond their usual life span, but also to ensure their safety as consumers. Millions of animals die each year for this belief.

The opposition to research using animals is not just one of the oldest but also one of the hardest animal rights issues to sell. People in the medical research establishment are suspicious of critics and, for the most part, convinced they are at perpetual physical risk from activists who break the law. They are also rarely challenged over their use of animals. Just as the activists who break the law are labelled terrorists, and case closed, so too have medical researchers long been considered sincere people of sound scientific intent who save babies and will, perhaps, one day save us all, with few questions asked. So far as politicians and most of the public are concerned, the main political issues surrounding them are their possible departure through a brain drain to the United States or their lack of research funds.

Few people listen with sympathy to animal activists' arguments that scientists and policy-makers are making little effort to find alternatives to the use of laboratory animals in Canada, that the "breakthroughs" made using animals are not proof that the gains had to be made that way. But then, few people know about what goes on in medical research or have any way of finding out.

For outsiders a visit to a lab animal facility is odd at the best of times. What you see are animals at rest, in their cages, big hallways with shiny floors, many doors (most locked), and curtains that billow with the outflow of sterile air. You don't see work being done on animals, nor can you read through the documents that explain what an experiment is supposed to be doing. Those matters are secret. The odd thing is that the very orderliness and precision are jarring rather than soothing. To a lay person, animals seem out of place in such a setting. On my tours, I had a sense of being overwhelmed: ducks in one room, rabbits in another, the baby incubator devices with mice through one doorway, the level, shrewd gaze of hogs meeting my eyes through the glass of another door. The professional pride of the trained staff who care for the birds, fish, and animals was obvious. The health of the inmates is often minutely monitored, until it's time for them to die so that the tumours or diseases or chemicals they have been given can be studied or the impact on some part of their bodies assessed or, simply, the project that required them can be wound up. The place can be as immaculate and impressive as the best of human health facilities but, in the end, it is a nightmare version of a hospital for the animal inmates.

For about two million animals in Canada each year, this is all there is to their lives, or to the last chunk of their lives, before their execution. Exactly what is happening to any of them, outsiders have absolutely no right to know, even if millions of dollars of tax money are going into the agencies that provide funding for much of the work or to the hospitals and universities, the institutions where much of the work is carried out. Perhaps it seems reassuring that places like the University of Alberta lab operate in a professional way. But in general research using animals is a private affair, and private labs in Canada can in practice do almost anything short of gross cruelty with little or nothing said about it. Even with labs that are inspected regularly, the system has been set up to ensure that the public never finds out if something unacceptable has been done, if the plug has been pulled on research because of how animals were treated. In this milieu, someone like Pat Milke is refreshing. She and a few others, such as University of Alberta veterinarian David Neil and, in Ontario, the University of Guelph's Denna Benn, stand out in a secretive world.

• • •

The law in Alberta stipulates that universities must use dogs from the city pound in their research. The dogs that go through Milke's facility, about 250 a year, are usually large and never properly trained or socialized. The bad-behaving among them go to projects that quickly end in death. The others go to projects that might last anywhere from six months to five years. One campus building has a roof area where staff sometimes take dogs out for air, but the noise can be prohibitive if there are a lot of hounds and huskies in the group. The university also has a farm where the long-term dogs can get some time in outdoor runs between tests. When I visited, the university was trying to set up a dog walker system, but not on campus. The weather outside is often too cold, and many of the dogs can't be allowed to pick up diseases. It is also not the greatest thing to have a lot of strangely shaved animals out on campus. They would be walking ads for the experiments being done on what were once pets, members of the family. The research has raised protests, for which Milke said she had no sympathy.

The facility allows three weeks at least between delivery from the pound and the start of research, Milke said. So, "If you want your dog back, you'll get it back. If not, you'll let it end up here." But in January 2000, university staff discovered that three supposedly unwanted dogs that were about to be used in research were very much wanted. The city pound had failed to reunite them with anxious owners, and only random checks by lab staff saved them. Horrified at what was clearly a flawed system, university officials stopped taking pound dogs and appealed to the province to change the law to let them buy dogs from a lab supplier. Those dogs are called "purpose bred." That they are born doomed, never have a chance at a home, and are treated as inventory by suppliers and research tools by labs is supposed to make a difference. The big difference is that no human hearts risk being broken by their deaths.

During my visit I could look through the window of one door and see a fluffy black and tan dog in a cell-like cage. Half of his body had been shaved for catheters to be installed. Bandages around his neck kept him from pulling them out. A drug could then be administered and blood easily drawn from the catheters for tests – one drug after another. A black and white dog, the only other animal in the room, watched intently from his cage, wagging his tail relentlessly, staring at the two faces looking in. Three times a day, handlers would enter the room to clean it. The dogs might be allowed to roam the hall then or be loose in the little room. The black and white dog was between tests and might get out to the farm for some time in the outdoor runs, but that would be about it. We didn't go into the room, and after we left his disappointed whining followed us down the hallway.

In a room around a corner, two ferret cages were empty. The residents were out for dental work, having their canines removed because they were going to be adopted. The ferrets were brought in for use in a video made to train lab workers. They didn't get many ferrets in the lab, and the fact that they were going to homes "makes us feel good," Milke said.

The steel cat cages were arranged in banks of four, each cage having a shelf on the side wall and a floor made of flat bars. The mice cages had little tubes for the animals to burrow into so they wouldn't hide in the bedding. One investigator was studying deluxe housing with mice, a bigger cage with extras – tubes, more bedding, and wheels that turn, with fixtures in different colours. The point of the study was to see if the brain developed more in mice with these extras, called enrichment, than in mice who didn't get as much to occupy them or to simulate normal mouse behaviour. Rats love to shred paper towels, it seems, so once a week a sheet of paper towel was left on the top of the cage and the rat got to decide what to do with it. The staff had to clear that first with the researchers, tell them the chemical content of the towels so that it didn't conflict with their research. Most of them, said Milke, had no scientific quarrel with giving rats a sheet of paper towel once a week to enrich their lives.

In animal research facilities, a lot of daily considerations like that depend upon the technicians. Milke spoke with pride of one change made at her facility because technicians pushed for it. With rodents, it is common to use orbital sinus bleeding, which means to take blood samples from behind the eye using a needle, because it is easier than finding a rat's vein. The problem is that the procedure is painful and some rats end up blinded. The technicians hated it, so now they anesthetize their rats and take blood from the jugular. "In animals, they may not be able to have a voice to say, 'Hey I don't want it there,'" Milke said.

At her facility, 90 per cent of the animals are rodents. They are the infantry of the research world and they are tailored for human research needs – inbred for generations, perhaps, or transgenic (having genetic material introduced from another species) – costing from $7 to $300 each. There are SCID rodents – severe combined immunodeficient – who are used for all sorts of research from AIDS to xenotransplantation (meaning between different species). They can't fight off anything, not even foreign tissue. So researchers use them to implant a human tumour, for example, or HIV. It is considered in the research world to be almost like having a little human to experiment on – or a live test tube. Opponents scoff, saying that there are almost as many reasons why mice and rats are not appropriate subjects for research into human diseases and disorders as there are ways in which they are used.[2]

The university lab also keeps primates and hogs. Despite all the talk of using fewer animals overall in research and proportionately more fish, larger animals are becoming an increasing feature in labs. While the number of fish used in labs more than doubled, for example, between 1989 and 1996, the use of non-human primates had also climbed back by 1996 to the same levels as in 1989.[3]

In Britain, despite government pledges to rein in the use of animals in research experiments, animal use figures in 1998 showed a huge increase of more than 25 per cent from the year before in the number of experiments on transgenic animals, to a total of about half a million. The leap in transgenics was so big that it pushed the total number of animals used in research up by 1 per cent overall, for the first general increase since 1976.[4] That was an ominous change from 1997, when the use of animals had been at a forty-year low. The uses ranged from developing animals with human diseases to "humanized"

pigs for organ transplant. Some 532,000 of the 2.66 million lab procedures were to breed genetically altered animals. The British national
Anti-Vivisection Society said that the use of animals in transgenic
experiments had increased by 500 per cent since 1990. That organization was pressing for tougher scrutiny to ensure that alternatives to
animals had been sought before experiments were approved.[5]

A lot of the action now is in organ transplant research. In this
field, pigs and non-human primates have been used in experimental
work for years. Scientists in London, Ont., are internationally known
for their leading work in transplants in both humans and animals.
One example was a liver transplant between a baboon and a rhesus
monkey in the early 1990s. In July 1998 Canada's first university
research chair in xenotransplantation was announced in London with
great excitement. Novartis Pharmaceuticals Canada Inc. had agreed
to provide an endowment of $1.5 million to bring the best minds in
the field to the project.[6] By April 1999 scientists in Guelph were at
work breeding humanized pigs, genetically altered to make their
organs more easily acceptable to humans, a step towards animal-to-
human transplants. By fall 1999 transgenic pig organs were being
transplanted into baboons at the University of Western Ontario as a
first step towards clinical trial with humans. The giant Novartis was
reportedly willing to put up to $1 billion into the work in hopes that
experiments would soon be possible using pig organs for people with
liver failure.[7] The multibillion-dollar market for drugs needed for
organ transplant subjects, another Novartis specialty, would seem to
have a glowing future.

In the United States, estimates put the potential value of the
animal-human organ transplant market at close to $6 billion by the
year 2010 – based on 450,000 yearly patients around the world seeking organs that would sell for U.S. $10,000 to $18,000 each.[8] With
that pot of gold shimmering in the distance, by 1998 companies were
reportedly spending some $100 million in research towards reaching
that goal.

New genetic technologies have opened a world of possibilities, all
of them promising the greatly increased use of animals. Early in 1999,

a Greek doctor based at a Japanese university announced a break-through in work on male infertility – he had grown human sperm in the testes of rats and mice. Another researcher in Japan then applied to use the sperm on unfertilized human eggs.

In Canada there has been growing concern that the largely unfet-tered world of research threatens to burst into our own daily life before the medical, ethical, or even humane concerns are raised pub-licly, let alone dealt with by government. A palpable excitement sur-rounds such breakthrough science. The stakes are in the multibillions of dollars for being first to the human transplant table. The chance that the plight of isolated transgenic pigs or the living conditions of non-human primates in labs might slow things down or mean more public scrutiny seems tiny at best. At most, the medical implications for humans may get discussed.

Research in genetic engineering has given us mice prone to such things as malignant tumours, sickle-cell anemia, cystic fibrosis, or Lesch-Nyhan's, a rare disease that causes self-mutilation. The idea is not to spread human diseases to other species, even if that is the basic achievement to date in some fields. It is to use other species for research that we wouldn't do on humans, so that humans might be cured. For example, heart and stroke researchers at St. Michael's Hospital in Toronto used mice engineered to develop blocked arteries from a diet rich in cholesterol and fat for experiments they announced in the spring of 1999. When the researchers injected the mice with some of the animals' own blood after it was treated with heat, ozone, and ultraviolet radiation, they found that the mice developed less plaque buildup in their arteries. They had plans to move on next to rabbits, but in Britain the treatment was already being tried on humans. These kinds of research, offering hope to humans, usually find public support, no matter what the cost in non-human animal life.

But beyond the traditional quest for cures, cloned and transgenic animals are considered potentially valuable for the business of devel-oping drugs, producing vaccines, and growing organs for transplant. Some of this might eventually be life-saving. But a lot of it is aimed at finding cheaper means of production by injecting human genes into animals to make them into little factories for therapeutic proteins or food that can be sold as health-enhancing.[9]

In agriculture alone, estimates of the worth of the global biotechnology industry by the year 2020 run from $75 billion to $700 billion.[10] Scientists have worked with the agriculture industry in searches for animals that resist diseases or produce leaner meat or more milk. There have been reports of experiments to develop featherless chickens (which, not surprisingly, turned out not to function normally), self-shearing sheep engineered to have wool that produced breaks as it grew (the animals got severe sunburns and heat stress), and pigs that grew much faster and were leaner (but suffered arthritis, infertility, and excessive gastric ulcers).[11] An official of Nexia Corporation, west of Montreal, reported that one bucket of milk from his company's goat – genetically altered to produce a human protein in her milk – would be worth between $20,000 and $25,000. The company, unwilling at that point to reveal what drug would be produced from the protein, put the value of the uniquely altered goat herself at about $20 million.[12]

Supplying all this research is another lucrative industry in itself. The crusading U.S. animal rights magazine *The Animals' Agenda* searched industry catalogues, annual reports, and trade magazines to come up with a sampling of prices for everything from animals to food and equipment. While they vary depending upon the animal's size, age, and other factors, some prices in 1995 and 1996 (in U.S. dollars) included: inbred mice, $8.80 to $14 each; a lactating mouse with litter, up to $106; guinea pig, $27.90 to $123; miniature swine, $300 to $720; rhesus monkey, about $1,200; restraining device for baboons, $3,000. Surgical alterations would cost extra: $8.35 to give a rat a vasectomy, for example, or $97.50 for an injection that would give an animal an Alzheimer's-like disease. Demands that animals be given a better environment in labs have added toys to the sales list.[13] In summer 1999 you could order rats or mice on-line from Charles River Laboratories at the cost of $65 to $200 each. Customers preferring to call could telephone 1-800-LAB-RATS to get through to the U.S. company, one of the world's biggest suppliers.

• • •

Animal activists are often told that they must make their case to the public and build a constituency for change. This is the logical, Canadian way. But, in reality, how does anyone make themselves heard in this world? What chance is there to compete with the message from a determined, multibillion-dollar and global industry whose future depends upon sweeping aside opposition?

Milke said she often feels people who protest research are ill-informed. (One exception she recalled was Darren Thurston, the "really well-informed" activist who toured the university before taking part in the ALF raid of 1992.) She said she has been asked if she tortures animals. The same people might turn around and agree that the research is okay if it helps humans and the animals don't suffer "too much." Even some technicians don't know that scrutiny of labs in Canada by the Canadian Council on Animal Care is voluntary, she said. The public probably believes, mistakenly, that someone somewhere keeps track of all the research and regulates it. The lack of knowledge is one of the reasons it is worth taking the time to tour people through the facility, Milke said. If nothing else, it gives people a basis on which to weigh the criticisms and form their own opinions.

"I don't want to make the decision for them. But I want them to have our side of the story," she said. "The public really should know what's happening. . . . I don't hide what I do. I'm justified in my mind in what I do."

Dr. Denna Benn, director of animal-care services at the University of Guelph, said much the same thing as she guided me through the central animal facility on a dazzlingly sunny afternoon in late October.[14] "We've always felt that if we don't talk to people, how are we going to get the message out?" she said. "I've never refused anyone."

The University of Guelph, Benn said, is using about one hundred thousand animals a year, 75 per cent of them chickens and fish. It has sheep, cattle, ponies, horses, and hogs. There are rats, mice, rabbits, dogs, guinea pigs, and not many cats, all spread over dozens of university facilities and rural properties in the province. The research protocols that explain the purpose of the work, the number of animals to be used, and what will be done to them are confidential, largely for fear that they will be taken out of context by "people with an agenda," Benn said. The University of Guelph had not experienced much trouble from people with animal rights on their agenda, at least until one day in July 1998, when a young researcher studying a new treatment for a canine skin disease found his car tires slashed in a campus parking lot. The following day someone smashed his windshield and spray-painted the initials ALF on the car. Slogans were also sprayed on the road near his home.

It's the sort of thing that everyone in the research community in the country knew about right away. It was the first real security problem for Benn since she had arrived as a newly minted veterinarian in 1980. She came to the job with a notion that the big picture windows in her office might leave her vulnerable. A run of attacks on labs by animal activists in the 1980s had sent a huge scare through the cloistered research community in North America. Institutions responded by installing better security systems, security guards, and doors with coded access locks. At Guelph, a major Canadian veterinarian and agricultural research centre, the university did not simply hunker down. It offered a spirited public defence of its facilities and its research.

Animal welfare groups in the United States had been advocating better conditions for animals used in research, teaching, or testing for years, and some abolitionist groups had long been opposed to using animals at all. But the arrival of animal rights advocates on the scene in the late 1970s confronted U.S. researchers with the most aggressive and public challenge to the basics of what they did.

In 1976 New Yorker Henry Spira, a veteran labour organizer and teacher, tackled the American Museum of Natural History in New York City over publicly funded experiments that involved mutilating cats to see how the changes influenced their sexual behaviour. His group picketed in front of the museum every weekend for eighteen months. Ed Koch, then a Congressman, related a conversation in which a museum researcher told him the U.S. government had paid $435,000 to determine that a male cat whose brain was first damaged would mount a rabbit instead of a female cat. The funding was lost, and the experiment ended.[15] Spira, a hero of the U.S. animal rights movement, was celebrated for the victory. It was the first time in more than a century of anti-vivisection efforts that a project involving testing on animals had been forced to close down.[16]

In the United States in the 1980s, Alex Pacheco and Ingrid Newkirk founded People for the Ethical Treatment of Animals (PETA), which would become a massive, well-known, and affluent animal rights organization. Within a few years it would have famous stars like Paul McCartney supporting it. It would also have a record of offering vocal support to illegal ALF raids, and a name that strikes terror (and provokes strong expressions of contempt, it must be said) in the hearts of much of the research community. In 1981 Pacheco wangled a job in the Institute for Behavioral Research in Silver Spring, Maryland, with researcher Edward Taub. The lab used macaque monkeys in what was supposedly research into why stroke victims sometimes couldn't move their limbs even if there was nothing wrong with them. Taub cut the nerves in the monkeys' limbs and then tried to get them to use the limbs by burning or shocking them or even throwing them against the walls of their cages. Armed with photos of terrible conditions in the lab and other documentation, Pacheco went to the police, who seized the monkeys. Eventually Taub was convicted of failing to provide proper veterinary care to the monkeys. Although the convictions were later overturned on technical grounds and the monkeys returned, Taub's funding was cut.[17]

In 1984 the Animal Liberation Front broke into a laboratory at the University of Pennsylvania and made off with hours of videotapes recorded by the researchers themselves. The gruesome tapes showed brain damage being inflicted on conscious baboons, the animals being mocked and operated on without anesthesia. ALF gave copies of the tapes to PETA, which produced a twenty-minute video that was shown around the world. By 1985 the lab was shut, though it reopened in 1993 with pigs as the new subjects for researcher Thomas Gennarelli.[18]

Canadian activists chalked up their own attacks on labs and, for a time, the media reported the actions in a way that reflected a sense of sympathy or admiration. The front page of *The Toronto Star* on June 16, 1981, carried a photograph of cat number 425, a nameless animal freed from a laboratory at Toronto's Hospital for Sick Children two days earlier. Two men and a woman identified themselves to reporter Paul Dalby as the ones responsible for the raid and as ALF activists. They described visiting the hospital's lab long in advance and later sneaking in when the security guard was elsewhere. They took photos and seized twenty-one animals, including guinea pigs, a rat, a rabbit with babies, and the cat, one of eighteen in the lab whose ears had been cut off. They described other animals, including piglets with burned backs, cats with electrodes attached to their heads, and rabbits with broken legs in slings. The hospital administrator was quoted as saying that animals were used only for essential procedures and "It's either this or use humans."

In fall 1984 activists – including Vicki Miller, just beginning her turbulent stint at the Toronto Humane Society – parked a mobile home in front of the downtown Toronto offices of the Ontario Heart and Stroke Foundation and staged a hunger strike in a futile attempt to convince the charity to end funding for medical research on a yellow baboon at the University of Western Ontario. On New Year's Day 1985, ALF raiders broke into another UWO lab and carried off a rhesus money and three cats. The research was again financed by the Heart and Stroke Foundation as well as the Medical Research Council of Canada. Acting UWO president Alan Adlington told reporters, "There's no doubt about it, we're in for a real battle between anti-vivisectionists and the research scientists."[19]

There were other episodes of vandalism at universities. Half of the faculties at the University of Toronto were targeted for vandalism or break-ins in the 1980s, said university veterinarian George M. Harapa.[20] But with better security, installed both to keep out intruders and to control quality, few incidents had occurred in recent years, he said. A former employee of McMaster University remembers how the casual access to the animal quarters of the medical centre came to a sudden end in the mid-1980s with the installation of electronic locks to control access even by staff from other divisions. The University of

Alberta lab raid in 1992 and a raid on the University of Minnesota in 1999 were unusual in the era of heightened security.

But in the summer of 1999, the Washington, D.C.-based Coalition to End Primate Experimentation launched a campaign to make life difficult again for universities and anyone else using primates in research. The twenty-four-city, three-month tour across the United States took a caravan of protesters to campuses, company offices, and even to the homes of researchers. Police made some sixty arrests before the high-spirited, civil rights style cavalcade was over.

Given the history of lab raids elsewhere, when Benn's photo appeared in the Guelph newspaper with an iguana in connection with her work, her friends told her she must be out of her mind to have posed for it. "It's scary," Benn said. "Do you know how scary it is? I've got nothing to hide yet I thought I'd be terrified." When two technicians went into the vandalized laboratory in the aftermath of the raid on the University of Alberta, Milke said, "I think they definitely felt threatened. I think all of us did." When the University of British Columbia was set to announce a new chair in animal welfare, the public affairs office was horrified at the suggestion from one professor that the announcement, with press present, be made in the facility where animal research is done.[21]

To their credit, some universities, like Guelph and the University of Alberta, did not flinch when incidents happened. Their willingness to speak on issues and to accept visits by outsiders continued. At Guelph, Benn worked hard to bring in outsiders to walk the dogs. True, it made the animals easier to handle in the labs, but it also gave the staff a boost to see the dogs getting out, and it showed that people did have access to the facility. When possible, dogs were given to adoptive homes after research ended, if they were healthy and psychologically fit. Rabbits and rats could be adopted too, but there wasn't much demand for them. Volunteers came in to visit those animals too – to talk to them and stroke them – mostly to make them manageable in the labs. Modern researchers are encouraged to be compassionate, Benn said, which is a change from the old days when being cold about the animals was considered proper and professional. Now no one mocks a researcher who feels blue when it's time to kill his or her subjects. Benn even had understanding words for the campus animal rights organization. They are young people who can come up with some good ideas, she said, even if she would never change their minds about research. When these same young people brought Ingrid Newkirk of PETA to speak on campus, they invited Benn to talk as well.

As I walked around the Guelph lab I spotted names on the cages of dogs: Baron and Lester and Julie and Lian and Janice and Iggy and Star. These dogs were being used for experiments with aspirin, in skin grafts and hip replacement. A technician's note on Wally's door advised that the anxious-looking Siberian husky with the pale blue eyes could be a picky eater and moody. "So if he is feeling down, please spend a few minutes with him." Vampy, a black Labrador-looking dog, like Wally a pound dog, was keen on bones. She wagged her whole body at a visitor. Big fluffy Moose desperately wanted out to play. One Husky with a shaved throat in another room was trembling and shy at the sight of a white-coated visitor. An uncertain-looking Troy, alone in her room with her pups, was barking and barking. A technician had written a note about the pretty black and white dog. "Please give Troy lots of love, she is lonely."

On another door was a warning about the "aggressive boars" inside. It advised you not to turn your back on them. Goliath and Floyd were big, perhaps 222 kilograms each, and "so smart," Benn said. Floyd was looking right back at us, making eye contact from under his pale lashes. It was a look that stayed with you. Transgenic hogs like Goliath and Floyd are killed when their research days are over. Their carcasses cannot be eaten, so they are burned. In another room prepared for hogs there were chew toys, objects made from rags and hose and hanging from chains. Like kids, Benn said, hogs get bored once they figure out the games, and the toys have to be constantly changed. These are animals considered so smart – in some countries pigs are pets, like dogs – that they need new toys. In the animal rights world, this point raises an obvious question. If they are so smart, how can we countenance treating them this way? In the animal welfare world, though, the same point means that they have to be entertained in the lab. The realm of animal welfare seldom designates a ground zero, a place where the human use of animals stops despite arguments of potential human benefit.

• • •

All of this – the concern about animal activists, the belief that research information can be taken out of context and unfairly criticized, the cutthroat big business of research – is the backdrop to what is undeniably a lot of secrecy. Animal extremists are the most often-cited concern, and patently the least real. (The concern, as we will see, can vanish whenever there is some advantageous breakthrough to announce.) Secrecy, to be sure, is not the word used by the Canadian Council on Animal Care (CCAC), the national body that oversees research, teaching, and testing using animals in Canada, to the extent that there is any national oversight. Some provinces have their own inspection systems, but they are limited in scope. The CCAC says that, to foster open discussion, all information concerning its assessments of labs must be "confidential."

In the United States, in the wake of activists' revelations about shocking abuses, politicians felt pressured by 1985 to pass laws dealing with animal research. In Canada, much earlier, the research community shrewdly acted on its own and therefore was not seen to be in need of government interference.[22] The CCAC was set up in 1968 as an independent body with financing – about $1 million a year – from two federal government agencies, the Medical Research Council of Canada (MRC) and the Natural Sciences and Engineering Research Council of Canada (NSERC).

The CCAC establishes guidelines for animal care and once every three years sends an assessment panel out to inspect labs that use animals. The assessment panel includes at least one scientist, a veterinarian, and, to represent the non-scientific community, a person appointed by the Canadian Federation of Humane Societies. If the inspectors decide that the labs are following its guidelines, the CCAC usually reduces that routine inspection in those cases to once every five years.

Members of the inspection panel get a list of a particular laboratory's research projects, with a brief description and data about the number of animals used, the species, and what is being done with them. Panel members can ask for more information from researchers when they visit or, if they want, they can ask to see the full protocols describing experiments submitted to the institution or granting agency for approval. Panel members look at how the university handles research proposals as well as at the particular projects. Then they sit down privately – "in camera," according to the CCAC – with institute officials and members of the institute's animal-care committee. They set out any serious concerns they have, make requests for immediate action to fix serious problems, and offer a verbal version of their findings.

Within ten weeks the inspection panel sends a written report to the laboratory, which is then supposed to reply to any concerns – in three months if the concerns are significant, in six months if they're not – with a proposed schedule for implementing changes. After the implementation report is in, the CCAC rates the institute: it can be found to be in compliance with the CCAC standards, in conditional compliance, on probation, and in non-compliance. The CCAC can report a finding of non-compliance to government and granting agencies. Getting to that point can take six months to a year, and that's before a lab has actually corrected whatever is found lacking.

In principle the MRC or NSERC can respond to a finding of non-compliance by cutting or freezing funding for the research. If a particular, offending project is funded from elsewhere, the whole institution can be cut off – a serious threat, because the MRC and NSERC are the main government research-granting agencies. Anyone doing contract work for the government is also required to be in compliance with the CCAC. However, in the CCAC's three decades, the MRC or NSERC has never frozen or cut funding because of non-compliance with CCAC standards, although some labs have been found to be in non-compliance. It is considered a penalty of last resort to be used only after persistent violations. (A CCAC official said the threat of stopping funds was made once, but that incident too remains confidential.)

Institutions inspected by the CCAC are required to have their own in-house animal-care committee made up of scientists, a veterinarian, staff from the institution who work with animals, and at least one staff member who doesn't. The only required outside presence is for one or more community representatives, usually appointed by senior administrators at the institution. These animal-care committees are considered very important by the CCAC, and they should be. The way the system works, with inspections by the CCAC only once in three years or even once in five, this in-house committee is really the only body that asks questions about what will be done with the animals used in research before it happens. And the committee has the authority to order an end to any research that it considers to be causing unnecessary pain or distress or that isn't following the originally approved use of animals. The committee is supposed to ensure that the institute has sought out possible alternatives to the use of animals, established the scientific merit of the work, justified the numbers and species of animals being used, and provided proper pain relief to animals (unless relief is not to be given for scientific reasons). The committee is to insist that the institute particularly scrutinizes painful experiments, provides enrichment for the animals in their lab quarters, and keeps up all the required forms and standards.

As part of this monitoring, the CCAC has established a set of categories, ranging from A to E, to be used by researchers to describe the invasiveness or severity of their proposed research. Both A and B involve little or no pain or distress. Category C is supposed to entail minor stress or pain of short duration, such as minor surgery under anesthesia or exposure to non-lethal drugs or chemicals. Category D covers moderate to severe distress or discomfort, such as prolonged physical restraint, radiation sickness, exposure to noxious substances with no escape, or the stress of maternal deprivation. The category covers a lot of territory, but stops short of death. Category E is for experiments that cause severe pain, "near, at or above the pain tolerance threshold of unanesthetized conscious animals," by CCAC definition. This category could include, for instance, exposure to painful levels of drugs or chemicals or studies on toxic substances or diseases that last until the animal dies. Some institutions do not do category E research.

The CCAC warns animal-care committees, in evaluating the research, to be especially cautious on a number of fronts: if the work immobilizes or paralyzes animals without reducing their pain, or uses electric shock; if it is intended to study their pain or stress; if it involves withholding food or water or pain relief after surgery; or if it uses exposure to extremes of temperature. A certain amount of pain or stress may well be a necessary part of the study, and it is accepted as such. The CCAC has set a few taboos, though. One is the use of drugs that immobilize but do not cause unconsciousness or relieve pain in surgery. Another is trauma that involves crushing, burning, striking, or beating without anesthetics. And while in the past experiments have been carried on until the animal dies – in cancer research or toxicology tests, for instance – the CCAC now calls on researchers to kill the animals humanely after signs of irreversible pain or distress appear – *if* the needs of the study can still be satisfied.

As for the secrecy of all this activity, the CCAC argues that information is fully shared among members of its panels, the institutions, and the CCAC itself, and is therefore not strictly secret. As the CCAC explains it in a policy paper posted on its Internet Web site: "*Confidential* can best be equated to *private*, and this is consistent with the understanding by the institutions which participate in the CCAC's assessment program. In this sense, confidential means that assessment information is private and not for general distribution." It is the public use of the material that is restricted, the CCAC says. In agreeing to serve, community members of animal-care committees at institutions and on CCAC assessment panels are supposed to accept this confidentiality. A particular institution may itself decide to make public the assessments, letters, or any information about the CCAC's rating, but first it must inform the CCAC that it is going to do so, and it must not release the names of CCAC panel members.

In practice, institutions rarely release information about the CCAC's findings. One exception was the University of Alberta's outspoken David Neil, who made public the CCAC's condemnation of the university's lab cages in the 1980s in a successful bid to get money to improve them. More significantly, not all of the facilities inspected by the CCAC have been willing even to have their names made public after being awarded the CCAC's Good Animal Practice certificate for obeying the rules – and that certificate is supposed to show off to outsiders the high standards of the institution.

The CCAC describes its role as working with the scientific community to ensure responsible animal use, to help achieve the best levels of animal care, and "at the same time being accountable to the Canadian public by providing accurate composite information on experimental animal care and use on a national basis." The CCAC gives out data about the total number of animals used across the country in the labs it inspects, the species used, the general purpose of the work (product testing or education, for example), and the category of invasiveness. It does not give out the names of the labs inspected, or the locations, nor does it offer any information about the kinds of research being done on animals or any violations of its standards. Despite its public funding, the CCAC is not covered by the federal access to information law.

The CCAC apparently fulfilled its accountability to the Canadian public, for instance, when it reported that, in 1996, the total number of all animals used in labs it inspected was 1,756,416.[23] (The figure would have been 1,952,045, but some animals were not included because the forms from a few institutions were incomplete.) The numbers were broken down to show how many animals were used in each category of invasiveness. At least 90,701 animals found themselves being subjected to the top category, E, the most painful, and another 414,436 at least fell into category D, the second most painful. The report listed the general uses of animals, showing that three hundred of them in the category E experiments were used in postsecondary education and training in facilities. Meanwhile, the CCAC guidelines say that painful experiments on animals solely for classroom teaching or to demonstrate established scientific knowledge cannot be justified.[24] Some 74,236 animals were used in category E studies to get products approved for sale, ranging from drugs to household products and cosmetics. Only 3,466 were used in category E work for studies for medical purposes relating to human or animal health. Some 12,694 were used for basic scientific research. No further details about the research are available.

Research community insiders have grumbled that the CCAC numbers are significantly lower than the number of animals actually used each year in research, teaching, and testing in Canada. Some animals, like the ones already dead and used in dissection, are simply not eligible for counting. Eyebrows have been raised over the actual number of animals killed off in efforts to create strains of transgenic animals, where success rates are less than 10 per cent. But there is no way to satisfy these doubts.

There is no way, then, that ordinary members of the public, who might want to express approval or disapproval on these matters, can know what labs are doing, unless the people doing the research volunteer the information, which they virtually never do unless they have breakthroughs to announce or results to publish. Most published results, unlike breakthroughs that make it to the newspapers, appear in scholarly journals that reach an elite audience, and, besides, they are difficult to understand. When breakthroughs are announced or results of work published, the reports might give details on the species of animal used and explain in general how the discovery was reached, but they probably won't give specifics about the procedures performed on animals or how painful they were. As a result, decisions about what can be done are left to a private, interested, and unchallenged group.

The all-important in-house animal-care committees are dominated by people who share the interests of the institution. They are by definition sympathetic rather than neutral when they judge the conditions of animals, the research plans, and the behaviour of scientists. They have little motivation to quarrel, for example, with the institution's star researcher. The so-called community members of the animal-care committees rely on the institution's invitation to be on the committee and to stay on it. They are outnumbered and can be intimidated by the scientists around them. They start at a disadvantage because they can't judge the accuracy of the scientific conclusions presented to them.

Brig.-Gen. Chris Snider (retired) of Ottawa was one such "community member." He spent thirty-seven years in the military and many years in assorted animal welfare organizations, including sitting on the boards of the Canadian Federation of Humane Societies and the Ontario Society for the Protection of Animals, where he became chairman. He also served for a decade as a community representative on the in-house animal-care committee for a federal government department. For the first while, he said, he felt useless because the jargon used in the field was foreign, and the research protocols were difficult to read.[25] Neither a shrinking violet nor a radical, he was not a critic of the system overall, but he said he believed that animal-care committees set up in private drug companies, in contrast to those in university or government settings, amounted to mere "sops." Even within Health Canada, Snider said, when it comes to a drug being tested for licensing by a private company, there has been a feeling that a company "customer" would not take kindly to having its research proposal turned down by the department's animal-care committee. After he refused to approve of several projects, he felt quite distinctly disapproved of by other committee members. On his animal-care committee, two negative votes could lead to the rejection of a research proposal. If Snider and the second community representative agreed, they could effectively halt the project.

Stephanie Brown of Toronto spent more than a dozen years serving on lab assessment panels for the CCAC and was given a citation of appreciation for her efforts in 1996. A former president of the Canadian Federation of Humane Societies and a former Toronto Humane Society president, Brown went on to edit a federation newsletter for members of animal-care committees. She found that the confidentiality requirements of the process undermined the results. "It betrays the concept of having a community member if you can't speak," Brown said.[26] She also came to believe that animal-care committees at institutions were not encouraged to be critical of research proposals. During a period when she served on one such committee at a Toronto hospital, she voted against renewing an experiment that involved putting metal bars into the backs of cats, immobilizing them. Rather than accept that the research was not going to be renewed because of her single obstructing vote, the other members of the animal-care committee simply decided that it would henceforth take two negative votes instead of one to veto a project.

Yet another flaw in the system has made it, in the words of a scientist who works within it, a paper tiger. If an institution or a private company lab using animals doesn't want to be inspected and judged by the CCAC, it doesn't have to be. And that refusal doesn't mean it still cannot go on doing research or testing using animals. Given that omission, in some parts of the country in certain labs there will be no one routinely inspecting the research being done or the conditions under which animals are kept, no one demanding that the use of animals and the kinds of things done to them be justified scientifically, no one even forbidding some research entirely.

"I can establish Dave Neil enterprises in most provinces in Canada to do animal research, using my own money and-or invested capital with *absolutely no controls or surveillance*, unless I am overtly and-or criminally cruel," the University of Alberta veterinarian Neil told the Canadian Association for Laboratory Animal Science ethics forum in Montreal in June 1997. "As it stands, Canada is a potential animal carte blanche shelter – like an offshore tax shelter system."

Neil stressed the urgent need for legislation that would make it illegal to conduct research or testing or do teaching in Canada using animals, except in institutions verified to be in compliance with CCAC guidelines. The proposal was hardly revolutionary, but there was no rush to join Neil on the barricades. CCAC sought a legal opinion on the issue and concluded that a federal law making its assessments mandatory and its standards enforceable was highly unlikely to work because of mixed jurisdictions. So the Council settled upon encouraging provinces to require adherence to CCAC standards and assessments and, at the same time, working on ways to make its standards national yardsticks through a body like the Standards Council of Canada.

Although some provinces have their own rules about animals used in research, in general provincial administrations appear to have no taste for making matters more rigorous for animal users. If anything, the push is towards less analysis of their practice. Ontario, for example, has its Animals for Research Act, which requires facilities using animals to have a licence. Its inspector, Dr. Bill Holley, is charged with policing the Act to ensure that the source of animals is legitimate, that care is adequate, and that the animals are not subjected to "unnecessary pain." But he is one person with some 142 facilities to inspect once each year – down from three inspectors and three visits a year in the past. He must base his policing on selective checks on work in progress rather than attempt to review everything a facility does.

Would it be better to model his work after the procedures of the CCAC? Not for the animals, it wouldn't. Holley can't question the purpose of the research. The law gives him no mandate to look at whether animals are used when alternatives are available, or whether they are used in repetitive experiments or in excess numbers. This limitation sharply restricts the interpretation he can put on "unnecessary" pain. Still, he does show up unannounced, with the clout of law behind him, and he does focus his attention on the care and pain of the animals. It's not that this Lone Ranger, as he's known, is putting anyone out of business. In his eighteen years on the job he has seen only one facility ordered to stop functioning while a hearing was held to question its conduct under the Act, and that event, with its details lost in the mists of time, was considered extraordinary. As far as he can recall, he has never seen a fine or a penalty imposed for breaches of the provincial law. But at least when Holley arrives, there is none of the advance primping and cleaning up and none of the fresh paint and cosy hospitality received by a preplanned CCAC inspection. He has tracked down at least two facilities doing research without a licence and given them twenty-four hours either to get the paper or close down. He has, rarely, ordered animals killed rather than let an experiment run to the bitter end.

"I've been on CCAC panels," Holley said. "They usually wine and dine them. . . . I don't get the breaks and the sitdowns and the muffins.

All's I get is 'Jeez, couldn't you come back tomorrow? There's three people off sick.'" Not, he hastened to add, that people are not generally nice to him.[27]

An advisory committee of vets, animal suppliers, and humane society representatives has been formed to push for a toughening up of the Ontario law – clarifications, Holley called them. One change could be to pin down what "unnecessary pain" means. Then Holley would be able to take stronger action. He would also like the authority to examine the purpose of research. He would like a facility's in-house animal-care committee to be required to get some outside expert to verify the scientific merit of the research. Without those items, the law is virtually toothless. But there is no indication of any intention to toughen up the Ontario law. Like ccac reports and findings, the Ontario inspection reports and actions are secret. However, a hearing, if some facility were challenged on its activities, could be public, said Holley, who finds the idea of openness sensible. By contrast, the notion of merging the collegial, gentle approach of the ccac with any provincial legislation seems a prescription for inactivity.

Stephanie Brown estimated that thousands of animals were being used in Canada with no oversight at all.[28] One recent, informed estimate put the number of labs not inspected by the ccac at about one hundred. Many of those labs were in the private, biotech industry. When asked, the ccac itself could not even say for certain how many existing labs it was not inspecting. Dr. Gilly Griffin, ccac information officer, said she believed the ccac was inspecting about 90 per cent of the country's labs.[29] Its Web site boasted in mid-1999 that it was inspecting more than 170 facilities.

While a university or some other public institution or a company doing government work would have to be inspected by the ccac to get public funding – which is a powerful incentive for universities to be inspected – increasingly even universities have been seeking partnerships with private companies to collaborate on research, a move that plays down the need for government funding. That significant change could undermine the overseeing system's already feeble impact. In earlier years, Neil said, the threat of losing funding was considered important to those within the system even if, to outsiders, the CCAC appeared to be toothless. He believed that adherence to the CCAC standards was, then, a serious business. According to Neil, the situation changed when the federal government decided to cut funding to NSERC and MRC. Those agencies in turn decided to pay for the costs of lab inspections only for academic institutions, which led a number of labs in private companies to drop out of the system and forego paying the CCAC's newly imposed fee of about $1,800 a day. Even within the lab community, the suspicion is that newer companies, especially in the biotechnology field, may be foregoing the costs and intrusion of CCAC inspection.

"A system which had to all intents and purposes become universal and successful was now exposed for the paper tiger it had always been for some," Neil said. "Furthermore, the very foundation of the assurance of laboratory animal welfare throughout the nation was shown not to be firmly established – that is, to safeguard animal welfare in good times and in bad – but rather to be vulnerable to policy changes, cutbacks, and quick decisions which virtually could pull the rug out from under the system."[30]

The CCAC's own attitude undermines the entire idea of a voluntary system. It describes its mandate as acting "on behalf of all Canadians" to ensure through programs of education, assessment, and persuasion that the use of animals, where necessary, is done to "acceptable scientific standards."[31] Given its own words, then, the Council is not there to act in the interests of animals; and it is a deliberate choice of words to ensure that "scientific standards" are applied to the use of animals. If you want to argue, for instance, that something cannot be done for ethical reasons, you must ground your argument in science or establish that it represents wide public feeling, what is socially accepted as ethical or unethical. You believe, for example, that keeping a dog in a room in a building with limited social contact and with brief excursions for exercise for five years is cruel. You feel sure that dogs need to belong to a group or a person to be happy. But you would have to prove that hypothesis scientifically. You believe it is unethical to inflict pain. How do you propose to do studies in developing pain relievers? The CCAC built its guidelines around when to step in to end distress or pain and how to chart the experiment in scientific detail, not on totally forbidding the pain or distress.

The federal government, for example, was urged for more than a decade to improve living conditions for a colony of monkeys that it owned and maintained, year in and year out, in facilities in Ottawa. Critics insisted that these social, intelligent creatures should not be kept without a chance to mingle and exercise with other monkeys, that they needed to have toys and variety rather than endure their lives in single or double cages. The CCAC was inspecting the government's labs, but the relentless haranguing for changes came primarily from outsiders, in particular the Canadian Federation of Humane Societies. As long ago as 1987, the Federation complained publicly about "intolerable" conditions, stacked cages with little or no exercise for the adult animals. The Federation said some would-be visitors were subjected to months of screening and tests that kept the public from knowing about the plight of the colony.

After its inspections the CCAC's confidential assessments apparently recommended improved conditions, but the Council obviously did not consider those conditions essential for the colony to continue.[32] Indeed, in more recent assessments of the primates the CCAC had blasted Health Canada. But harsh words said in private aren't heard by anyone else. Small surprise, then, that they had such small impact.

Public criticism by the Canadian Federation of Humane Societies – and the relentless efforts of Brown in particular – added a new layer of unpleasantness to some of the exchanges between the government bureaucrats in charge of the colony and the Federation. Correspondence exchanged between the Federation and Health Department officials shows that cost estimates in the millions of dollars for brand new quarters for the colony dwindled by 1991 to subdued talk of spending in the thousands for more basic improvements. By 1996, group housing rooms were reportedly being built for some of the animals. Over the years, many of the standard 24-inch by 28-inch by 34-inch cages had been modified to 72 inches by 28 inches by 34 inches to allow two adult females and babies to be housed together. Demand for the monkeys, both internally and in sales to private and university labs, was also dropping.

As the government-Humane Society dispute over the monkeys continued, the CCAC published its own report in a 1989 newsletter, pointing out that females and babies were given from eight to sixteen hours to enjoy larger exercise cages (72 by 84 by 32 inches) "every two to three weeks" and more changes of ambient air each hour than most human office workers. The colony's facilities, the newsletter reported, met CCAC standards.[33]

The monkey colony – made up of about seven hundred and fifty cynomolgus monkeys in the summer of 1999 but in earlier years numbering more than one thousand – had been established in 1983 when India cut off the supply of rhesus monkeys. Canadian government veterinarians went off to the Philippines to oversee the capture of some eight hundred of the cynomolgus from that country's forests to be used to repeat quality tests of polio vaccine. At least a hundred of them died in the process of capture and transport. Back in Ottawa, they were kept and bred and, at times, sold off to other researchers. When, some fifteen years later, the government decided it would no longer duplicate the manufacturer's tests of polio vaccine, it no longer needed the expensive monkey colony. At that point the administration was still promising, but had not yet delivered, group housing to satisfy some of the monkeys' social needs.

The government asked the Royal Society of Canada, an association of scholars and scientists, to recommend courses of action. In November 1997 the Society came back with a report stating that Ottawa was responsible for the animals and that while the colony was one of the most valuable in the world there was a dwindling call for them in research. It recommended that the monkeys who were not needed for legitimate research in CCAC-monitored facilities should go to less restrictive living conditions in a sanctuary, as should any of the survivors of current research. The Canadian Federation of Humane Societies urged the government, in fairness to all the animals, to provide the money needed for a sanctuary. Failing that, the government should kill them humanely.

By the summer of 1999, little had changed. Some of the 754 monkeys in the government colony were still being used for testing. One hundred of them were potentially destined for a sanctuary at the University of Montreal, if negotiations underway succeeded. Once there, they could be used for some tests, but the stated intention was that research be limited to observation, Health Canada officials said. For the rest, most would live on in Ottawa in new group housing, still not ready. Even when housing became available, a few monkeys would have to remain alone in cages, because they were too infected to mingle with others or prohibited by research requirements from joining in. If other government departments or private laboratories wanted them for experiments, they remained available. Those other labs, said Health Canada, would have to be "sanctioned" by the CCAC.[34] The Canadian Federation of Humane Societies' newsletter, a tough semi-annual publication, added an ominous note to the ongoing saga of the monkey colony. The newsletter, *caring for animals*, had acquired a letter from Health Minister Allan Rock to the Royal Society in February 1999. The letter noted that the government was putting more money into health research and that "there is every indication that this new research will stimulate a demand for non-human primates."[35]

Dr. James Wong, CCAC director of assessments, was one of the two government veterinarians who had gone abroad to trap the monkeys. As an employee of Health Canada, he had spent two months in the Philippines, working to capture and then ship back the monkeys. "I became quite close to two of them," Wong said. "They're remarkable animals. You can't help it. You know, you come in and they're dancing around." He waved his arms in wide greeting gestures.[36] In the end his two special monkeys were shipped off to aid research into Alzheimer's disease or some such thing, having grown too old for the breeding program. He shrugged: "What are you going to do?"

Disputes between animal advocates and the scientific establishment are seldom about whether or not some research procedure hurts animals physically. More often they revolve around what is accepted as fact about animals' physiological needs, their feelings and their ability to suffer emotionally and psychologically. Advocates first have to establish that a need or feeling exists, then argue successfully that the need or feeling should be given priority over the potential benefit that the research might bring to humans. Only then would scientific standards be influenced. This happens, but very slowly, as the gradual change in conditions for Ottawa's primate colony shows. And if information on what happens in labs is available only to insiders, the scientific work needed to assess the impact of research on animals' needs or suffering depends upon insiders who have some reason and enough stamina to pursue that work.

To a certain extent the attitude of the CCAC is in tune with that of researchers. The Council believes that research using animals needs to be done and that science must guide what is acceptable. The CCAC's attitude, obviously, comes from the views of its membership on how its rather vague mandate should be interpreted into actions. Its members include five federal government departments with scientific interests; representatives of academic faculties of medicine, dentistry, and psychology and universities generally; associations representing scientists and specialists in animals used in laboratories; three federal agencies that give research grants; two charities that give research grants to study human diseases; and zoologists (a group oriented towards research).

Another important member is Canada's Research-Based Pharmaceutical Companies, a new name for an umbrella group that used to be called the Pharmaceutical Manufacturers Association of Canada (PMAC). A press release issued in April 1999 said the name change was made to reflect the industry's role as "the leader in health research in Canada." According to the release, the group of some sixty-plus companies accounted for 42 per cent of the total medical research and development in Canada and would spend more than $900 million on that work in 1999. The release also quoted Dr. Henry Friesen, the president of the Medical Research Council of Canada, which is supposed to be the final arbiter of financial penalty in cases of research found wanting by the CCAC. Friesen stated, "The research-based industry has made invaluable contributions to Canada in the past decade."

Significantly, in late 1997, when the group was still called the PMAC, the multinational companies' spokesperson Judy Erola was quick to pronounce bomb explosions at Biochem Pharma Inc., a Quebec company, the likely work of animal rights extremists. To the contrary, though, police tied the bombs to stock speculators trying to manipulate the market. The incident revealed much about PMAC's view of animal rights and the speed with which the threat from activists could be invoked. In Canada the research community considers anything beyond the Canadian Federation of Humane Societies as being radical.

Essentially, these members of the CCAC, the body supposedly riding herd on research, are all from groups with a direct interest in the business of carrying out research, of using animals if they deem it necessary. Many of them represent the institutions or companies doing the research. They have, at the very least, an in-bred reason to look kindly on science and unkindly on criticism or negative publicity. Cynics might say they have a conflict of interest or an interest in making the CCAC act in as uncritical a way as possible, short of seeming so ineffective that there are calls for the establishment of a mandatory, outsider-dominated oversight body. The CCAC considers this setup to be a voluntary process of assessment by peers, which is another more benign way of describing it.

The CCAC also includes the Canadian Federation of Humane Societies, which supports research using animals where alternatives are not available, and the Royal Society of Canada, whose member scientists and scholars are interested in promoting research and learning. Clement Gauthier, who was appointed executive director of the CCAC in early 1999, was in 1992 founding director of the Coalition for Biomedical and Health Research, an agency set up by the academic and commercial research sector and the drug industry to boost public spending on research. The Coalition has complained that the government is too slow to allow biotech products onto the market, and it has pushed for a separate agency to take that authority away from Health Canada.

Given that almost all of its members and its executive director are either doing research or have been actively promoting it, it would seem highly unlikely that the CCAC would bring a tough approach to the task of monitoring research and, when warranted, of penalizing or even mildly criticizing it. The organization understandably plays down the issue of secrecy. It notes that its animal-care committee system has been copied in other countries, including Britain, Australia and the United States. The CCAC has powerful admirers, at least in the research establishment.

In the United States, freedom of information laws make the details of laboratory work much more available. For example, the California animal rights group In Defense of Animals was able to keep running tabs on the deaths of chimpanzees during research in labs at The Coulston Foundation: on the number of charges, of violations logged by U.S. regulatory bodies against the company, and on the kind of research being done. The animal group was able to make public all of this, plus the identity of the client for the potentially crippling research done on chimps by Coulston in testing a new spinal device.[37] In the case of labs getting federal funding, U.S. information laws provide for access to the federal inspection reports on facilities; to approved protocols for experiments that explain the procedures, species used, anesthesia planned, and reasons for a project; to correspondence between a lab and the Agriculture Department; and to annual reports on the number of animals used and to records of what happened to all of them. For private facilities, reports of inspections, annual numbers of animals used, and correspondence with the federal Agriculture Department are available. While the U.S. regulation of labs may have its bad aspects – it exempts rodents, for example, from its coverage of laboratory animals – at least these information laws are in place and can be tightened up periodically, as they have been. It isn't necessary to start from ground zero each time to fight the same old battle about why the state has any right or need to interfere.

Britain, a country with one of the oldest laws on animal experiments, requires licences for projects using animals and for those doing the experiments. British law, according to research done for the Law Reform Commission of Canada, is far clearer on what is accepted as "necessary pain" to be inflicted upon animals in the course of a research project.[38] Under Britain's Animals (Scientific Procedures) Act of 1986 (which replaced an 1876 law on cruelty), pain, suffering, distress, and lasting harm are said to include "any material disturbance from normal health," defined as the physical, mental, and social well-being of the animal, as well as "discomfort, disease, injury, physiological or psychological stress" either immediately or over a longer term. The law allows the minister to revoke licences and provides for prosecution and fines or, in extreme cases of violation, jail terms. It requires that the potential harm done to animals based on a research proposal be weighed against the likely benefits to humans, other animals, or the environment. Experiments that produce severe pain or serious injury without anesthesia are not to be licensed, nor are those that use dogs, cats, or *equidae* (horses or donkeys) unless it is established that no other species are suitable. The continued use of the same animal in other experiments needs specific approval.

The British government has banned the use of animals for testing alcohol, tobacco, and cosmetic products. It will issue no more licences for tests using great apes, except in special cases, and it now requires ethical reviews and more animal welfare experts to be included in the process of approving research.[39] In Europe a 1993 directive of the European Parliament said that member states would ban animal tests for finished cosmetic products. A ban on testing the ingredients was delayed by a failure to approve acceptable alternatives. Canada is one of the few Western countries without any sort of legislation on animal experiments.

In Britain, as in the United States, more information about research using animals is available to the public than is the case in Canada. In Britain the law requires that data on the numbers of animals used in testing be compiled in an annual report, which is put before Parliament. Although they do not reveal names of researchers or laboratories, the reports do record the number of violations of the law, the nature and severity of those infringements, and the actions taken as a result. They also detail incidents in which research that would not normally be allowed is granted a licence as a special case –

for example, the country's Defence Department project to use eight marmosets to compare therapies for exposure to chemical weapons.[40]

•   •   •

In Canada, "It's up to the institution to decide how much of what they're doing they want to discuss," said the CCAC's Gilly Griffin. "I think their concern is principally security, perhaps in response to what has happened in other countries." The CCAC's James Wong said most institutions have a policy of talking to the community about the research they do using animals. While most people wouldn't know specifically what research is being done in institutions, he said, most universities do permit visits, although they might be wary of visitors with a known animal rights connection.

Still, when I attempted a random, admittedly unscientific sampling of universities and hospitals across the country I found them less than open to visits by members of the public. Some simply didn't reply to my letters of inquiry, or they promised to reply and never did – like the University of British Columbia, the University of Western Ontario, and Toronto's Centre for Addiction and Mental Health (formerly the Clarke Institute of Psychiatry). A suspicious few immediately contacted the CCAC office when they received an outsider's requests about visits and asking for other information.

The University of Alberta and the University of Guelph were exceptions. They actively invited a visit and spent the better part of a day answering my questions. The University of Toronto was open to visits with a week's notice but required a signed statement pledging to keep confidential the nature of the research and the names of anyone involved in any animal use or in funding it. The statement also required a sweeping promise never to publish or circulate any "defamatory" comment about "any person who, or institution which, is involved in or associated with the activities, operations or facilities referred to herein." Slip up on this, the university form warned, and it could mean legal action.

The universities of Calgary and Saskatchewan were not open to visits by the public to their facilities, although both were generous in answering written questions in detail and with care. A visit to the University of Calgary animal facilities could be arranged with the approval of the director of the Animal Resources Centre. The director of the University of Saskatchewan's Animal Resources Centre, Dr. Ernest Olfert, replied at great length to questions about research at his institution and included relevant policy papers. Since 1995, for example, the university has had a policy for cats and dogs kept for long-term research that calls for a minimum of one-half hour of exercise three times a week for dogs (daily exercise outside of a pen, ideally) and loose-housing for cats (exceptions to be justified). Sunnybrook and Women's College Health Sciences Centre in Toronto willingly answered questions but were not open to visits by other than scientific researchers. "As you have already ascertained, there is no standard policy across Canada for access to research facilities," wrote Dr. Miles Johnston, a professor and director of the trauma research program at Sunnybrook.[41]

As for the CCAC, its record is certainly not one of condemning the use of animals in research or testing. According to Wong, it is not an advocacy body and not in the business of recommending the phasing out of tests using animals. But it has always quite definitely been an advocacy body for the research community.

For example, in 1980-81 the CCAC swung into action in the face of what it saw as an upsurge in animal rights protests against the use of animals in research and testing. Beyond straightforward suggestions to labs on how to safeguard security, the Council contacted every Member of Parliament to warn about the attacks and to offer to answer any letters they got critical of research. Many MPs and government departments took them up on it. When critical articles appeared in Toronto or Calgary newspapers, the CCAC made sure to get rebuttals printed. When people complained about Defence Department radiation studies using dogs and rats, the CCAC circulated a rationale for the work by cancer specialists. When the use of dogs from municipal pounds in research became controversial, the CCAC contacted municipalities in Metro Toronto and even a dog club on the east coast to argue the issue.[42]

In 1986 the CCAC decided to share its files with a pro-research lobby called Canadians for Health Research. The CCAC files, with a rapidly growing section on animal rights activists, were undoubtedly a useful resource. When the organization prepared a warning document assessing animal rights and welfare groups, the CCAC helped to distribute it. Wong said the group's publication discussed security issues, which would interest those on the CCAC mailing list. Since the mailing list was confidential and couldn't be loaned, the CCAC purchased and distributed the organization's document itself.[43]

A remarkable little book published in 1997 by Memorial University professor and scientist Sam Revusky, a psychologist, details his tumultuous contacts with CCAC inspection panels as he experimented on rats at the Newfoundland institution from 1971 to 1990. By no means an animal rights advocate, Revusky plainly rejected the notion of any oversight of scientific research beyond general laws governing any other kind of animal use or treatment. But he also dismissed the effectiveness of how the CCAC performed its oversight in particular. Experimentation, he wrote, is "more vulnerable to cheap morality than other uses of animals because it is publicly funded and its rejection interferes with individual human rights less obviously than regulation of other uses of animals."

However, Revusky noted, most scientists can get around the CCAC quite easily. Indeed, he said he knew of no scientist who ever explicitly sought alternatives to animal use, as allegedly required. He railed against the secrecy of the CCAC process, arguing that it was wrong for universities to act as "secret societies" and to forbid community representatives from publicizing the inhumane treatment of animals if they saw it. The CCAC, he said, had been used as "a public relations ploy against animal rights activists and as leverage by which to obtain animal facilities that might not otherwise be considered worthwhile by those who must pay for them."[44]

So foreign is the notion that the public has any right to know about anything done in labs, even those on "public" university campuses, that someone who asks for it can become engaged in absurd, circular paper debates. For example, many people have asked, as I did, that the Ontario government provide them with information about the total number of animals used in research, testing, and teaching in specific facilities and institutions in the province. After all, a significant amount of research and testing using animals in Canada goes on in Ontario. The information must be filed annually with the province. But all that the province was willing to provide was annual, composite totals.

For example, the information officer of the Ontario Ministry of Agriculture, Food and Rural Affairs provided on request a summary of the total number of animals – broken down into species – used in research, teaching, and testing in the province for the years 1993 to 1997. Primate use ranged from 483 animals in 1993 to 1,483 in 1997. Fish and mice, used by the thousands, dropped considerably in totals over the same time period. Some 1,841 dogs and 791 cats were used in 1997, with 753 of the dogs and 276 of the cats coming from municipal pounds.[45] In all, over four million animals were used in Ontario in the years 1993 to 1997. But if you want to know what the dogs or the primates were used for, or what labs used the cats, you cannot find out. If you want to know who paid for the research on any of these animal species in particular, that information is not available. If you want to know what animals a specific, public university lab used, you are out of luck.

The provincial government's data on a great variety of subject-matter can be pursued under Ontario's freedom of information laws, if it is not given willingly. But the government officers deny requests under that law for information about animal use by specific institutions – or even the individual annual reports from institutions on how many animals they used, even with their names and identification removed and no purpose specified. The denial is based on provisions in the law dealing with the life or safety of persons or the security of a building that might reasonably be expected to be endangered if the information is released or if disclosure could cause financial or scientific harm. When such requests for information are made to the Information and Privacy Commissioner, the CCAC has weighed in as an intervenor to argue against its release.

This position has been upheld through a decade of appeals and even though, after one appeal in 1997, ten unnamed institutions or facilities agreed to provide records of their total, annual individual animal use if their identities were not disclosed. Despite the views of the anonymous ten, the CCAC, the government, and many of the other institutions and facilities argued against that directive, saying that it wouldn't be hard to figure out which animals were used by which facilities. The Ministry and unnamed others provided the Information and Privacy Commissioner with "examples of the activities of some of the extreme factions of the animal rights movement which use violent and illegal methods to promote their cause. These activities include harassment, death threats and bombings. They also point to specific acts which have occurred over the past several years, some quite recently, involving research facilities."[46]

Unfortunately, the Ontario Ministry of Agriculture, Food and Rural Affairs was unwilling to provide any information even about these extremists' threats or bombings or harassment in the province, some of which (particularly the bombings) must have escaped public attention or police notice because they do not seem to be reflected in media reports. When I asked for information about those extremists whose actions were cited to the commissioner, I was told that the information was private. Even the information that the government gave to the commissioner setting out the government's specific reasons for not releasing the data was not available. This makes it hard indeed to present a counterargument. The Ministry's freedom of information officer said that no other information exists in its files about this serious problem of animal rights extremists, except in the briefs prepared for the commissioner, which are inaccessible.

Appeals to the commissioner to treat publicly funded institutions differently than commercial, private operations in releasing information have been rejected. One appeal noted that this sort of information was once released on animal use in the 1980s with no dangerous results. Doesn't that counter the argument about danger? The government does not need to prove that harm will result from disclosure, the commissioner replied, only that it might.[47] When I contacted the commissioner, I argued that the law required that expectations of harm not be "fanciful, imaginary or contrived." Since the government didn't take the whole issue seriously enough to keep real files, since institutions gave out much greater detail about the animals they specifically used when they published reports on their research, and since granting agencies like the MRC and NSERC posted on their Web sites details about the kind of research they were funding, often providing specific details, how could anyone sincerely contend that less detailed, less specific information would be dangerous to give out? The appeal was rejected.

• • •

Just about the time the commissioner was, for reasons of security, upholding the need for secrecy for this anonymous information about unnamed Ontario institutions, the University of Toronto courteously replied to a request by mailing a report on its animal use for 1996 and 1997. The two pages, identifying the university by name, were exactly the pages the commissioner and other institutions said could not safely be made public, even anonymously. University of Toronto veterinarian Dr. George Harapa said the university had been releasing the information for about seven years. The campus ombudsman had received a student request years ago for a mass of confidential information about the university's research and, after discussions, those involved decided that this particular data wasn't among the material that could be properly kept secret. Had it caused a problem to release this information? I asked Harapa. "Not at all," he said. Since the numbers over several years show a decline in animal use, he said, you could argue that it helped, because it highlighted the university's effort to cut back on animal use.[48]

When outsiders pose questions, much is made about the research community's need for secrecy. But when there is a scientific breakthrough to announce, that doesn't seem to be a problem – even though the published results of experiments are undoubtedly useful in providing information about what animals are used, for what purpose, and in which labs.

For example, the Canadian Federation of Humane Societies has regularly reported on the selected use of animals in specific research projects in a newsletter for members of animal-care committees. One issue, for example, noted that two McGill University investigators had reported in the journal *Pain* in 1996 that they suspected bee venom would help provide a valid test of pain in animal experiments. They thought this because, using money from NSERC, they had injected gradually increased doses of honey bee venom into the hind paw of a rat: more venom, more pain, lasting from ten minutes to more than an hour. The researchers used aspirin and morphine to provide pain relief. In 1999 University of Toronto researchers reported on their experiments administering repeated shocks to rats.[49]

NSERC, on its Web site, informed the world that in 1997 it gave $43,000 to a University of Toronto psychology department investigator to do brain research using rats; $10,000 to a Wilfrid Laurier University psychology department study of rats' appetites; $17,000 to a York University study of memory and cognition in non-human primates, and $10,000 to the same institution for a project in great ape cognition; $13,000 to C.D. Rollo of McMaster University's biology department for a facility to raise transgenic mice. The newsletter *Animal Research Digest*, circulated among animal rights and animal welfare people, culls many scientific journals to offer information about research projects either underway or completed. Sometimes the information is provided in press conferences, as it was when the University of Western Ontario announced in 1992 that to study drugs to combat rejection it planned to work on organ transplants involving baboons and monkeys.

The point is that ordinary people, considering how the system works, might conclude that there is something beyond the fear of terrorists at work in the refusal of the research community to be open. The real goal, it seems undeniable, is to bolster the mythology that those who pursue animal issues, whether they are animal rights or animal welfare advocates, are too extreme to be given any credence. This mythology eliminates the necessity of full-scale public scrutiny, of possible public criticism of what is being done to animals, and, as a result, avoids inconvenient government interference. The theory is that, if you give an inch, if you give animal groups any credibility or acknowledge any criticism or any right to question or regulate, you only invite more. Then, perhaps, you stand to lose control of the easily manipulated, industry-dominated system now in place, the best that any business or researcher could hope for.

Government interference, for instance, raised its head when Ontario's New Democratic Party government of the early 1990s made plans to ban cosmetic testing on animals and any use of the so-called Draize test. The Draize test is nasty. It involves dripping chemicals into rabbits' eyes to establish the extent of irritation and damage caused by the ingredients in cosmetics and other household products. Such a test is not required by law in Canada. Manufacturers decide what tests to use to satisfy the government that their products are safe. The NDP, which was delivering on a proposal it had made in opposition years earlier, was also responding to a strong public campaign organized by the Animal Alliance of Canada. Practically, it was an easy governmental step that meant changing some regulations under existing law rather than passing new legislation.

Ontario Agriculture Minister Elmer Buchanan promised the changes in the spring of 1993, a year after he had first promoted the plan inside government.[50] The province would have been the first North American jurisdiction to take such action, although the European Community had already begun similar action. Besides, Ontario had estimated that at most two hundred animals were being used each year in Draize tests and fewer than one thousand in all consumer product-testing.

In November 1998 Britain ended all animal tests for cosmetics and toiletries in that country. By then, only a small number of animals – about three hundred rats, guinea pigs, and rabbits – were being used there for those purposes, most of them for skin and eye irritability tests and only by three companies. There had been a voluntary ban the year before for animal testing for suntan products and toothpastes. In the mid-1980s about fifteen thousand animals had been used in those tests annually. But the ban was modest. It applied only to products made in Britain and not to imports, including those from France, where some twenty thousand animals were being used for tests each year. The ban did not cover individual ingredients on the grounds that some of those ingredients were used in medicines. And despite its pledges before winning office to hold a royal commission on the need for animal experiments and to allow animal tests only when essential, the British government had failed to undertake a harder look at the medical and scientific use of animals when jailed animal liberationist Barry Horne went on a dangerously long hunger strike to draw attention to that pre-election promise.[51]

But in Ontario the government plans fell through, despite relentless campaigning by Animal Alliance program co-ordinator Andrea Maenza and others. The Canadian Cosmetic, Toiletry and Fragrance Association wrote to one MPP to warn against the international animal rights movement and argue that companies must be allowed to decide for themselves what animal testing, if any, was necessary. An Ontario ban, the association said, would "communicate an inappropriate message."[52] Opposition to the idea was strong among university researchers, Buchanan admitted to reporters, because they feared that "the next step will be to ban animals completely."[53] Maenza's efforts to meet with Premier Bob Rae were rebuffed, and the subject was referred back to Buchanan, who told her in a short note that he "remained supportive" but couldn't say when anything might happen. He made a vague reference to the legislative agenda, even though only a change in regulations was involved.[54]

It's not that a ban on testing was scientifically impossible. At the University of Saskatchewan, the committee on animal care puts limits on the use of Draize tests and the LD-50 acute toxicity test. (In the LD-50, an ingredient of a product is force-fed to a group of animals until 50 per cent of them die, thereby helpfully providing a level at which the scientists can determine toxicity.) Before accepting research that uses either of these tests, the university requires a written statement from a regulatory agency that the test is necessary and proof from the researcher that alternatives are not acceptable and that the research is not duplicated elsewhere. At the University of Alberta,

Pat Milke said, the LD-50 is not used because their policy is not to wait for animals to die lingering deaths. Her institution had, she said proudly, turned down a contract for Draize testing, a procedure banned in some states but still carried out in some Canadian facilities despite existing alternatives. It was good to know that money was not the only thing that mattered at her university, Milke said.

Internationally, the animal movement has fought a running battle with the research world over the scientific validity of using animals in experiments. There is abundant literature on each side over drugs that proved lethal for humans despite reassuring animal tests (and denying the truth of this), over which medical breakthroughs did not need animal use (or did need it), and over the availability of alternatives to animals. For instance, when saccharin was more or less exonerated by the National Institute of Environmental Health Sciences in the United States in May 2000, after two decades of the product being declared a likely human carcinogen, animal rights advocates seized upon parts of news reports in which officials explained that the bladder tumours that the artificial sweetener caused in lab rats were now judged "not relevant to the human situation." One certainty is that Canada lags behind other countries in efforts to find alternatives to animal use.[55]

Critics of the animal movement often complain about the amount of money that the groups have available to devote to their campaigns. But the groups with the largest amounts of money are the traditional animal welfare organizations, which are the gentlest of critics. Other groups, such as the Animal Alliance of Canada, are much more hand-to-mouth. With some twenty thousand supporters across the country, the Toronto-based Animal Alliance has four full-time staff members paid about $18,000 each a year, plus four part-timers and volunteers. Paid employment in the animal rights side of Canada's animal movement is not the norm. If the issue is research, the pockets on the other side are deep indeed. As a study in a U.S. journal noted, big companies have increasingly been on the attack against their critics. A multinational drug company in 1998, for example, fought in court to prevent the release of a report on heart drugs and lost, but only after forcing a Canadian regulatory agency on the other side to use up a hefty chunk of its annual budget in the battle.

This is the setting in which big-stakes research in transgenics and xenotransplants is being carried out. The CCAC has developed guidelines for transgenic animals. The Canadian Federation of Humane Societies has complained that those guidelines put no limit on the pain that genetically unique animals might experience. The Federation expressed concern that these animals could be born facing lives of painful deformity or unanticipated misery. If nothing else, the stark, uncontaminated conditions in which they must be kept, for the safety of humans as much as to protect the research itself, promise lives of inevitable loneliness and deprivation. Will the misery of a pig or a sheep or an ape count for much in this new world of research? Who will know about it or have the power to object?

Jacqui Barnes, a director with Animal Alliance of Canada, made a public demand in a January 13, 1998, letter to the editor of *The Globe and Mail* that seemed both logical and almost pathetically hopeless, all things considered. If, after rigorous scientific and ethical discussions, Canadians decide that xenotransplantation, like human cloning, is immoral and unethical, Barnes wrote, "We must send a clear message to the industry to stop all xenotransplant research." In the United States a coalition of U.S., Swiss, British, and Dutch medical and animal groups tried another tack, threatening legal action against Health and Human Services secretary Donna Shalala if her agency did not respond to their legal petition asking for a ban on animal-to-human transplants.

Research was already racing ahead. Scottish scientists stunned the world with the first successfully cloned mammal, Dolly the lamb, in 1997. That breakthrough was followed quickly by cloned mice in Hawaii, calves in Japan, and, in South Korea, a human embryo that was stopped at a cluster of cells. By 1998 Japanese scientists and agricultural officials were looking at the cloning of cattle to solve the country's problems of depending on foreign beef. Gradually, with cloned vegetables already in the markets and cloned goldfish on sale in pet stores, the early public fuss about the ethics of it all died down, nor was there much attention paid to negative reports. That lack of attention to the downside of such scientific adventures might explain, in part, why public debate quickly faded. Dolly made front-page headlines, but by early January 2000, when British scientists found that sheep cloned like Dolly grew up with dramatic differences in their appearances and behaviour, for reasons unknown, that story turned up on the inside pages of the newspapers.

When troubling findings began to mount, *The Toronto Star*, for example, chose a modest corner of page nine for a striking news story from London, England, in May 2000. It said that cloned animals were reported worldwide to be developing unexpected tumours, excessive growth before birth, with tragic consequences, or abnormal developments in internal organs, not a happy note for the prospects for animal to human transplants. In Japan, four of eight cloned cows died soon after birth despite appearing normal. An official from the institute where Dolly was cloned even noted that researchers were warning that the technology was new and unsafe.[56]

In Canada, some people were taken aback by the announcement that genetically altered pigs had already been imported from Britain with no involvement by Canadian health authorities. The pigs arrived at Montreal's Mirabel Airport in April 1998 and were inspected by agriculture officials as any other pig would be, after much negotiation between drug-maker Novartis Corp., Novartis's subsidiary Imutran, and researchers for three Canadian universities. In Britain there was public controversy over the shipping of transgenic pigs (intended to breed pigs for future use in pig-human organ-transplant experiments) to some six other countries. The action was seen as a way of avoiding British laws regulating experiments.[57] The European Union's bioethics committee had recommended that clinical trials of pig-human transplants not proceed at that point. In Canada no decision had been made or publicly discussed. That raised the question, noted Montreal professor and ethicist Margaret Somerville, of whether there should even *be* imports of these pigs bearing human genes if no decision had been made to allow anyone to conduct trials.[58]

In late April 1999, when Nexia Biotechnologies Inc. of Quebec made headlines with the cloning of three identical goats, the federal government quickly announced it would soon bring in legislation dealing with the issue. By mid-summer officials were predicting that legislation would be ready for debate by the end of the year. The proposed laws would deal mainly with human reproductive and genetic technology, including a ban on cloning. Meanwhile, had any researchers applied to Ottawa to move any of this work from the lab to the outside world, for clinical trials or production? The federal government would not comment on whether it had received such applications. With three public universities and industry already involved in the transgenic pig project, the federal government was still at work on the theoretical implications and ethics of xenotransplants.

A draft of the set of proposed federal standards for xenotransplants was posted on the government's Internet Web site in the summer of 1999, inviting public comment.[59] The introduction of the standards raised ethical questions. The draft said that primates might offer fewer rejection problems as a source of transplant organs for humans, but they caused other worries about ethics, because of their genetic closeness to humans. Pigs, the draft asserted, were less of a problem in that way, because humans already eat them. The government was proposing a National Review Board to assess the safety and ethics of all clinical trials with animal organs. Facilities involved must be inspected by the CCAC, it said, and follow its guidelines. Those guidelines say that animals shouldn't be subjected to "unnecessary" pain or distress and, if it is necessary, efforts must be made to lessen the pain and distress. Animals used in such transplants, the draft said, must be bred and raised in captivity, kept in facilities with highly restricted access, and have no contact with other animals.

"Though pigs are curious, gregarious creatures, those bred to supply organs live in sterile conditions designed to minimize exposure to outside pathogens," Stephanie Brown wrote in a newspaper article.[60] "Their lives are unnatural and short. Piglets are caesarean-delivered, fed by hand in incubators, not suckled by their mothers, at the

University of Guelph. Pigs 'pharmed' for spare parts have been genetically engineered. . . . Besides eroding the integrity of the species, transgenesis is an uncertain process in which only one in 100 animals may carry the added gene, with the remaining 99 animals unwanted and wasted. Frankensteinian deformities can occur, with organs oversize or missing, or in wrong places."

Such concerns, unfortunately, seem unlikely to change the course of research in Canada. By defining anyone who wants to critique the condition of animals in research as strange and dangerous, the medical and research establishment has left little, if any, room for discussion. The public has been more or less shut out of the activity, admittedly with little protest. Government has not only tacitly agreed to this state of affairs but also periodically pitched in to help fight off objections. Activists face a vicious circle. They have little or no information available to help them convince the public that their criticisms deserve a hearing. The industry will not sit down at a table to talk with people it labels dangerous. Even its contacts with conservative animal groups are grudging. Is it a surprise that labs remain the target of illegal activities? And that activists are increasingly turning their attention to the numerically largest use of animals, agriculture?

CHAPTER FOUR

Agriculture
Keeping Humans Fed

In the summer of 1999, cows near the picturesque southwestern Ontario town of Elora were involved in settling a serious agricultural question. Rubber rings had been fastened around their tails so tightly that the blood was cut off. After a time the blood-starved, deadened lower part of tail would fall off. Then, with their stubby, twenty or so inches of tail, these cows would presumably help the world discover if it hurts much to have a tail mutilated like this, whether it keeps on hurting, and how difficult it is for cattle to keep flies from driving them nuts without a long, tasselled tail to whip across their flanks.

The reason that a respectable researcher was hard on the trail of this bit of science was that up to 20 per cent of cattle in Ontario were having their tails chopped off. Many farmers have become convinced that shorter tails will somehow *reduce* the problem of flies – the theory is that less tail means less dirt and germs to attract flies – and that shorter tails will be out of the way during milking.

To many of us, it might seem obvious that it would hurt to have a tail treated this way, that it would be more difficult to keep flies off, and that a shortened tail would surely matter to an animal, especially in the stifling days of summer in less than pristine barns or even in fields. To a researcher like Ian Duncan, who was conducting the tail-docking study in Elora, the research was necessary to convince an industry of the need for change. After all, the agriculture industry, like other big businesses, is not going to give up a particular practice that it believes boosts profits, unless it has to or is convinced that the practice is not helping. And the agriculture industry itself is pretty much in control of how animals on farms are treated, and it intends to keep it that way.

It is an industry more used to being respected than challenged in Canada. It is one thing to learn to live with regulations governing the chemicals that are sprayed generously over fields or fed to animals to speed their growth. Those rules are grounded in scientific studies, although that doesn't mean they are accepted without challenge or complaint. But it is quite another to hear people who do not raise animals on farms talk about the lives of these animals. That, it seems, is often taken as an insufferable insult. For if outsiders have their stereotypes of the farm world, so too do agricultural insiders have stereotypes about the people who don't live or work in farming communities. While some city folks might see the farm world as peopled by rubes in manure-caked boots, more seem to hold romantic, vague notions of people close to the soil, more admirably straight-talking and hard-working than a lot of us. That flattering image does not go unnoticed in agriculture, where farmers are sometimes urged to draw on their good standing with the public to back their calls for aid in times of economic trouble or to combat critics.

Some city people – urban dwellers, as they're often called when they're about to be found wanting – might be a little surprised at the caricatures of themselves: they think meat comes from plastic packages. They make endless, often silly demands about farm products and then whine about paying. They believe what they see in children's movies about animals and everything animal activists say. They're intolerant of farm noises and afraid of manure. The animal activists among them hate humans – or think animals are just like humans. Urban dwellers should be educated by the school system to see things from the farm point of view and, failing that, should keep their noses out of what isn't their business (farming). They should, however, support significant government aid to farmers when they are told it is needed. These were just some of the casual remarks offered to me as I conducted interviews, sometimes with people who refused to be identified. Outsiders' views about cutting off cows' tails, I concluded in the course of these discussions, would not count for much.

Duncan, an internationally respected scientist and chair of animal welfare at the University of Guelph, had his proposal for the tail-docking research turned down by the university's animal-care committee. Committee members believed it was obvious that the rubber bands on cows' tails caused pain. The industry disagreed, said Duncan, on the grounds that there were no obvious signs to prove they hurt. Milk production did not fall off along with the tail, for example. If animals produce, the agricultural industry concludes that they are therefore not in distress. Failing proof to the contrary, the dairy industry was not prepared to stop tail-docking. But it was prepared to put money into the research, and because the dairy industry is "fairly sensitive," Duncan said, it might well act on the results of his study.[1]

The same sort of research had already been done in New Zealand, a major agricultural nation in which tail-docking was once common but has gone into decline. Scientists there studied five pairs of twin cows, one member of each set of twins with a docked tail and one without. Three times a day, once a week, all during the summer and fall of 1994, the scientists watched one side of each animal for six minutes at 7 a.m., six minutes at noon, and six minutes at midnight, noting the fly-induced behaviour (muscle reflexes, front and rear leg stampings, tail flicks) and counting the number of flies settling on the front and rear of the animal at each time of day. The findings: consistently more flies on the rears of tail-docked cows than those with full tails; more tail flicking and leg stamping on the docked than the undocked cows. The scientists noted that these findings were consistent with similar research in 1992.

A summary of research concluded that very little difference existed between cows with full and docked tails when it came to the convenience of the people in charge of milking, but a considerable difference existed in the cows' ability to deal with irritating flies. The studies did not support arguments about docked tails being healthier or increasing production. Maybe, noted researcher Lindsay Matthews, it would do simply to trim the long tassel at the end of the tail in spring and let it grow back over the summer when flies are at their worst.[2]

Duncan doesn't particularly like conducting research into matters such as tail-docking. As an animal welfare scientist, what he finds engrossing is trying to figure out what makes animals tick. In the summer of 1999, for instance, he was at work on an engaging project to find out more about hens' dust-bathing, that routine wriggling on the tummy and breast and general sprinkling and fluffing with dry dust that some birds use instead of water to clean themselves, as if the dust were dry shampoo. Duncan wanted to find out how important it was to hens to be able to do this every few days.[3]

According to Duncan, animal welfare scientists who have been busy with the basics of finding ways of decreasing obvious suffering are now seeing value in activities that give animals pleasure. He believes that some animals clearly suffer from boredom – like pigs who are curious and want to explore. This sort of knowledge has implications for intensive farms in which pigs have little if any room to walk indoors, never mind going outside to lie down or wander in a field where they can watch the seasons unfold or the birds and clouds pass by.

The poignant thing about the kind of work Ian Duncan does is that, even if he were to discover beyond a shadow of a doubt that chickens value dust-bathing highly, that this is, next to eating, what makes them happiest, the discovery isn't likely to make a big difference in how they are treated. He would also have to prove that if the industry catered to chicken happiness, it would pay off in more eggs or faster growth or cost savings. He would have to prove that some sort of dust-bathing could be arranged for the huge, caged indoor world inhabited by egg-laying hens or the crowded indoor floor world inhabited by broiler chickens. The changes would have to come at a cost that would pay off enough to more than offset the costs of disrupting an already profitable system. Then, and only then, the industry might finally act on his research.

. . .

Agriculture is big business in Canada – 276,548 farms with a capital value of $156.5 billion in the 1996 census and more than $70 billion in goods and services produced by the wider agrifood industry of farming, processing, and service. It represents the single largest human use of animals. The numbers range from over 102 million hens and chickens to some 865,000 sheep and lambs, with pigs, cattle and calves, and turkey in between, each numbering in the millions. Not surprisingly, agriculture has also increasingly become the focus of attention from both animal rights and animal welfare groups.[4] There has been a growing sense that the world of agriculture has shifted from its traditional ways – from farms owned by one family, its livestock limited by pasture and capital – into something quite different and bad for animals. In the 1960s Ruth Harrison's book *Animal Machines* so stirred the British public that a parliamentary committee began to examine conditions in big, intensive farm operations.[5] In the United Kingdom, legislation was passed in 1968 to allow the minister to set codes of practice for raising farm animals. By the 1970s a farm-animal welfare council was toughening up those codes. By 1999 Britain had outlawed the widespread practice of keeping sows in narrow, individual stalls or crates or tied by tethers that severely restricted their movement for prolonged periods of time. It banned that same kind of close confinement for veal calves. The European Council decided to ban cages for laying hens by the year 2002 in all new or rebuilt egg farms in member states and set standards to make life better for hens remaining in cages in older operations. Cages would have more room and offer nests, perches, and areas for pecking and scratching. Veal crates – individual stalls allowing little room to move – were to be phased out in all European Union states by the end of 2006. In Australia, some politicians were in favour of a ban on cages for laying hens. In New Zealand, consideration was being given to changing stalls for sows because of public complaints. The protests came later to North America, but they came.

The first national codes of practice recommending – but not enforcing – basic conditions for rearing animals on farms in Canada were published in the early 1980s. Still, despite a federal Health of Animals Act, passed in 1990, that makes it possible for the federal government to regulate how animals are treated on farms, Canada follows the same voluntary, self-policing approach that the country has taken on almost everything lucrative that involves animals. Britain, by contrast, has a State Veterinary Service conducting farm inspections to ensure codes are followed. In 1998 its officials checked on 6,592 farms and pursued investigations in 212 of them. One mink farmer was fined thousands of dollars for violating the rules.

Canada does have regulations on the transport of animals to slaughter and on what happens in the abattoirs themselves. But relentless budget cuts and a government distaste for regulation have led to limited enforcement of the rules on the treatment of live animals. Efforts to deal with recognized weaknesses in slaughterhouse or transport systems have depended upon the enthusiasm of overworked civil servants willing to buck a trend. The federal mandate appears to be a hands-off, after-the-fact sort of surveillance instead of on-site monitoring. The agriculture industry has not been the subject of shrewd government scrutiny. Instead, it has become a collection of clients for whom the rules are tailored and from whom fees are collected. For animals, that has proved a deadly attitude. The emphasis has been on cost-saving and partnership.

Perhaps as a result, the lives and deaths of animals used for food have increasingly become a priority issue for the animal movement. Activists are targeting key features of modern agriculture: the indoor confinement of animals (some of them never get outside except on their way to death); the mutilation of animals (some have their toes or bits of beak or tails lopped off, tailored to accommodate machinery or crowded conditions in big farms); the millions of animals who arrive dead or near death at slaughterhouses because of how they have been treated; and the low priority accorded animal welfare in slaughter. The industrialization of agriculture, the shift from what used to be small businesses to megafarms, to "factory farms," is as much a part of the debate as whether or not you think certain animals exist only to be eaten by humans. Today you can drive through the countryside, through centres of agricultural production, and see relatively few animals. They are mostly indoors, which is why these operations are called factory farms. The name rankles the industry, where it is seen for the epithet it is meant to be.

As the 1990s came to a close, in Halifax Beth MacKenzie Kent and Gail Zwicker of the Nova Scotia Humane Society were plotting a visit to slaughterhouses to document the daily, legal business of killing for food. In Toronto, the Animal Alliance of Canada was distributing a newsletter on food animals edited by activist Stephanie Brown. In Winnipeg, the group PAAL (People Acting for Animal Liberation) was searching for the best way to tackle farm issues in a province in which the hog industry was rapidly expanding. If they could only show people "how the packaged corpses arrived on their table," said PAAL co-ordinator James Pearson, the public would understand the activists' cause.

In Vancouver, the no-nonsense Tina Harrison of Canadians for the Ethical Treatment of Food Animals (CETFA) was carrying on a long-time crusade to bring attention to the plight of animals raised on farms. A poised, dignified city woman made radical by her experience in protesting the seal hunt in the 1980s, Harrison had set out to educate herself on the issues of agriculture. Her group's efforts include a shocking little publication: the confessions of a livestock trucker who in 1996 unburdened his troubled conscience and described the dismal conditions of animals being carried to their deaths. The CETFA booklet contains none of the rhetoric of the animal movements' usual literature. It is only the graphic, blunt words of one Canadian truck driver, more distressing for being unadorned.

The agriculture industry tends to see this new attention as an unwanted and unwarranted attempt to interfere in an age-old occupation. Animals today, the industry says, are well protected from harm and the elements, are better fed and monitored, and avoid the diseases animals suffered in old-style farming. They are also part of an assembly-line, big-business approach to production that, according to the industry, simply wouldn't work or be affordable any other way.

Canadian chicken farmer Bruce Weber put some of the animal activists' complaints down to a combination of too much Walt Disney and Bugs Bunny. The way in which animals are shown in film and television fiction makes people anthropomorphic, he said. They project human qualities onto chickens. The truth is that, "this is an instinctive being and we like to think we're intellectual."[6] Weber blamed animal rights people for spreading a combination of hatred and ignorance, and he attributed much of the problem to the urban-rural divide. "Today, many people have seldom, if ever been to a farm, much less know anyone who lives on one," he wrote in an essay on the issue. "These people are open prey to emotional and perhaps embellished stories about what happens on the farm. And, when they hear that modern agricultural practices are no longer as they were in the old storybooks, it is as upsetting as the fact the Eskimos no longer live in igloos."

One succinct, if opposite, assessment of the reaction to changes in agriculture was offered by U.S. author and professor Bernard E. Rollin. The major reason for keeping animals has always been for agriculture, and one truth of agriculture was always that if animals thrived, producers thrived, he said.[7] Animals only did well if they were kept in conditions that suited their nature. But with the marvels of science and technology, this is no longer true. You can raise thousands of chickens or hogs inside one building. You can keep calves in crates or stalls all of their short lives. Antibiotics, vaccines, hormones: these allow farmers to raise animals successfully in ways that are convenient for production rather than suited to the animal's nature, Rollin said.

"If modern agriculture no longer guarantees the respect for animals' natures presupposed in traditional agriculture," Rollin writes in his book *Farm Animal Welfare*, "that role must be taken up by law and regulation. This is the sense in which animal rights is a mainstream notion for assessing animal treatment. It is, in essence, a vehicle for preserving the ancient contract in the face of radical change in animal use."[8] Indeed, according to Rollin, when Sweden passed a law in 1988 to forbid intensive confinement of animals on grounds of efficiency alone and required that agriculture accommodate animals' natures, the Swedish public saw it as a return to traditional values rather than some radical, animal rights sort of move. The law said farm animals were to be guaranteed adequate shelter, access to hay and straw and litter at all times, separate areas to eat, sleep, and defecate, and access to outdoors. It would mean phasing out intensive, confinement systems.

An Alberta agriculture official, Dr. Terry Church, had a different view of the Swedish experience. He told a 1990 symposium on farm animal welfare held in Edmonton that the Swedish legislation would compel drastic changes in farm practices. It was passed in the name of humane treatment of animals, he scoffed, but it was "almost entirely the result of lobbying by an 87-year-old author of children's books, Astrid Lindgren." He also warned, "We may not like them, but we should be very aware that animal rights activists are intelligent, articulate, well organized and funded, and they are committed."[9]

For the animal movement, the timing for a focus on farm issues would appear to be good. There is a potent mix of fears loose in the public realm, fears fed by the development of genetically altered foods, abuse of antibiotics, and frictions even among rural residents over the odours or threats to water quality presented by big, intensive farms. This is fertile ground for the animal movement to find support. Just as animal activists are not squelched by being dismissed as uninformed or sentimental, other members of the public have not been quieted by being told their fears are groundless. After drug and blood tragedies, on and off energy shortages, food contamination scares, assorted toxic spills, and a long campaign to convince people they were helpless before the giants of the corporate world, the credibility of government and of big business is shaky.

"I'm not the biggest expert," independent Winnipeg businessman and animal activist John Youngman said cheerfully. "The public has been told that their opinion isn't valid because they're not experts. But you can say [to producers], 'Whether I'm right or wrong, you're the one who's going to pay. I'm the consumer.' "[10] Youngman, a member of the boards of the Winnipeg Humane Society and Canadian Federation of Humane Societies, joined Humane Society executive director Vicki Burns on a committee with the Manitoba pork industry to discuss the treatment of hogs as that province's hog industry went through a decade of unprecedented growth. "One of our roles is to get people to open their eyes and ask if this is the way they want society to go," Burns said. "It's time to start balancing ethical questions with scientific research."

As a Humane Society official, Burns was included in a government-industry discussion about what the voluntary code of agricultural practice should recommend for horses kept for the collection of their urine to make drugs. Why shouldn't the code stipulate that these mares be allowed outside for exercise at least once a week? Burns asked. A veterinarian on the committee told her there was no research to prove that exercise outdoors would be better for the horse. To Burns, it was obvious that horses needed exercise. The need for research to prove it, she said, struck her as "ludicrous."[11]

According to Ian Duncan, "Progress in animal welfare is excruciatingly slow." Progress is also a relative concept. In England and Wales, for example, progress for the industry might be finding ways to challenge the ban on slaughtering "red meat" animals within sight of each other. That ban does, after all, slow down the slaughter line by a few seconds per animal. One study published in the English journal *Animal Welfare* reported on "An Assessment of Stress Caused in Sheep by Watching Slaughter of Other Sheep." The researchers divided up forty-four sheep into pairs and killed off one of each pair while the other one watched. They tested the survivor for heart rate, ran blood profiles, and concluded that it would be just fine to kill them in front of others.

In a later issue of the same journal, researchers were detailing their "Lack of Evidence for Stress Being Caused to Pigs by Witnessing the Slaughter of Conspecifics," which is to say stress caused by fifteen pigs forced to watch other pigs being slaughtered. If the killing line could be streamlined and speeded up in this way, the researchers noted, the process could reduce the "high percentage of pigs showing signs of recovery" when they had supposedly been stunned into the required unconsciousness before killing. Apparently the alternative of improving the operators' stunning methods was not of interest to the researchers.[12]

Perhaps what qualifies as progress for someone like Ian Duncan does not seem to be progress to some farmers or other people in the agriculture industry. Agreeing on certain basic facts about animals – on how they feel and what they experience and what they require for mental as well as physical well-being – becomes a complicated task when sides have been drawn and unwelcome research results are seen as an attack. Some parts of the agricultural industry, Duncan said, "see me as the enemy, trying to put them out of business. I criticize some of their practices, but it's to protect them from criticism."

Canada has guidelines, called codes of practice, for the care of farm animals. But they are voluntary. Even at that, the industry-dominated, non-profit body that co-ordinates the development of codes – the Canadian Agri-Food Research Council (CARC) – is reluctant to impose any strictures upon farmers. Manitoba is an exception, in that it has made adherence to the codes a legal requirement. New Brunswick was at work in the summer of 1999 on legislation that would make the codes mandatory, although the expectation was not that inspectors would be seeking out violations; instead, the codes would be used as standards to guide cruelty inspectors and others.

Both Duncan and Frances Rodenburg, the executive director of the Canadian Federation of Humane Societies, have served on CARC's Expert Committee on Farm Animal Welfare and Behaviour. Since 1995 CARC and the Federation of Humane Societies have been updating existing codes of practice and developing new ones. Aside from basic criminal laws against outright cruelty to animals, these voluntary codes are all there is to govern how animals are treated on farms. But cruelty doesn't cover what is considered normal farm practice. Cruelty would be castrating your dog without anesthetic. Castrating your piglet that way is just normal farm practice.

On only one occasion in some fifteen years of work on these codes – which are supposed to be the product of consensus among CARC and its committees, including the Federation of Humane Societies – did the Federation insist on adding one footnote to one code, and that had to do with deer raised on farms and the removal of the soft new antler growth called velvet. One item said that removing velvet – live tissue – from deer or elk required the supervision of a veterinarian and care to minimize stress and ensure the animal's welfare. The Federation also insisted on adding a footnote stating that, as an animal welfare organization, it considered the practice of removing velvet antler growth to be "ethically wrong" and that acceptable techniques to prevent unnecessary stress to the animals were not available.

"Industry didn't like that," Rodenburg said.[13] "Most of the commodity groups don't want that to happen again. Now those guys say, 'We can't trust them. They're going to fill the codes up with footnotes.'"

It's hard enough for the Federation to be providing what is essentially a stamp of approval from the animal movement, albeit the conservative part of it, to codes that sanction battery cages for hens and crates for calves. If the industry had decided to refuse to allow the Federation to register its serious dissent in a footnote, Rodenburg said, the Federation should have pulled out of the process. The footnote dispute was almost entirely symbolic. It didn't change what farmers could do, but it did suggest that the industry would brook no interference and that the animal welfare input was tolerated rather than respected.

In themselves, the voluntary codes offer a few surprises, both for what seems to have to be written down, lest it not be done, and for what the industry holds out as respectable, good practice in animal care. In the case of sheep, for example, the code of practice says that the castration of rams (if they aren't to be sold before puberty) should be carried out with a rubber ring plus a crushing device or accomplished by cutting before the age of seven days. Castration of older rams should be done by a veterinarian and under anesthetic. The code says that, usually, long-tailed woolly sheep "benefit from tail docking." Like castration, tail-docking should be done before seven days with a heated docker, a rubber ring, or a crush and cut device, or a combination of these. It says that the "assessment and control of pain associated with castration and tail docking is currently an area of intense research interest. Present recommendations may well change in the next few years." The sheep code was written in 1995, and by the summer of 1999 CARC was still reporting no new recommendations on the subject.[14]

The castration procedure for young sheep might seem barbaric enough, but it is a far sight more civilized than what the sheep code says is an "unacceptable" method called a "mules operation" to control a problem called blowfly strike. This procedure, developed in Australia, involves cutting the skin off parts of the thighs and around the anus and vulva. When the area heals, the scarred, bare skin surfaces will supposedly be less prone than woolly skin to fecal and urine soiling. Less soiling should mean less likelihood of the nasty maggot infestation known as blowfly strike.[15]

Critics argue that even shearing can be hard on sheep, often leaving animals with cuts or vulnerable to chill or sunburn. They blame breeding for creating health problems in the pursuit of profit. For example, sheep with heavier wool yields may also have excess skin, with more folds where moisture could invite maggot infestations, or so much wool that vision is obscured. Rubber-ring castration or docking can leave open wounds or cause tetanus. Ewes are sometimes sent to slaughter at age eight, perhaps half their possible life span, exhausted from overproduction. When their nursing lambs are taken away and put on grain feed to boost their weight for market, sometimes the mothers suffer from an inflammation of the udder.[16]

Calves raised for veal have been one of the agriculture industry's most controversial and high-profile issues because of their continuous confinement and restricted diet. These calves are a by-product of the dairy industry, the result of keeping dairy cows pregnant so they will produce milk. These little by-products are sold young – officially, they can be sent to slaughter as young as nineteen weeks of age – before their flesh gets toughened by age or exercise.

Milk-fed veal – the lightest coloured meat – comes from calves slaughtered at the age of about five months. After their first week of life, and weighing as little as ninety-five pounds, they can be shipped on trucks to farms where they are raised either in individual stalls or in pens with other calves, fed rations of milky liquid feed. The code of practice recommends that the individual stalls be twenty-seven and a half inches wide if the calves are not tied at the neck with a tether, and thirty-one and a half inches if they are tethered. For larger, older calves, the code recommends stalls thirty-five and a half inches in width and sixty-five inches in length. The code says that if calves are tethered, the tether should be long enough so that calves can stand and lie down, but not so long that it can tangle and choke them. In the European Union, where veal calves have also been a hot topic, stalls are supposed to be used only to eight weeks of age. That stipulation is absent from the Canadian code. By 2006, Europe is supposed to have phased out individual crates.

Calves this young, left in group pens without their mothers to suckle, often suck on the ears, tails, navels, or scrotums of other calves. The habit can lead to injuries or to drinking a lot of urine. Sometimes when they are taken away young they are fed from buckets, or they simply don't seem to be satisfied with the amount of sucking they get from the artificial teats used to deliver their liquid diet.

Mike Cooper, marketing director of Grober Inc., Canada's largest producer of milk-fed veal, said neck tethers are not used anymore on calves in Canada.[17] In the United States, unlike Canada, operators use double stalls with a short divider in the middle instead of individual ones. At $200 a stall, this is cheaper, but tethers are necessary to make sure that each calf gets to eat only its own ration of feed. In Canada, small, individual stalls are still common. Although group pens are cheaper to build, in those cases more dominant animals can shove smaller ones aside, making it hard to ensure that each of them gets fed properly. In an attempt to make group pens more efficient, Grober installed a $48,000 computerized, automatic feeder in its Cambridge, Ont., operation, the only one of its kind in North America. When the calf puts his head through the slats of the feeding station towards the nipple, a computer reads his ear tag and causes his individualized portion of white liquid feed to swirl down into the bottle so he can eat. The computer will not dispense more than his daily ration.

• • •

At Grober's operation, quiet, seven-week-old calves clustered at the feed station or huddled on the floor against the wall while a man in shirtsleeves emerged from a glass-enclosed office to check the machine. At that point the machine's durability was still open to question. In another part of the Grober operation, calves nearly ready for slaughter milled about in a windowless, room-sized indoor pen. The bare, slatted floor was scattered with their almost-liquid droppings. The long-legged babies with their bewildered, mild eyes had turned into rounded, less gangly youngsters with nothing much to do except to nose each other or stand. They had nothing to chew or to see. When they went outside, it would be for a trip a few miles down the road to the company meat-packing plant, where they would be turned into packages of chops or scaloppini.

Grober produces its trademark Delft Blue Veal in three "crops" a year of eight thousand animals each. The company wants a consistent quality and size of animal so that the meat is uniform. Consistent quality means a steady supply and more equipment than an individual operator could afford, so there are very few independents in the business. The 1970s and 1980s saw a big drop in the market, largely due to criticism of how the calves were raised. Cooper said the industry let the criticisms go unanswered and paid the price. "We stuck our heads in the sand," he said. It would have taken work just to stay even, what with immigration patterns bringing people to Canada from parts of the world where veal is not a common food. Now, he said, they try as an industry to chip away at negative consumer attitudes. There is an export market to serve in the United States, where Grober rates in the top ten of producers. Although other countries have banned veal stalls where the animals spend their whole lives, Cooper does not expect such action in Canada. Here, he said, people sit around a table and work things out.

The Woodstock area of southwestern Ontario is Canada's biggest veal-producing centre, and the calves there are either being raised under contract to Grober or are on Grober's own farms. Still, although the area has miles of rolling, lush fields, when you drive around it there is not a veal calf to be seen. When I arrived at Grober's own farm, an attractive, modern set of buildings with air vented through peat moss and waste water recycled to stop odours, there was nothing to tell me that hundreds of seven-day-old animals arrived there weekly, some after an eight-hour truck trip. If they are younger than seven days, they die off too easily. They have their blood checked regularly with the help of a $50,000 machine to decide if they need iron supplements — a special precaution because the anemia of milk-fed calves is a long-standing complaint about the industry. The farm has its own veterinarian and round-the-clock staff and leading-edge technology. The place is state of the art for North America and as good as it gets for calves. It isn't typical for calves elsewhere.

What is typical for hogs is, increasingly, massive farm operations that house thousands of animals indoors. Pregnant and nursing sows are commonly confined in stalls, in which they are sometimes unable to turn around for months on end. The goal with nursing sows is, by restricting their movement, to prevent them from crushing their piglets. Operators also find it simply easier and cheaper to confine large numbers of animals in single pens than to pay for enough skilled workers, who would know what to watch for and when to intervene if some animal is bullied or is getting less than her share of food, to manage hogs in a group pen. The economic argument, especially when farms are operating with huge numbers of animals, is a prime consideration for determining conditions for all kinds of animals.

The Canadian code of practice says holding units should allow pigs to move forward and backward and to lie down. It does not recommend the use of tethers and suggests that producers consider changing their confinement systems for pregnant sows when they are renovating or building, "because the use of stalls is a contentious welfare issue." It promotes the use of pens of about eight square feet instead of narrow stalls for nursing sows. (Sows can be over six feet long themselves.) By contrast, in Britain, in 1991 the government banned both tethers and stalls for hogs and gave the industry an eight-year period to adjust.

The tether ban was to match regulations in Europe, but the stall ban was a stiffer measure. The European Community then decided to ban confinement crates for sows by the year 2004.

The developments in Europe have made the industry edgy, according to Laurie Connor, who chaired a review of the farm code for pigs. Connor, a professor in the University of Manitoba's Department of Animal Science, said the industry was not convinced that the same regulation would come to Canada.[18] David Fraser, one of two professors of the ground-breaking animal welfare course at the University of British Columbia, said it would be "terribly unwise" for the industry to continue to use such close confinement when it is so publicly unacceptable. There is no reason a stall couldn't be wide enough for an animal to turn around, he said.

Welfare issues in agriculture are important because a healthy, contented animal is productive, said Manitoba Pork spokesman Ted Muir.[19] Crates are used for reasons of health and meat quality. No farmer is going to risk his expensive operation without a cost-benefit analysis, and banks are even less likely to take the risk of financing them, Muir said. They like to stick with what they know will work. In Manitoba many of the biggest of hog operations have expanded to serve largely export markets, and they were built up according to the familiar confinement stall systems, with the operators obviously not convinced that any new regulations were going to interfere.

Here again, science would be a battlefield given any move to limit how producers confine their animals. Fraser and fellow U.B.C. professor Dan Weary head their university's new animal welfare program, which has funding from the agriculture industry, government, and the British Columbia Society for the Prevention of Cruelty to Animals. The professors said they considered themselves to be on no particular side, neither producer nor animal protectionist, but simply in search of answers to questions being posed about animal welfare.[20] "How does it really affect the sow if she can't turn around for three months?" Fraser asked. Everyone knows that castrating pigs is painful, Weary said, and the farmer does not enjoy doing it. With more knowledge about how the animals feel, he said, better ways of doing things could be found.

But, again, if everyone knows that castrating pigs is painful, why is more study needed? Either you believe that pain matters, and you do something about it, or you are saying you don't think it is important enough to deal with. Anesthetics do exist, even if administering them takes time and money. Similarly, there is no proof that turning around hurts a sow, and surely you don't have to be an animal extremist to think that natural activity is better for an intelligent animal who has just about nothing else to do. The industry says it is concerned about control over feeding and possible fighting among animals in group pens. But when a larger style crate that allowed greater freedom of movement appeared in Ontario, it didn't sell because it seemed to offer no economic benefit.[21] It is hard not to conclude that economic benefits are the true test in agriculture and that the stress on gaining more scientific knowledge is often an excuse to make it harder to challenge farm practices. The assertion that we don't know enough about animal minds or feelings, a scientific lacking, is used to defend conditions for animals that, in earlier days, would have seemed out of place as a matter of common sense. It puts the onus for scientific proof on those who would limit what is done to animals on farms.

The codes of practice say that castration and trimming the top quarter of piglets' sharp teeth should be done in their first few weeks of life if, as usual, it is to be done. The end third of the tail is often trimmed so that other pigs won't chew on it in close quarters where there isn't a whole lot else to chew on. Boars get their tusks trimmed to the gums, though the code warns about avoiding gum damage. (In Britain, pig tail-docking is supposed to be an exception rather than routine.)

Bob Hunsberger's southern Ontario hog farm would not be considered a big one now. Size seems to be measured in units of 1,250 sows these days, he said, with labour costs kept low, individual stalls for each animal, and artificial insemination. Modern large operations have biotechnology security, which means that visitors to a big pig barn must shower first. Hunsberger has four hundred sows and a set-up that was more common in the mid-1970s to mid-1980s. His animals spend most of their time in group pens with sides that could open to the outdoors for natural ventilation and daylight. His sows are kept in individual stalls for up to two weeks after breeding to ensure they are pregnant, but the stalls have hinged, shared sides so that the animals can turn around by pushing the end of the middle wall temporarily into the neighbouring sow's space. In the last three or four weeks of their pregnancies they are again kept in individual stalls to control their feeding, then once more for three or four weeks after giving birth and while nursing. In the group pens the animals can mill about in a limited fashion, and the hogs all defecate at one end, away from the feeding and resting area. They watch visitors without alarm and turn their snouts to investigate an offered hand. It is not a megafarm operation, but Hunsberger does not criticize that way of raising animals.[22]

His sows are in pens for much of their time, he said, because he likes it that way. "I like seeing pigs in pens. I don't have scientific reasons." He likes to throw a slab of hay into the pen and watch as the animals play with it. As for the European bans on crates, he said he doesn't believe it is right or scientific. Probably sows in stalls are healthier, he said, and the economics of stalls are certainly better. The stall ban in England was influenced by people who believe sows would be better off out of stalls, but it's just because they believe it, he said. "When we make a decision that they are better outside, we mean *we* like it," Hunsberger said.

While agriculture in the past probably made too many decisions based on economics rather than the welfare of animals, he said, there is now recognition that not enough is known about animals. But he knows of nothing in modern agriculture that amounts to intentional animal abuse. Does the industry not fear regulation or consider it advisable to move away from stalls in this latest, massive expansion? In Canadian agriculture, he said, the attitude is to build for what the producers believe is best and to trust that they can ultimately explain that to the public's satisfaction.

Critics of the hog industry aim their fire at operations larger than Hunsberger's, at operations in which animals are routinely kept in stalls and stand over slatted floors beneath which their smelly wastes accumulate. For both workers and animals, the gases from the wastes can cause respiratory problems. Critics say this confinement set-up is cruel for an animal as intelligent as a pig. In Cape Breton, the Nova Scotia Network for Animals co-ordinated a letter campaign for tougher standards for massive farm operations after several fires in huge hog barns killed thousands of animals at a time.

The B.C. Society for the Prevention of Cruelty to Animals tried a positive approach in 1996, giving an award to a local hog farmer whose carefully planned four-hundred-hog Eco Barn operation was a study in industry contrasts. Cors de Lint's hogs had full, undocked tails and roomier twenty-pig pens with fresh air, sunlight, and deep sawdust flooring to root in. The farmer, a former veterinarian in Holland, told the BCSPCA that he knew the pigs would clean the pens themselves if they were given the chance, and they did. The animals organized their space into eating, sleeping, play, and waste areas. They pushed the waste, less smelly than liquid manure because of the sawdust mixed in, into a trough by themselves. A mechanical scraper carried it off. His system drew European interest because stricter welfare conditions there had farmers searching for alternative systems that work.[23]

Animal activists call the egg industry one of the most systematically cruel. For that, they are generally accused of inflamed rhetoric, of putting the worst spin on things. But even a reading of the code of practice, the one written by industry itself and held out as admirable, can make an outsider blanche.

The voluntary code of practice for poultry recommends that chicks not be thrown or picked up by their heads. When producers want to dispose of the unwanted chicks, they can use a high-speed macerator that chops them up. It is important, the code says, to be sure there is no backlog at the entry point of live chicks waiting to be shredded, or it would not be a humane death. Decapitation or neck-breaking is not practical in a big commercial operation, and drowning or piling chicks in disposal containers to suffocate is not considered acceptable. Chickens raised on the floor as broilers should be able to stand, turn around, and stretch their wings normally without difficulty. Cages for chickens (egg layers) should be at least eight inches long and sixteen inches wide for a single bird and twelve inches by sixteen inches for two. This is where they spend their entire lives.

If the producers withhold food and water to force chickens to moult and to manipulate their egg-laying cycle, they should try not to have the birds lose more than 30 per cent of their pre-moult body weight, the code says. There are more deaths than usual during a forced moult, it notes, but if mortality reaches 3 per cent of the flock in fourteen days, it should be ended. Feather-pecking or cannibalism among chickens can be a substitute for the normal activity of searching for feed, which the caged bird no longer has to do, the code says. You can reduce the pecking by increasing food, reducing the group size, and adding distractions, like straw. In some cases it may be necessary to trim the chicken's beak. But that measure, as in the removal of parts of toes, should only be taken if necessary to prevent injuries.

Bruce Weber said his 12,600 chickens were content in their cages. It is the only domain they know; they have everything they need and are not in fear of predators. This cage system, he said, produces eggs that are cleaner than ever. As for beak-trimming, he called it minor surgery. He does it with a hot knife, cutting through the beak. For a day or two afterward the chicks cut back on eating, he said, and for a week or two their beaks might be tender. But he believed it was absolutely necessary to keep chickens from cannibalizing each other with this procedure and argued that, since it costs ten cents a bird to trim beaks, farmers would not spend the money if it were not necessary.

Critics say this procedure is cruel, unnecessary, and can cause chronic pain. Some of these charges "contain a grain of truth," Dr. Peter Hunton of the Ontario Egg Producers' Marketing Board told a U.S. industry magazine.[24] The issue came under discussion in the magazine after a trial project found that birds with intact beaks ate better and, left with untrimmed beaks, represented no economic disadvantage. Hunton observed that most commercial producers would not be willing to risk changing their practice. In Britain, research is being pursued into dust-bathing and other natural activities for chickens as a way of reducing pecking and cannibalism and perhaps making possible a ban on beak-trimming.

Some studies suggest that beak-trimming – or debeaking, as critics call it – causes chronic pain in the nerves of chickens' beaks. In the agricultural industry this worry tends to be dismissed with the observation that the chickens eat and lay eggs, so they must be happy, or happy enough. Sometimes supporters note that at least debeaking is not as bad as older efforts at controlling aggression in chickens, including ill-fated experiments with red contact lenses that left birds with painful eye damage or blinded. There is talk within the industry of efforts being made to breed for less aggressive birds, which would decrease the need for debeaking. But skeptics note that breeding for heftier breasts or plumper thighs gets the priority because it boosts revenue, while aggression can be cheaply dealt with by chopping off a chunk of beak.

Indeed, breeding seems to be going in the opposite direction. Temple Grandin, a U.S. professor and internationally respected expert on slaughter and livestock behaviour, said she is concerned that genetic experiments are producing problem animals. She cited the example of super-big killer roosters who seem to have lost their courtship rituals and simply attack, rape, and harm or kill hens. There are hogs so nervous that they cannot be handled by the usual systems. Grandin, an assistant professor of livestock handling and behaviour at Colorado State University's Department of Animal Sciences, predicted that issues of confinement may be dwarfed in future by unexpected genetic problems.[25]

The egg-laying industry is one of the most highly mechanized of farm sectors. Chickens for egg-laying are hatched in incubators and shipped immediately to farms. (The males are not wanted, which is why the code of practice deals with how to kill chicks.) In Weber's operation the cages stretch down the windowless building in rows, perhaps three cages high on each side. Diet and lights stimulate hens in cages to lay more eggs. The only activity the chickens have is eating from the troughs outside their cages. Their droppings fall through the mesh floor and are carried away. Weber's farm has someone to collect the eggs from the little gutter they roll into, but on larger farms, where it is possible to have one person run an eighty-thousand-bird operation, that job is done by machine. The lack of exercise and the continuous egg-laying mean that the calcium-depleted bones of the hens are fragile and easily broken. At twelve to eighteen months they are called "spent" and considered of little value. The whites of their eggs tend to get runny and their bodies worn down, although they have a potential lifespan of many years. At this point they will have laid perhaps three hundred eggs, compared to a few dozen a year that they might lay in a natural setting, where they would nest and scratch for seeds and dust-bathe. In the end they are trucked off to be slaughtered and used in soups, pet foods, or processed human food.

Broiler chickens, raised on crowded floors until their slaughter at about forty days, are often so engineered to grow quickly and produce a lot of meat that their legs cannot properly bear their weight. They may suffer breast blisters from the floor, where waste accumulates in the increasingly soiled bedding.

Forced moult is a more common procedure in the United States than in Canada, and one that activists there are aggressively challenging. However, there is no reason why producers in Canada couldn't use it if they wanted. "It's not so bad," Weber said of the forced moult process, although his operation, he said, did not need it. "People go on diets. With this, you withdraw water for a day, then food for six, and then phase it back in. It's nothing that I have a conscience about." In Ontario producers have recently given consideration to trying the food deprivation procedure to boost egg production, which would in turn supply increased demand from large processing companies. The idea is to shock the birds into stopping egg-laying for a brief time, after which they could come back into production for another stint. But the trials run by the Ontario Egg Producers found no economic advantage to the approach. In the United States, forced moult has been the subject of an intensive campaign by animal activists, who want the practice banned. They argue that it is inhumane, that it causes severe suffering, increased deaths, and, possibly, more danger to human food safety by weakening the hens' immune system.

Industry codes of practice are also in place for other kinds of animals raised on farms – for beef and dairy cattle and horses. Fur farms have their own codes with recommended sizes for the cages in which mink and fox live.

The code of practice for horses kept for the collection of pregnant mares' urine is a gently phrased document. Horses should be allowed "as much exercise as is necessary." The stalls that the very largest mares stand in for months should be five feet wide. Others can be narrower. The code stipulates water quantities, suggesting that water "should" be offered several times a day. Foals should have "adequate shelter." Tougher codes could actually make a real difference in this particular industry because at least one province, Manitoba, has made it a legal requirement for agricultural operations there to follow existing codes instead of leaving adherence to them as a voluntary option.

As it happens, Brandon, Manitoba, is the Canadian centre for Wyeth-Ayerst Laboratories' Premarin facility. The province is also home to a large share of the more than four hundred plus farms involved in collecting millions of gallons of urine a year from pregnant mares for the giant multinational drug firm. Wyeth-Ayerst uses the urine to make Premarin, a drug that, in pills, creams, injections, or patches, has been on the market since 1942 to deal with the symptoms of menopause and to diminish the risks of osteoporosis and heart disease in women over the age of fifty. Premarin has an enormous, billion-dollar market around the world and, with the sixty million or so women in North America expected to enter menopause by the year 2000, it would seem to have a rosy future. But there are plant-based alternatives for this drug, and animal activists are determined to promote them.

The extraction of pregnant mare's urine (PMU) – used especially in the production of estrogen supplements and birth-control pills – had been an Ontario industry for decades, until flack about the squalor in which foals were raised and the brutalization of mares pushed the Ontario government into passing regulatory legislation in the 1960s. The industry shifted to Manitoba. Animal activists around the world have given Canada much unflattering publicity over the horses, arguing that they suffer from lack of exercise for half of each year, from September to March, when they are kept in stalls for urine collection. They say the horses often develop sores from the collection devices strapped to their hind ends and that they are kept on skimpy rations of water while they serve in what is contemptuously called the pee line. (Less water makes estrogen, the important ingredient, more concentrated in the urine.) In the third trimester of the mare's pregnancy, when estrogen content in her urine drops, she is turned out to pasture to foal.

Even more than the complaints about barn conditions, it is the plight of an estimated forty thousand foals born each year to these pregnant mares that is seen as the real tragedy of the industry. The riding-horse market can take only so many. So, usually early in September, at just a few months of age, the foals are taken to sales to be auctioned off. Many of them are briefly fattened up and taken to slaughter. The U.S.-based HorseAid organization, a long-time foe of the industry, has followed the foals to meat markets in Japan.

Wyeth-Ayerst has repeatedly rejected the criticisms, saying the company's suppliers give mares the best of care and that many foals go to riding stables and farms. The North American Equine Ranching Information Council, an organization representing some 440 ranchers and farmers who raise PMU mares in North Dakota, Saskatchewan, Alberta, and Manitoba, has devoted itself for years to combating what it considers inaccurate criticisms. The Council argues that no more than one-third of the foals go to the meat market and that this international trade would exist whether or not PMU foals were available. It says that vets under contract to the company visit farms at least three times during urine collection, and that company inspectors also make the rounds. The company insists that farmers follow the code of practice and that the horses get plenty of water and exercise as needed. The Council's Web site offers testimonies to the quality of care that the mares receive, including an excerpt from a 1995 report by Tom Hughes's CanFACT, the Canadian Farm Animal Care Trust.[26] CanFACT was established in 1989 to focus on the conditions of animals on farms, and stresses on its Internet Web site that it is neither vegetarian nor in support of "antisocial" tactics.

Hughes, a combative veteran of the animal welfare movement, has come down on industry's side in this issue. The 1995 CanFACT report on PMU farms came after a tour by experts, Hughes said. The report found the farms much improved, with the horse care as good as in any other part of the horse industry, and Wyeth-Ayerst sincere in its claims about good care.[27]

Winnipeg animal rights activist and PAAL co-ordinator James Pearson did not share this assessment. He predicted that farmers with contracts to supply mares' urine to the drug-maker would eventually find themselves rudely dumped when Wyeth-Ayerst itself decided to produce a synthetic product to compete with the alternatives already on the market. He told about having his car followed after he and other activists were seen observing farms from the road. Some of the farmers want to intimidate critics, he said, and at auctions activists have reportedly been bullied by other buyers when they have come to bid for foals. Their unwanted interventions drive up prices. Vicki Burns of the Winnipeg Humane Society described the industry as "ridiculously touchy" and said her office's requests to tour horse farms went nowhere.

• • •

Farmers – the producers in the agriculture system – are not the only ones virtually left on their own to regulate themselves. Government has steadily backed away from regulating other parts of the system, even when rules are on the books. The transport of animals, for example, is one area that makes crystal clear the scant value placed on the lives of animals raised for food. For example, at just the federally regulated slaughterhouses between two and three million animals arrive dead or dying or so ill they must be destroyed – year after year after year. That figure does not include the number of injured animals that arrive and, if they are still considered fit for human consumption, are sent directly to slaughter.

Provincially inspected slaughterhouses, where meat is produced for domestic consumption, are considered to be generally less demanding. According to one Ontario official, in the face of efforts to upgrade towards federal standards some meat packers were warning that they might be forced out of business or even into a black market, where they would operate illegally without a licence and uninspected. This raised the fear that, should it happen, the government could lose control over enforcement.[28]

For years now the industry and members of animal organizations have been discussing the problem of animal transport. The federal government has also, however slowly, recognized the existence of a problem. In 1987 the Federation of Humane Societies produced a survey indicating problems and the need for more enforcement, and years later, in 1995, Ottawa produced a one-year project that revealed serious transport problems, particularly for hens. A sampling of federally inspected abattoirs in 1995 and 1996 found that, on average, 2 per cent of each load of hens arrived dead. More than 5 per cent were dead in 7 per cent of the loads in 1996 and 11 per cent in 1995. The conclusion drawn was, "Inadequate transportation practices are an industry-wide problem."[29]

Other numbers support the need for action. Statistics from federally inspected slaughterhouses alone show that, in 1991, 2.6 million animals were dead on arrival, including 2 million chickens, 15,967 hogs, 113 horses, and 14 deer. In 1994, a total of 3.3 million transported animals arrived dead at their destinations, including 4,000 rabbits, 2.3 million chickens, 12,867 hogs, 602 cattle, and 401 calves. In 1997 there were 3.2 million dead in total, including 2.3 million chickens, 15,836 hogs, 2,542 mature turkeys, and 36,939 young turkeys.[30]

A plan was eventually drawn up to deal with what was seemingly the worst problem, spent laying hens – more than a decade after the government was urged to act for the sake of millions of birds dying miserably each year on their way to slaughter. By sometime in the year 2000, the promise went, there would be automatic investigations in cases in which 3 per cent or more of a load of spent laying hens arrive dead at federally inspected slaughterhouses. In fact, this program was supposed to have been in place as early as 1998. The discussions, and delayed plans, are part of a slow, deferential process in Canada's federal Department of Agriculture, which speaks volumes about the lack of importance attached to the hardships of animals. The federal trend has been to stay away from on-site monitoring and to step in only after a problem has been identified statistically.

That hands-off attitude only shows signs of growing stronger, which bodes ill for any attempt to improve more than the worst transport outrages. The attitude also marks a complete turnaround for the government's role over the past twenty years. In the 1970s an Agriculture Canada more engaged in improving things than in recording data had developed a program to cut the deaths of cattle being transported from west to east in Canada. It succeeded in reducing mortality rates by 50 per cent, a record that was seen in economic terms as a good thing. (Spent hens, alas, are considered of little value.) The progress with cattle led the government to pass laws allowing it to regulate the transportation of animals to ensure humane treatment and to cut diseases related to the hardships of shipping. Across the country, federal programs were then developed to actively monitor animals moving within provinces and across provincial borders. It was a neat fit with the scrutiny accorded animals being imported or exported.

In the mid-1980s, citing something called emerging fiscal pressures, Ottawa decided to redesign the system as part of its plan to cut back on the civil service. In other words, the system was slashed. The changes left federal veterinarians in slaughter plants much less aware of transport problems that should be investigated. Before that time, for instance, trucks had been inspected on the highways to ensure that transport regulations – originally put in place because of a high rate of illness and death among cattle shipped east to Ontario – were being observed. By the late 1980s this inspection had dwindled to periodic visits to slaughterhouses and some assembly yards. Now all that remains of the transportation checks is a single inspection station at the Ontario-Manitoba border, where there is also a provincial weigh scale. The future of even that lone federal inspection post remained up in the air in the summer of 1999, according to Dr. Gord Doonan, head of the federal Humane Transportation Program. Roadside checks are done now sporadically and randomly. The government's intent was to put the onus on transport companies to comply with regulations rather than have their behaviour actively monitored, Doonan explained.[31]

At the same time, changes were underway to the Meat Inspection Act to drop a ban on shipping animals under the age of fourteen days. It had only ever been considered a factor in terms of meat quality, rather than a way of protecting young animals who were barely past the newborn stage and, like sad spent hens and other older animals, considered fragile. It had become clear, Doonan said, that there was no connection between meat quality and the age of shipping. So Doonan was scrambling in late summer of 1999 to prepare a regulation that could be enacted simultaneously under the Health of Animals Act and would forbid transporting animals to slaughter at less than seven days of age. That age suited the veal industry.

The Canadian Food Inspection Agency, Ottawa's enforcement body for the Health of Animals Act, had talked some years earlier of setting a graduated scale for inspections to keep a lid on abuse of animals during transport from farm to slaughter. The idea was that, if 3 per cent of the truck load of animals or birds arrived dead or died before slaughter, a cursory check would be made by the government inspector at the slaughterhouse to see what had happened. It seems hardly a radical idea, considering that it would mean a significant number of animals in a single shipment had died in ways they weren't supposed to have. The inspector would run over how long the trip had taken and other facts already on hand to be sure that regulations had been followed. At 4 per cent dead, the inspector would do post-mortems on some of the dead animals to find out the cause of death, in case further action was needed. At 5 per cent or more dead, outside labs would be asked to study specimens of some animals, a precaution in case charges were laid and neutral evidence was needed in court. The plan was that this graduated scale would be implemented for all kinds of animals, perhaps with injuries or bruises rather than deaths on arrival to be used for other than chickens. Other species – goats, pigs, cattle and calves, horses – suffer injuries more often than die compared to birds.

For Doonan, who was being told repeatedly that there was no staff left to perform the extra duties this graduated scale would require, extending the system to other species seemed a distant goal. "Whether we'll actually manage to do it, I don't know," he said. In any case, he remained confident that the case of spent hens, at least, would soon be covered after endless rounds of consultations with the producers. In Quebec, he said, inspectors had already taken it upon themselves to put the new system in place, but that had not happened elsewhere. Similarly, some inspectors had picked up on the idea of unannounced visits to auctions to check on conditions for animals. Doonan said he also hoped that more of them could be encouraged to look at the animals in the receiving areas of abattoirs more frequently than just a couple of times a day.

"You know, they're just hens and nobody cares about hens," Humane Society Federation official Rodenburg said of the staggering numbers of hens dead in transport. "They're suffocating on the trucks and they're freezing to death. People have such double standards. If that had been horses or dogs!"

It seems unlikely that the agriculture or trucking industries will have to quake at the idea of a crackdown. There are only ever six to ten prosecutions related to transport injuries a year, and only the most severe injuries get that far. A Chilliwack, B.C., producer, for example, was fined $1,500 when nearly 12 per cent of a load of chickens died in the cold of a January 1996 day during a trip to a federally inspected slaughter plant. That case had depended upon complaints from the public at the sight of dead and dying chickens on a ferry run. A Guelph truck driver was fined $2,000 in July 1998 after 10,444 chickens suffocated on his vehicle.[32]

Instead of prosecutions for clear breaches of the law, Ottawa decided it preferred something called administrative monetary penalties. Court cases can take up to two years, Doonan said, and this approach could work much more quickly. It would also mean that the company, trucker, or farm producer would be spared a conviction on his or her record and the embarrassment of a court hearing. It involved a sliding scale of potentially steep fines and a written agreement for the offending party to fix things up. However, signing such an agreement could mean the fine would be lowered. An outsider might also see the approach as an indication that the offence was not such a big deal. "We feel to get compliance, we have to get to people's hearts," said Doonan.

Tina Harrison of the Vancouver-based Canadians for the Ethical Treatment of Food Animals has come to wonder if hearts are involved at all. The booklet that her organization produced – an Ontario trucker's testimony about hauling livestock – makes disheartening reading. Fearing for his safety, the driver asked that his identity be protected. In the interview he described flouted regulations, tormented animals arriving at slaughterhouses ill or crippled or unable to walk off the truck (these ones are called "downers"), and indifferent slaughterhouse inspectors and humane societies. Pigs with broken pelvises, called "spreaders," are not officially allowed to be dragged off trucks live with chains attached to their legs, because that causes unnecessary pain; but the trucker said he had seen it done. The sick or injured animals are supposed to be killed humanely, but the trucker said he had never seen such a thing done.

"I've had nine pigs dead at one time and there's other drivers who have had 30. One fellow that I know had 35 pigs dead, out of a load of 200," the trucker said.

> And for that fellow that had 35 pigs dead, he had been out partying the night before and pulled over on a 30-31 degree day and fell asleep for six hours. Inside the trailer was probably about 50 degrees because of the heat, you know the metal being heated up. And they basically just roasted. . . . So I was so bothered by this I called the humane society the next day. I called the Hamilton SPCA. No, I called the Toronto SPCA first. They referred me to Burlington, I think it was. They referred me to Hamilton. Hamilton said, "I don't know why you're calling us." And they said, "call the head office." And I called the head office and finally I gave up.

The day the driver with thirty-five dead pigs arrived at the processing plant, the trucker said, an inspector was present. But no charges were laid on the death of the thirty-five pigs, and the inspector only glanced into the vehicle. (Companies pay the government for the services of veterinarians to oversee slaughter. Their work is assisted by government inspectors as well as company employees who supposedly draw suspect animals to the vets' attention. All animals are supposed to be seen before slaughter by a federal employee.)

On another occasion, when pigs were being made to jump several feet down to get off of a truck, with some ending up crippled, the trucker called the Humane Society anonymously. He later heard that, for two days after his call, inspectors checked loads and told drivers to put a 150-pound ramp onto the trailer for the pigs to walk down. The truckers found the ramp too heavy, and they soon did away with it. But, the trucker said, it might appear on any related paperwork that a problem had been fixed.

The trucker talked about animals frozen to the metal floors of trucks because of a lack of bedding in cold weather; or animals piled up, injured, after one had fallen down en route. The only way to get an animal on a truck back on its feet if it has fallen, he said, was to jolt it repeatedly with an electric prod through the air holes on the truck sides. But that doesn't work with pigs, he said. He told about having a dead pig explode as the other animals stepped on it during unloading.

"When a pig explodes, I mean what happens when I'm unloading, is that all the other pigs scurry to get off. Well, you're prodding them so they don't have any choice. They all run over the dead pig or jump over it and it's just like an explosion. Well, I mean, it's the first time I've ever been sick to my stomach from it. Because there are pieces of pig all over the sides of the trailer and all over you and it's disgusting."

Once the trucker hauled a bull that collapsed near the front of the trailer sometime during the trip. At the destination, with three or four men jabbing at it with electric prods, the bull tried to drag his useless hind quarters to the rear of the truck. After forty-five minutes the animal reached the ramp at the rear of the trailer and fell off, smashing onto the ground below. Again it began to drag itself along. The trucker asked the crew why someone didn't kill the animal, put it out of its misery. He was told there was good meat on it and it had to be got inside the building. An hour later the bull was inside and the workers were streaming out for the end of the shift. The trucker was left feeling sure the injured animal would be lying inside all night.

Once, he said, another trucker was fined for arriving at Sault Ste. Marie with injured horses – several with broken legs had been left on the truck overnight – and after that incident he was himself warned that it would be bad news if he got involved in alerting the Humane Society. He thought of that warning as he prepared to talk to Tina Harrison. "I said to Tina, before I was so scared to come forward even to talk to her about it, I just couldn't sleep at night. I had nightmare after nightmare. . . . There was so much on my mind. I wanted to tell someone and I couldn't. I was so scared that, once I did contact her, it's just been a constant worry. What if I was ever found out? . . . My life would be in danger."[33]

Given that the government admits that problems do exist in transport, what critics of the system want is fairly simple. They want genuine inspections and an accounting for transport deaths and injuries, with offenders going to court. They want, in effect, several million unscheduled and often agonizing animal deaths and injuries each year to be considered a serious issue.

• • •

What happens after animals arrive at slaughterhouses can be as troubling as the problems in transport. Once again, poultry leads the way. Federally inspected facilities – those allowed to ship meat abroad – are said to have the best conditions and most diligent government inspection, compared to provincially inspected plants for domestic sales and small, local abattoirs. Provincial systems vary across the country, and in some provinces animals may not be inspected at all before slaughter.

In late June 1999 front-page news stories in Toronto charged that meat from four slaughterhouses there was being sold abroad as federally approved even though veterinarians had seen neither the live animals nor the carcasses, as required. An internal letter surfaced in which veterinarian Dr. Jacques Caron of the Canadian Food Inspection Agency (CFIA) complained about two plants operating for several days at a time off and on from December 1998 to spring 1999 with no federal vets present. As Caron complained, the system had become yet another "paper tiger."

The CFIA had, like every other official body dealing with animals it seems, slashed its staff in a move towards more self-policing by industry. A B.C. vet reported around the same time that he had been asked to sign forms approving meat from chickens, even though he had not seen the birds. The CFIA replied that vets did not need to be on site to supervise the work, that their services needed only to be accessible. But export regulations require that animals be under "veterinary supervision" before and after slaughter.[34] Not long after the news stories had died down, Caron, chair of the veterinary group of his union, the Professional Institute of the Public Service, found out that one of the same plants had begun slaughtering animals early one morning without a federal vet present.[35]

With staff shortages and the obvious priority being post-mortem safety of the meat for human consumption, the condition of the live animals on arrival or while they move through the slaughter system appears unlikely to be occupying anyone's mind for very long. Caron, a hog specialist, said that some days he had time only to see the animals set aside by government staff, and no time to view the unsorted new arrivals himself. The routine is for plant employees under federal inspectors' scrutiny to screen arrivals and pull out those that are not walking or have visible abnormalities to show to the vet on duty for approval or rejection for slaughter. At federally inspected plants government inspectors are also present, so that all animals are supposedly viewed by someone other than company workers. The company's desire to protect its reputation and fear that a stressed animal produces bad meat, at least in the case of pigs, can add a measure of protection to the animals' welfare, Caron said. The policy, once again, relies heavily on self-policing, based on the premise that everyone involved holds as much commitment to obeying the rules as to improving the company's bottom line.

One problem, Caron said, is that slaughterhouse employees who deal with the animals when they are still alive are not as well paid as others who handle their carcasses. Those with experience usually move on to the better-paying positions. If they don't, it's usually because they do not have the necessary skills.

One undramatic little story of everyday routine speaks volumes about the lack of urgency attached to the welfare of animals as they are put to death and about the deference accorded the facility supposedly being policed. The records of the CFIA – the federal inspection agency – require that pre-slaughter conditions be policed and problems reported. In keeping with this practice, on December 9, 1993, a federal vet at a B.C. slaughterhouse noticed a pen of veal calves being showered with a fine spray of water. The animals had been sprayed for several hours, non-stop, with cold water inside a cold barn. The vet contacted his regional supervisor and said it seemed inhumane to spray cold water inside a cold facility onto such young animals. The owner, when contacted, said the method was used to calm calves and make it easier to clean their hides. He noted that an Ontario slaughterhouse also did the same thing. The vet contacted an Ontario colleague, who told him that in the Ontario operation the water used was a warm spray and was turned on thirty minutes before slaughter began in a heated barn under conditions that were almost tropical.

A week later the B.C. vet went back to the plant and tested the conditions by having the water spray turned on without any animals under it. The pen was drafty, about 6.5 degrees Celsius. Even when hot water was shunted into the line, the temperature did not rise above that of the ambient air. "It was decided that, on an interim basis, we will let the calves be sprayed for at most one half hour prior to slaughter," the vet wrote in a report to his supervisor.[36]

The authorities decided to seek more information so that other conditions might be laid down for the plant. The vet didn't like simply to monitor the calves to see how chilled they were getting, because it seemed too ad hoc. He said he believed the question of their well-being in this case was beyond his expertise. The thorny issue made its way to the highest levels in the federal chain of command. On January 20, 1994, the chief of regulations and procedures for the Meat and Poultry Products Division at CFIA headquarters in Ottawa wrote to the federal regional manager of meat products in British Columbia to say that the spraying of the calves in the B.C. facility was unacceptable "from a humanitarian point of view" and should not be allowed. The CFIA chief suggested that warm, uncrowded pens with food and water would calm the calves and that the hides could be cleaned after slaughter. He added, in reply to a suggestion from the slaughterhouse manager, "We do not see how the practice of spraying calves will improve meat quality." The letter indicated that the Division office would seek guidelines on spraying veal calves.[37] The whole process had taken about six weeks, plus the time of several professionals and senior consultations – all to tell a company to turn off the cold water.

Among the most disturbing of slaughterhouse complaints are concerns about poultry – especially laying hens considered no longer of much value. Ian Duncan blames the egg industry, saying it shouldn't be allowed to operate in such a way that, at the end, these birds are considered to be the "garbage."

Temple Grandin, who can boast that half the cattle killed in Canada go through systems she has designed, is regularly invited by authorities to inspect facilities in Canada. On one such tour in 1995, Grandin visited twenty-one slaughterhouses in Ontario, British Columbia, and Alberta, all of them small- to medium-sized cattle, sheep, poultry, hog, and horse operations. Her inspection visit was pre-announced, and the poultry plants surveyed had expressed an interest in being included. Even with that level of preparation, advance notice, and good will, three out of the fourteen cattle, hog, sheep, and horse facilities visited did not pass the grade for humane slaughter. Of the four poultry places Grandin visited, two did not pass muster. In one chicken abattoir, as many as 3 per cent of the chickens missed the pre-slaughter stunning: they were killed conscious, against the regulations, because they raised their heads. In this type of operation, chickens are shackled and attached, upside down, to a moving line so that their heads pass through an electrical stunning water bath for some seconds. If they lift their heads too much in a natural effort to right themselves, and if the water is not the correct height, some of them may miss being stunned and go on, conscious and still alive, to throat-slashing and even scalding. Fixing this problem was a simple matter of adjusting the level of the water bath carrying the electrical charge, but it was a solution that no one had bothered to put into effect.

In one turkey operation Grandin visited, the birds all passed through the stunning process but some began blinking afterward. At three plants some turkeys were dirty. At one the turkeys had blisters on their breasts, and in two others many birds had bare breasts where their feathers had been worn off. These problems are caused by overcrowding on the floor of the barn where they were raised, and by a lack of clean new bedding, Grandin reported. The reason, she concluded: "The grower gets paid the same price for both clean or dirty turkeys."[38]

Grandin described conditions as "terrible" at one plant she visited that was under provincial jurisdiction for inspection. As a sideline, the plant supplied sterile blood for the production of blood agar, used in lab tests. To collect the blood, the operators tied up seven sheep at a time. Two of the sheep, fully conscious, were strapped to tables with seat belts, with the others waiting their turn on the floor. On the tables the sheep were being bled to death with a catheter and without pain relief – the idea being to keep their hearts beating to facilitate bleeding. The restraint, Grandin reported, is even more stressful for the animals than slaughter. The employees told her that this was standard procedure for the blood agar business. The plant failed her inspection. Despite her long experience in the business, Grandin later admitted that the sheep-bleeding operation was "gross" and had shaken her.[39]

After Grandin's visit, the farm press reported on the sheep-plant situation. In Ottawa the press coverage brought the matter to the attention of the federal minister of agriculture, although his department had no jurisdiction over that particular operation. A deputy minister assured the minister that, following Grandin's visit, provincial officials had reported that changes – of a sort – had been made. Now, "Only two animals are being restrained at one time instead of six or seven," the bureaucrat wrote. "Thus restraint time for each animal is much less."[40]

Grandin's tour included stops at four ritual slaughterhouses, two kosher and two halal. Two of the four did not have proper restraint devices so that the fully conscious animals' necks were bent too much before their throats were slashed. Grandin also reported that throughout her tour she saw no sick, crippled, or emaciated sows or cattle. Rather than consider this encouraging, she called it surprising, and said she was worried that those animals were "being diverted to provincial plants." At one plant, she said, workers told her about a provincially inspected operation where sheep were stunned before slaughter by being bashed on the head with a board.

Grandin maintains that, properly done, slaughter can be as humane as any form of euthanasia. But, she said, while improvements could be made, especially for poultry, the industry puts too little money into research and development. Europeans, for example, use a mechanical "rubber fingers" system in which chickens are gently picked up and carried on conveyors to be loaded, rather than grabbed by hand by crews of catchers and shoved into cages. A U.S. company tried the European system briefly, but found it did not mesh with the massive computerization of its existing operation. "The design problems are fixable but somebody has to pay for it," Grandin said.

Ian Duncan has been promoting the use of argon gas to stun chickens, a system used in Britain, because he is troubled by "horrendous" problems in chicken slaughter. In the gas system the chickens are killed in cages with a gas that appears to cause them no undue alarm, as opposed to the system of being yanked out of their cages alive and going through the electrical water bath, which often fails to do the job. The use of gas would even make the jobs on the line in slaughterhouses much better, Duncan said. It is the one change he would order if he could wave a wand and have it happen. But for gas to catch on, it would have to be sold as an economic benefit beyond the capital cost of changing machinery, and Duncan is not holding his breath. The poultry industry, he said, is "one of the worst" in accepting changes that improve the welfare of animals.

The Canadian industry is well aware of the argon gas system. A fact sheet posted on the Internet Web site of the Poultry Industry Council in the spring of 1999 explained the divergence between the North American and European systems of slaughter. A high percentage of birds missing the stunner caused concerns in Europe, the fact sheet said, and as a result operators there tried a higher voltage of current. That did not fix things, and carbon dioxide gas caused too much stress. Argon proved successful with poultry and pigs, the fact sheet reported. It caused no meat quality problem and was easier on both birds and workers. No doubt its use would be monitored from North America, but "animal welfare is not as important a concern in North America."[41]

· · ·

On one clear spring morning Danielle Divincenzo of ARK II went off to a suburban Toronto high school to show more than one hundred students a selection of real-life horror movies. One of the movies, a short video on slaughterhouses made by PETA, featured an agonizingly long scene of a cow being dragged by one leg from a truck, her eyes uncomprehending with pain. In another scene terrified pigs had jammed themselves in a small chute trying to escape an electric prod. When the light came on in the auditorium, one teenager, aghast, demanded to know why the police didn't do something about this.

While Canadian slaughterhouses may be better than those in the United States, as Grandin reported, outsiders have little opportunity to see this for themselves. Divincenzo told me about her own efforts to surreptitiously film a Toronto hog slaughter operation in which staff wore ear and nose plugs and the lavish use of electric prods added to the chaotic atmosphere. When Tina Harrison decided, in her logical way, that she needed to see inside slaughterhouses to know what she was talking about, she set out with a teacher friend to do just that. Respectable-looking women, they managed to talk their way into slaughterhouses to watch, although at one place they were brusquely escorted out. "We got back into the car, pale and knees quivering," Harrison recalled. "We said, 'Where do we go from here?

We have our own experiences to call on.' We decided to say exactly what we saw in our newsletter."

When Vancouver filmmaker Jennifer Abbott began to make a documentary in 1996, she telephoned and wrote to sixty slaughter-houses explaining her plan for a film on culture, meat, and animals. All of the plants refused her entry, and her requests to film slaughter were refused. On May 17, 1996, she crawled under a fence at Intercontinental Packers in Saskatoon to film a dead cow left lying outside, about thirty feet away from her. Plant security called police and she was arrested for mischief. Although the charge was dropped, she said, "It proved my point. The doors really are closed."[42]

The pattern in slaughter, as in agriculture in general, is too much self-policing and too little importance attached to what happens to the animals as living creatures. Too often the issue is what is considered worthwhile in dollars. These are not equivalents that should be balanced: the tormented death of a terrified bird being scalded against the cost of a delay in the processing line.

In efforts to gain public sympathy, animals raised for food are a much harder sell than is proper care for kittens or puppies. It's as if, once they are labelled "food" animals, whatever comes their way in the business of feeding the population is deemed acceptable and necessary. But animal activists have gained new allies as intensive farming has stirred up more general protests. The alliance of animal activists and other critics has sometimes been cemented by manure – or "nutrients," as it is called in the industry. In limited quantities, manure can be a useful fertilizer, but in excess or poorly managed it can damage soil, sink into groundwater, or wash into waterways. The intensive farms seldom have enough open land to allow all of their huge stores of manure to be spread as fertilizer, which means they have to store much of it in underground tanks or lagoons. Sometimes it leaks. Often it causes awful odours. In these cases urban dwellers find common cause with rural residents, and animal activists.

In Huron county in Ontario, one of the pig centres of the province, bitter battles have broken out over leaks from the storage tanks of one modern big farm. The leaks appear to have found their way into Lake Huron. The same kind of environmental concerns have been echoed across the country, from the Maritimes to Saskatchewan to Alberta's cattle feedlots – as happened in May 2000 in the small Ontario town of Walkerton, when one of the worst outbreaks of E. coli bacteria in recent Canadian history killed at least seven people and suddenly put factory farming and manure in the spotlight. In the United States, farms have come to be seen as major sources of water pollution – from hogs in South Carolina to chickens in Chesapeake Bay. Efforts to control manure application and regulate pollution have been complicated by jurisdictional disputes and the power of agricultural lobbyists.[43] In Canada, when the issues flare up, rural municipalities often discover they have little room to act either to limit the number of big farms, which seem more like industrial development plopped down in the countryside, or to impose controls any stiffer than might be considered necessary for small, traditional farms. That is partly because provinces across the country have enacted right-to-farm legislation that effectively puts the operations out of municipal reach as long as they can claim to be doing what is established farm practice, a catch-phrase usually left undefined.

Animal activists also find allies in serious public concern over increasing resistance to antibiotics. Warnings about the use of low levels of antibiotics to boost animal growth have been around since the 1970s. The practice had begun in the 1950s and caught on as increasingly intensive operations used the drugs to keep animals healthy in stressful or crowded situations. After a salmonella outbreak in the United Kingdom killed seven people whose illness proved resistant to the usual treatments, Britain established a committee that recommended, in 1971, that antibiotics be banned from livestock feed. As Orville Schell documented in his thorough and tough-minded book *Modern Meat*, drug companies in the United States responded by lobbying farmers to protest such "speculative" measures and to hang onto their handy chemical tools.[44]

In 1989 the Agricultural Institute of Canada published a book that reported the "growing concern over the practice of using so-called sub-therapeutic doses (of antibiotics) over extended periods of time to increase productivity."[45] The worry, the book noted, was that about half of all antibiotics made in Canada were being used on animals and that this use could allow a resistance to antibiotics to develop. Health Canada had made a half-hearted effort in the early 1980s to get companies to prove that the use of antibiotics was effective, but when the companies didn't bother, neither did the government.

By the late 1990s the debate about antibiotic resistance had reached a wider public. The World Health Organization called for cutbacks in the use of antibiotics in feed in 1997. In 1999 an advisory committee told the British government that antibiotics used on animals were to some extent responsible for resistance in humans and called for more control and care. The British Medical Association welcomed the report. Elsewhere, studies in medical journals linked farm use of antibiotics to resistance, and some defenders of the agriculture industry responded by saying it was getting too much blame. While Ottawa warned that it might crack down, the industry began to demand scientific proof. As the farm press explained, it is a common practice for large chicken, hog, and beef operations to head off illness by adding antibiotics to feed, but, after all, humans were also making inappropriate use of drugs.[46]

Ottawa responded in June 1998 with a workshop that struck all the right poses without actually doing anything. As a later memo explained, the workshop ensured that everyone had a say. Next would come a National Steering Committee to look at the agriculture and food part of the anti-microbial resistance issue, which would "dovetail" with the work of a co-ordinating committee. To succeed, this must feature "partnerships among many different stakeholders" to reach "science-based" approaches, and it must all be done through a "consultative process." The inactivity produced by this mind-numbing sort of exercise may well drive increasing numbers of people into the camp of the animal activists.[47]

In Australia a report from an advisory committee to the government raised the same issues in August 1999. Charged with reviewing scientific evidence on antibiotic resistance, the Joint Expert Technical Advisory Committee concluded that antibiotics used on livestock threatened food safety and human health. It recommended that the use of antibiotics as growth promoters be reviewed and phased out if not strictly controlled. Earlier, a report in the *Medical Journal of Australia* set the tone when it documented evidence that the use of avoparcin had fuelled resistance to a similar human antibiotic, vancomycin. Dutch researchers reached similar conclusions in 1997 after a study of forty-seven farms using avoparcin on turkeys found that farm workers and even residents in the farm neighbourhoods showed signs of resistance to vancomycin, a drug of last defence against some serious infections.[48]

What will the agriculture industry in Canada make of the increasing criticism from activists? Parts of it will undoubtedly follow the example of the research community and declare that there are dangerous animal extremists at large. But agricultural schools are adding more discussion of animal welfare issues to their curricula. U.B.C. professor David Fraser remembered that, in 1971, he couldn't get a journal to print an article saying Canada needed to take farm animal welfare seriously. By 1981 he held the animal welfare job at the federal government's experimental farm in Ottawa, and by the late 1990s the University of British Columbia had two positions in animal welfare, and faculties across the country had at least half a dozen others. "It's a growth area," Fraser said.[49]

Tom Hughes does not share those feelings of progress. For farm animals, he said, things have only become worse.[50] In his forty-five years in the animal movement he has seen enormous change in some areas, such as the treatment of pets. But for farm animals, things are worse. "We've robotized them. Now they are simply no more than robots. They're being treated as machines, not sentient creatures."

In Winnipeg, Laurie Connor said some of her university colleagues were startled at the idea of animal rights people being right on campus, some of them taking courses for veterinarian studies. While her department offers no animal welfare courses, it does make room for discussing the codes of practice and issues of animal welfare. Connor co-ordinates a seminar on farm issues, and she arranged for the local Humane Society to tour some hog farms, a measure she hoped had created "somewhat mutual respect."

The agriculture industry often charges that what animal rights advocates want is for everyone to eat only vegetables. (The hostility of this accusation is curious in one respect, given that farmers, after all, do grow vegetables and the makings for the notorious tofu.) But the more conservative animal welfarists would be content with taming the style of modern farming, with altering its brutal confinement systems and assembly-line approach to animals. The most significant change has to come first in attitudes to animals raised for food. If animals kept for companionship deserve protection, why don't animals raised for food receive the same consideration? People believe that some of those animals, such as pigs, are as intelligent as dogs. It is the role humans have assigned them, rather than their own qualities, that makes animals raised for food appear to be different than pets. Animals destined for the plate are rarely allowed to register in human minds as individuals, let alone be admitted to a relationship, as a pet would, that shows off their personalities or potential. Without that basic recognition, it proves difficult to develop a more generous attitude from humans. Instead, attitudes seem to be hardening in the opposite direction. The current practices are declared to be the normal way of farming, with the "normal" attaching to how humans behave rather than how animals live.

The animal welfare side of the movement has encouraged a more traditional approach to farming, putting forth the idea of a seal of approval for farms that take account of the natural habits and needs of animals. They promote a version of "Freedom Food," the label used in Britain to designate meat, eggs, and dairy products from farms that don't use the factory set-up. Stephen Huddart of the BCSPCA, B.C.'s CLAW, and Hughes of CanFACT are convinced that Canadian farmers can be successful by serving a public increasingly interested in the contents of food. According to Hughes, the British experience shows people are prepared to pay significantly more for food from animals raised in a more natural fashion. He proposed a "Freedom Food

Canada" label to be issued to producers, truckers, or abattoirs, after inspection by his organization, if they meet rules that include more space, no hen cages, outlets for normal animal behaviour, and speedier transport to humane slaughter. But efforts to get such a program off the ground here became locked into a revolving door of potential food industry backers, who first wanted proof of supply, and producers, who first wanted guaranteed markets. "That's why I'm still sitting here seething with impatience," Hughes said.

In France a "Label Rouge" version of chicken had developed sales of more than $259 million U.S. by spring 1999. Plans were also in the works for free-range eggs. The label certified that birds had more room on the floor indoors than they were getting in intensive operations; that at least eight weeks of their growing period allowed access to outside runs, with food and water placed to encourage them to go out; and that the use of drugs was limited.[51]

Activists give the idea of legislation to enforce on-farm conditions mixed reviews. Rodenburg, speaking for the Humane Society Federation, said voluntary codes are probably better because any acceptable legislation would most likely be too weak, given the public's lack of understanding of the issues. Harrison of CETFA is fed up with voluntary approaches and wants some law laid down in farming as well as tougher, enforced rules in transport and slaughter. The industry tends to see legislation as unwarranted interference and rejects it on the grounds that it would take away the flexibility that allows the voluntary system to change with new information. "Freedom Food" labels have attracted limited interest. Pearson of PAAL in Manitoba warns that legislation can be deceptive. While giving the impression that things are better than they are, it can build in loopholes, like the notion of "normal" farm practice. Doonan of the CFIA in Ottawa said that there would never be enough staff to enforce legislation.

Most activists, regardless of their views on eating animals, are willing to talk about changes that would improve the lot, if not the fate, of animals on farms and in slaughterhouses. One impediment is that, other than the Canadian Federation of Humane Societies and some SPCAs, animal activist groups are treated as hopeless nuts or dangerous radicals by the agriculture industry. Farmers might want to consider that animal activists, even the most radical, often make more sophisticated distinctions among kinds and systems of farming than the agriculture industry makes among its critics.

The Ontario Farm Animal Council (OFAC), an industry association set up in 1987 to deal with a perceived threat from animal rights proponents, is an example of blanket hostility aimed at all but the most conservative of animal advocates – effectively, at anyone who offers serious criticisms of how animals are treated in agriculture. The Council's annual meeting held in Guelph in April 2000 featured a speech by Steve Kopperud, president of the Animal Industry Foundation, a U.S. agribusiness lobby group funded by the powerful and affluent agriculture sector. Ironically, it is the power of animal advocates to attract donations from supporters that most rankles the AIF, along with efforts to elevate the legal and moral status of animals in Western society. Kopperud appeared to see little difference between the outright illegal actions of a small minority of animal activists and the legal protests of animal rights advocates. He complained in his speech not only about the movement's young and radical nature and its illegal actions, but also, and equally, about legal media campaigns promoting vegetarianism and law courses focusing on animals. He urged farmers in the OFAC, "our sister organization to the north," to use their credibility with the public to fight back against the "danger" spilling into Canada from the U.S. animal movement. Although he stressed the need to explain publicly how well agriculture conducts itself, he also counselled: "There is nothing to be gained from sitting across the table from someone who is dedicated to putting me out of business."

Esther Klein's Animal Defence League of Canada mails vegetarian and vegan recipes from its Ottawa base, along with newsletters and information kits on a whole range of animal issues. Klein has spoken to farm audiences, parliamentary committees, and the media. When she called for legislation to protect animals raised on farms, she said it might also form a protection for farmers who want to operate differently but believe they can't beat the intensive systems and so must join them.

"In a civilized society we have minimum wage laws and other labour laws to prevent the exploitation of our more vulnerable members of society," Klein told a farm audience. "In the same way, no farmer should be forced out of business and out of competition because he is being undersold by someone running an Auschwitz for animals."[52]

Then too, there is one form of farming in Canada for which even the conservatives of the animal movement tend to draw the line. It's called hunt farming, and by the turn of the century it was a growing, and nasty, business.

CHAPTER FIVE

Extreme Agriculture

Rob Dunham might have come from the central casting office. He was ruggedly handsome, with an aw-shucks little grin that broke out when he stopped himself from swearing in front of the mixed audience at a conference of deer and elk farmers in Guelph, Ontario. (He was only going to say "shit.") He was wearing plaid, and he hunted elk for a living. What could be more Hollywood Canadian than to face the wild outdoors, to stalk those big, serious creatures with the soaring antlers?[1]

At his High Calibre Ranch in Lloydminster, Saskatchewan, Dunham actually *shoots* elk, something a bit different from hunting them, and mostly he lets rich Americans do the shooting. When Dunham talked about the intricacies of getting provincial governments to do what farmers wanted them to do, he gave a rueful shake of his boyishly tousled head. What could he tell the audience about this bureaucratic stuff that would make sense of it? After all, he said, "I shoot elk. That's what I do."

What was he doing talking to farmers on a raw March day, this Canadian shooter of elk? Well, that was the odd thing. His business is not really about stalking big game, facing the danger of tracking those magnificent brutes on their home turf for a man-to-beast showdown. It would mortally offend Rob Dunham and his counterparts to hear it put this way, but what they are doing is more like shooting fish in a barrel. On Canadian hunt ranches, no matter how hard they run or how smart they are, the animals can never escape.

These ranches are something more than simply a new kind of farming – or yet another form of hunting. They are about fox, mink, wild boar, and emus, among other wild animals, being turned into produce. They are about deer kept captive (they are never tame) for their urine and meat, about elk being held down so their furry, sensitive new antlers can be sawed off at the base to provide all manner of products for the lucrative health food market.

In Canada this is a relatively new, and growing, industry, so far largely concentrated in Alberta and Saskatchewan. The Alberta Department of Agriculture licensed 117 game farms in 1990. By 1996, the total was 305. In 1996, of the nearly 26,000-strong Canadian herd, Alberta was home to 12,000 elk and Saskatchewan to 10,000.[2]

For most of the game farms that sprang up in the 1990s, elk was the animal of choice. The primary market was for breeding stock – with 1997 prices of about $2,500 for a bull calf, $20,000 for a cow, and up to $5,000 for an elk bull. The furry velvet antlers – hacked off in June each year after no more than eighty-five days of growth – were going for about $40 a pound in the spring of 1999 and reselling at up to $500 a pound in Korea. A mature elk stag might produce twenty to thirty pounds of velvet a year.[3]

Once you have turned wildlife into produce – and Canada is well on the way to doing that – hunt farms are the logical conclusion. In some ways, they are necessary. If wild animals are farmed produce, then there must also be marketing plans, and with those plans solutions to problems. For example, what does a farmer do if the cost of venison from his stock of white-tailed deer is too expensive to compete with venison from other kinds of deer or other meat? If the stock is "wildlife," he does not have to do anything. If the animals are valid farm livestock, then he has a problem to solve, and that is where hunt farms fill the bill. They are fenced places where deer can be shot for fun rather than slaughtered for food. White-tailed deer have a cachet for hunters. They are big and beautiful. They make a handsome trophy. To refuse to allow hunt farms, it follows, is to deny that white-tailed deer are valid farm livestock, that there remains some question about that.

The same principle holds for fuzzy, new-growth antlers. Prices are notoriously volatile and controlled largely from abroad. When prices plummet, as they did in 1998 and 1999, what are elk farmers to do? The answer is hunt farms. They can deliver, almost to order (like a pizza), the size of elk antlers that a hunter wants as a trophy. And when elk get old, or if they prove troublesome, or if their antlers are not producing as much velvet antler as they should, farmers should not be expected to take a loss. If these animals are producing antlers as a farm product, the situation calls for a marketing solution. These same elk could be sold for valuable hunt-farm targets.

A farmer faced with such deer or elk problems could sell the animals he had been feeding and vaccinating to places where they would be hunted, just as if they were wild and wary of humans. This transaction could be built into the system for farmers raising animals that were once considered wildlife. It could be a kind of safety net for those years in which meat or antler prices fall. Perhaps it might even be argued that this is a more dignified end, a death more fitting a wild animal – although that thought raises the issue of their wildness, and assumes that there is something dignified about hunt farms.

Once deer are being raised on farms anyway, it is no great leap to an industry that produces a hunt scent product derived from deer urine. Or if some people think that drinking tea or swallowing capsules made from the velvet taken from deer or elk antlers is going to make them feel better, there is good money to be made there as well. South Korea is the prime market for the world's major velvet producers: Canada, New Zealand, China, and Russia. Koreans have long used velvet for tonics for everything from kidney disorders and anemia to low sperm counts. The new consumer products now include Dr. Sim's Velvet Antler Bar or pure Canadian Elk Antler capsules to improve mental functions, athletic performance, and natural immunity.[4]

Hunters with access to the Internet can search out Gary Tank's Fatal Attractor, a bottle of deer urine said to be 100 per cent pure and special because it is from one animal only rather than a mixture.

Choose from doe or buck urine at $9.95 a bottle in U.S. funds, plus shipping and handling from the Minnesota entrepreneur. The exact size of the bottle isn't given, but how much can you need? In suburban Toronto you can pay $7.45 for a 113 millilitre bottle of buck scent. Hunters can use it to lure a deer of the opposite sex, or a rival buck, or to cover up human tracks.

At the Guelph conference the assembled farmers listened to Professor Jeong S. Sim explain that the active ingredient in velvet is glycosaminoglycan (GAG), that rabbit and rat tests are showing that GAG has healing properties, that the Velvet Antler Bar he has developed is a good pick-me-up. They aren't going to be claiming that it treats ailments, just that it is a food supplement, he told them. He had another piece of advice to move their antler velvet into the new high-tech world: "Don't call it velvet . . . I don't like it." Sim's own product names sound either more scientific or more macho. His long list of accomplishments include his Designer Eggs, Designer Omega-Bar, Designer Ovo-Cal, and Designer Antler Bar, all of which are already on the market. He is also the CEO of two spin-off companies, including Dr. Sim's Designer Food Concept Inc.

Sim came to Guelph from something called the Designer Food Concept Research Group in the University of Alberta's Department of Agricultural, Food and Nutritional Science. He was excited about an international symposium, the first ever, planned for April 2000, in Banff. The idea was to put together the scientific foundation needed to boost antler velvet as a "nutraceutical," or a food that enhances health. The problem so far had been "incomplete understanding" of the active properties of velvet, he explained.

Talk of elk antler snack bars does rather take the edge off the romance of the restoration of wild elk herds, that perennial project in Ontario. For the better part of the twentieth century, the province tried to restore the elk that once roamed wild but were wiped out in the late nineteenth century. A reintroduction program in the 1930s worked until the idea took hold that elk were to blame for a disease in cattle, after which most of them were killed. By 1993 the Ontario government, with the eager backing of hunters, was trying again to restore the herds, with animals brought from Alberta parks for release around Sudbury. A news report described the new effort as a yearning to hear the bugle of the wild elk again echo across the north.

In a way, the gulf between animals as live creatures and as the agricultural products we make of them is easier to see in the case of deer or elk farming than it is with hogs or cattle. Most of us don't yet consider deer to be a farm animal. Most of us might feel a bit uneasy at the business of immobilizing them to hack off the sensitive, live tissue that is velvet antler so that someone can down a supposed health tonic or hope for a better sex life. Most of us don't regularly eat venison or hanker after a chance to shoot elk. So for most of us, these are still live animals and not yet products. They haven't yet become synonymous in our minds with food, in the way in which we turn pigs to spare ribs or cattle to beef or hamburgers. When we look at them, we still see animals; and we see animals that we picture as having lives apart from our own – places to go, young to raise, and lives that have no connection to being useful or money-making for us. Some of us even find them graceful or beautiful. In effect, people tend to see them more in the way in which many animal activists see the entire animal world, including pigs or cattle. We don't ask who these animals belong to or what purpose they are serving. They just *are*. And we don't think it's nuts or sentimental or extreme to see elk or deer in that way.

The start-up costs of deer and elk farming can be significant, but they are less overwhelming than for some other agricultural operations. With special, high exterior fencing running to $12,000 or more a mile, a squeeze device to hold the big animals still for sawing off their antlers or for vaccinations priced at up to $5,000, water systems at perhaps another $5,000, plus stock costs, trucks and a freezer, fenced holding pens, and land, a farmer could end up investing more than $300,000 in an eighty-acre farm. The figures are different for raising stock to sell than for selling antler velvet, but the expectations are still for both operations to turn a profit at the end of ten years, clear of the huge machinery costs usually carried by other kinds of farms. Given the financial burdens of more traditional farm sectors –

the big capital costs for machinery, for example – and given that elk and deer need much less maintenance and can use more marginal land – an acre that might support one beef cow is considered sufficient for three to five elk cows – it was no wonder that the audience at the Guelph gathering of deer and elk farmers also included Ontario dairy farmers, quietly listening to every word. Meanwhile, in Saskatchewan, there has been talk of bison and elk replacing grain as a crop for hard-pressed farmers.

"Did you know," asked a headline on page nineteen of the Ontario Deer and Elk Farmer's Association eleventh annual convention booklet, "A White Tail urinates 20 oz. to 25 oz. per day and [this urine] sells for $18.99 U.S. per ounce." In the booklet Great Canadian Whitetails is advertising a seminar on white-tailed deer farming for venison, embryo sales, or urine or semen sales. "Urine is a $150-million market in the U.S.," Harm Spangenberg, president of the Ontario White-tailed Deer Producers association, told the farmers at the Guelph Holiday Inn. "It's a by-product, gross as it might sound to some of you."

• • •

Rob Dunham was also tossing big figures around. He told the farmers in Guelph that they could be on the edge of something big, on the verge of a brand new industry in Canada.

In October 1998 the Saskatchewan government conveniently amended the regulations of its provincial game-farming law to make them match what was already happening on the farms. The province's law already allowed on-farm slaughter of farmed deer and elk by the operator or a veterinarian. Animal activists tend to consider on-farm slaughter more acceptable, especially when it spares animals ill-suited to being trucked to a slaughterhouse. But that wasn't quite the point with the Saskatchewan change, which was to allow the killing job to be delegated legally to another party. It effectively meant that the farm owner could hand over the so-called "on-farm slaughter" to a hunter, who would need only to follow proper firearm safety rules. Because the animals in question are not wild animals – they are officially farmed animals – there would be no need for a hunting permit. This is slaughter, literally.

As Dunham explained, hunting on the province's deer and elk farms had already been occurring for at least three years before the law was changed. The key had been getting permission for on-farm slaughter. Then it was a matter of waiting for the government to clear up a "grey area" about who could do the killing. Dunham was now forecasting that up to six more elk operations would soon open up shop in Saskatchewan, and he mentioned talk of a Toronto company bringing in European hunters. If you added in the prospect of white-tail deer hunting, the sector was set to explode.

Dunham said he had more than eighty clients aiming for some one hundred elk in 1999. In 1998 his clients shot seventy-eight of the eighty-seven animals killed in the province. His High Calibre Ranch would soon be doing a million-dollar business, with a lot of that money going back to animal breeders who could supply stock. For three or four months of the year, he employed three people full-time. Hunt farms are a long-established business in Europe, he said, and an accepted business in the United States. He showed the Guelph audience slides of his deluxe guest accommodations (6,000 square feet, five baths, sleeps nine). The quality was what his clients expected when they were paying thousands of dollars to hunt his animals.

Dunham might charge $3,000 to take hunters after white-tailed deer in a normal hunt in the wild, but it would be double that to hunt elk on the farm. A record-setting rack of antlers from a big trophy bull could bring in $18,000 – in U.S. money. Dunham had two Toronto doctors come up to hunt on his farm, at $12,000 U.S. each. Animals that Canadian breeders were selling for $1,500 each were going to the United States, where hunters were paying $8,000 to kill them, he said.

Toronto doctors, thousands of dollars: this is the kind of folding money that farmers can take seriously. The slides showed the shop at Dunham's ranch, where a local man made some $27,000 in six weeks carving animals killed by hunters into slabs of meat. There were maybe eleven or twelve new applications for hunt ranches (they don't call them farms) in Saskatchewan, Dunham said. A hunt operation could take the old elk bulls off farmers' hands, take the ones that are too difficult to manage, the bad actors. Instead of $1,000 for hamburger, he said, farmers who hooked up to supply a hunt ranch might have a $10,000 "trophy product." The animals that were not great producers of velvet could turn out to have spectacular antlers if the racks were allowed to grow out instead of being cut off to be processed and powdered into tonic capsules and tea.

"It's going to be a very big economic boom for elk and deer farmers," Dunham told his attentive audience. "What I'm trying to do is get the industry going."

(Elsewhere, hunt ranches were advertising package deals with prices in the $5,000 range, in U.S. dollars. A Nebraska ranch priced its elk by the size of the antlers, beginning at $3,380 U.S. for the smallest animal, excluding any other charges.)[5]

Tim Toeppner, a licensed Northern Ontario black bear outfitter who had just lost out on much of his livelihood when the provincial government cancelled the spring bear hunt in January 1999, was also at the conference. He had been hired as a hunting consultant by the Great Canadian Whitetails company. The company's investors had set up for deer urine collection and embryo research and, Toeppner told the farmers, they wanted his help to convince Ontario to allow hunt farms. He wanted the farmers' help in the form of an endorsement of the idea, because now was the time to strike, he said. The provincial Conservative government felt obligated to deliver some sort of relief after cancelling the bear hunt. Quebec already had its hunt farms. Saskatchewan had them and was set to take off. An estimated sixty-five were operating in Canada, perhaps one hundred counting part-time operators. What was to stop Ontario?

Well, there is that problem with what Dunham calls public perception. Boone and Crockett – the U.S. sporting club that sets North American standards for such things as trophy measurement and the definition of "fair chase" – would not consider this particular activity to be a "fair chase," Dunham admitted.[6] The hunt farms don't have at least one open side. There are fences all around. There is no escape.

Real fair chase would be free-range and involve animals that had not been handled by humans, animals living wild. Still, he said, in one corner his 1,700-acre property has more than three hundred acres in bush, with no cross-fences and patchy bush elsewhere. He knows where the elk are, because he lives there. But the hunters don't know, and they have to work their way through some thick bush at times.

"I get in trouble saying this," he told the audience. "The way we grew up, it's not really hunting." But, he added, to the customers it is.

A public image – particularly ugly in the United States – of shooting animals in pens or former circus animals or tamed creatures trying to hide under trucks or cowering in bewilderment has not helped the cause. While that image may not be widespread in Canada, where hunt farms are new and have had little public attention, the problems of perception will undoubtedly grow along with the industry here. After all, promoting the idea of hunt farms as a solution to dips in the market for farmed animals, and then insisting that these are creatures wild enough to be hunted, make for a difficult sell. In the United States attention has focused on what are called "canned hunts," which offer animals that are sometimes so tame around humans that they watch hunters approach. This does not provide the classiest, most heroic image of hunters. It's right up there with hunters shooting mother bears who have their heads in buckets of bait and cubs waiting for mum to come back – a scenario that killed the Ontario spring bear hunt dead. The cognoscenti call shooting animals in pens on farms "collecting." "There's always some guys going to do it," Dunham said. "There's a market for collecting."

What Dunham would like is a set of strictly voluntary guidelines for hunt farms, even on the issue of collecting or shooting animals trapped in pens. Pretty soon the market would rule out this collector business, he said. It is the same argument made in other forms of agriculture: that farmers know best, that regulation is unnecessary, and that whatever the market supports is appropriate. It is an argument that recognizes no place for the interests of the animal as a live being to be considered or for the question of the ethics involved.

In the United States, at least five states have banned canned hunts. In July 1999 New York took a run at the issue in a curious bit of law-making that left some hunters and some animal activists equally out-raged. The intent seemed to be to get rid of "collecting." The state law would mean that, after November 1, 2000, it would be illegal to kill animals hobbled or caged or tied to posts, all of which had been tak-ing place. Cast-off zoo animals – sick, old, or tamed – were being hog-tied or penned so that "hunters" could shoot, spear, or otherwise kill them – "collect" them, presumably. In outlawing this kind of activity, the state added the proviso that it would be acceptable to hunt these animals on operations with more than ten acres of land, which would in effect legalize hunt farms. To some animal activists, it seemed a worthwhile step to get the collectors outlawed, but to oth-ers, legitimizing hunt farms was too big a price. You only need to scan the advertisements to see that a market does exist for hunt farms in the United States. One New Mexican operation offered a hunt for trophy elk designed for hunters with physical handicaps. It boasted that in 1998 a paraplegic in a wheelchair shot an elk using a rifle trig-gered by a mouth-operated switch.[7]

At the Guelph meeting, Dunham did not mention the annual meeting of the Alberta Fish and Game Association held just weeks before, in February 1999, when the angry group of traditional hunters and fishers attacked proposals to allow hunt ranches. With velvet prices dipping still further, Alberta elk farmers were pushing for the acceptance of deer and elk hunts on private land. For those animals, velvet and sales of breeding stock are the only real markets, and hunt ranches could repair the damage of the price drop. But the traditional hunters weren't swayed. "This is largely an issue of ethics and the definition of fair chase," the Association's president Dave Powell said bluntly. "The concept is just repulsive to me, to the public and to real sportsmen."

For Powell and other politically attuned hunters, hunting on farms is an idea that could be poison. Already a minority interest, hunters could only be hurt by being publicly seen as guys who shoot captive animals. The sport might rank in the public mind with a big-game hunt of calves or piglets. Those animals might already be in line to be slaughtered, but this shift would make a game of their plight. In the wild, Powell argued, animals are wary creatures, unlike those from farms who live every day with the knowledge of humans. "The bottom line is simple: if the animal has a reasonable chance of escape, it's hunting," he said. "If not, it's killing an animal in an enclosure and not much different from butchering a cow."[8]

Ian Thorleifson, executive director of the Canadian Venison Council and the Alberta Elk Association, didn't mention Powell's comments to the Guelph farmers either. Instead, he just complained that, as long as they did it humanely, farmers ought to be able to do whatever they wanted with their animals. He left it to Dunham to gloss over the opposition and to Toeppner, the hunting company consultant, to complain cryptically that the powerful Ontario Federation of Anglers and Hunters was one of the biggest obstacles to hunt farms in Ontario.

· · ·

In Ontario the Conservative government overhauled fish and wildlife legislation at the beginning of 1999 so that elk and white-tailed deer, native species, could be farmed – but not hunted – in captivity. The rules effectively mean that only non-native wildlife, animals like European boar, can be hunted in captivity. Wild boar are not a real public relations problem, since they're not romantic or even familiar to most of us, and some farms in the province were already offering them as hunting targets. The province's fish and game laws are also no obstacle to hunting red deer, fallow deer, sikka deer, or mule deer in captivity because they are not native species, like elk or white-tail. Some native birds, as well as pheasants, have been hunted on farms for years, and this can continue, Ontario government officials said.

Ontario meat inspection laws could form an obstacle to this activity. Essentially the law prohibits any meat from being sold for human consumption that has not been inspected, which means the meat would have to go through an abattoir. A farmer can slaughter an animal on his own property for his own consumption, but a paying hunter on his farm could be considered to be buying the meat. But it might also be argued that a hunt farm customer who took a deer home wasn't participating in the retail meat market. Provincial officials are working largely on theory and legal opinion at this point. Game farms have only recently begun to grow in the province, and the new legislation is the first real crack at regulating them. That is enough to keep government officials busy. If hunt farms, featuring non-native deer or other animals, catch on in a big way, officials predict considerable pressure for letting the public have a say. As well, work has been underway to develop a national meat code so that all provinces would have similar inspection laws for meat retailed inside the country. When this code became ready for public discussion, officials said, hunt farms might figure into the debate.

The issue gained currency in December 1999, when the International Fund for Animal Welfare announced it had priced animals on a farm north of Toronto, where a hunter could shoot a wild boar for $300 and a big-horn sheep for $18,000. Where the animals came from remained unclear, but the OFAH condemned the practice. The province announced a review of hunt farms.

The Canadian Federation of Humane Societies has urged its supporters to find out about the hunt-farm legislation in their own provinces – it varies from total bans to British Columbia's ban on anything but boars to New Brunswick's allowance of pheasant hunt farms – and to express their disapproval to the minister in charge. The Animal Alliance of Canada has made a similar call for opponents to recognize game farms as "a very real threat" to wildlife and a practice that should be ended.

The Canadian Wildlife Federation denounced hunt farms years ago as the hidden agenda of game farms – where animals most of us think of as wildlife are raised as livestock – and called for a ban on all game farms. Like many conservation groups, the CWF disapproved of game farms on principle. It said they were a contradiction to conservation because they put a market value on wildlife and allowed both its private ownership and its frivolous use.[9] Poaching can also become a problem when wildlife is farmed, because it becomes easier to market illegally taken animals and to add them to existing farm stock, the Federation said. Quaint as it sounds, poaching doesn't just mean someone killing an animal or two. Poaching also means business-scale trafficking. In Alberta, two big poaching busts in 1998 resulted in more than four hundred charges against more than fifty people after two years of undercover police work. Hundreds of wild elk, deer, and moose had been killed for illegal meat sales.[10]

Even in Rob Dunham's Saskatchewan, all is not calm. The Regina Humane Society, convinced the public had no idea that some sixteen hunt ranches were operating in the province, began to raise the issue in 1999, with the help of the International Fund for Animal Welfare. While the Society is "definitely middle of the road" and not anti-hunting, said the Society's executive director Cathy Lauritsen, the issue is ethics, not hunting. If hunt farms were allowed, she said, there was no reason that there wouldn't be pressure to hunt more exotic, lucrative animals, like leopards. Game farms have argued that their animals are not wild, Lauritsen said, so how can it be fair to hunt domesticated animals?[11]

Critics of game farms also argue that the Canadian public can end up paying the costs, because to prevent the spread of the illness whole herds must be killed when disease is found in any animal. This triggers compensation payments to farmers that run into millions of dollars. In April 1999, for instance, the federal government ordered five hundred elk killed at an eastern Ontario farm because of an outbreak of tuberculosis. This was one of the largest culls due to TB since the 1970s. The disease can spread to other animals and to humans. The herd owners argued that the $1 million offered in compensation would leave them with a huge loss.[12] Periodic escapes of farmed animals are also inevitable, and critics see this as both a threat to native wildlife and another expense in the mandatory tracing, capture, and testing that follows.

Other wildlife can suffer when game farms are established, because natural predators and even the wild cousins of farmed animals are suddenly ranked as competitors and troublemakers. At the Guelph conference, deer and elk farmers talked about the problems of wild deer and elk approaching their fences, drawn by the animals inside. Sometimes the animals charged and damaged fences as the wire wrapped around their antlers. A few farmers grinned knowingly and said that, in the west, they had found the best thing was to make a deal with a local Native reserve whose members who could shoot the wild troublemakers without needing a hunting permit. An Ontario government employee at the conference shifted uncomfortably, saying that Ontario was trying to restore wild populations and wasn't all that keen on anything that added to the kill.

The animals, it seems, don't understand the distinctions drawn by farmers about the differences in life on each side of the wire. At the Guelph meeting, one angry voice called out from the floor that speakers should stop referring to "wildlife." These are farmed deer and elk, not wildlife, he said. Game-farm associations explain that even though farmed elk and wild elk are the same species, the farmed ones are very different in behaviour because generations of the animals have been raised behind wire. (This argument is not advanced when hunt farms are the subject.) The Chinese are said to have farmed deer for thousands of years and, it seems, the Roman were old hands at it too.

The Winnipeg Humane Society was a strong opponent of elk farming when the Manitoba government passed a law in 1996 allowing it. Vicki Burns argued that the provision to allow the capture of some wild animals for Manitoba farms was cruel, that the taking of velvet antlers was painful and traumatic, that sales of velvet to the Asian market contradicted efforts to halt the sales of other wild animal parts, such as bear gall bladders, and that disease could threaten the province's wild elk population. Moreover, she expressed her concern about reports of a version of mad cow disease found among North American elk in Saskatchewan and the United States. The provincial agriculture minister, Harry Enns, replied that her concerns about transmissible spongiform encephalopathy or chronic wasting disease on a Saskatchewan game farm in 1996 referred to one imported animal, which was killed and burned. Another thirty-four animals that had been in contact with it were killed. Enns told her that the new law on elk farming would have strict controls and there was no concrete evidence to show that the disease could be transmitted to other species.[13]

Since 1996 chronic wasting disease has been diagnosed in another elk operation in Saskatchewan, after a bull died in 1998. Some animals on that farm were destroyed as a result, but others from the herd were not. Afterwards they were monitored at six-month intervals. Three other elk farms in South Dakota reported cases, as did elk farms in Nebraska, Oklahoma, and Montana. Citing these cases, Dr. Ian Barker of the Ontario Veterinary College's pathology department called for better surveillance in Ontario of wildlife populations for signs of the disease, plus mandatory reporting and identification systems for farms, including automatic autopsies for animals that die on their own.[14] Some slaughtered animals could also be included in the brain examinations, he said. The cause of the disease is unknown, the incubation period in mule deer and elk is about fifteen to eighteen months, and transmission among animals is by contact. According to Barker, because other forms of this disease are suspected to have passed from sheep to cattle and, more certainly, from cattle to people (Creutzfeldt-Jakob disease), it should be assumed that eating meat from infected animals could be hazardous.

In January 1999, after fears were raised that a man who donated blood might have eaten infected deer or elk, the federal Health Department dismissed concerns that some sort of mad deer disease might have entered the human blood system. News reports included assurances that there was no known case of a human contracting mad deer disease.[15]

The Manitoba decision to legalize elk farming did not come without public opposition, particularly over the provision that wild elk could be captured for farm stock. James Pearson of PAAL said he and other activists travelled six hundred miles north to protest in an area where elk were to be captured. Some of his group, he admitted, went north with the idea of sabotaging the effort. But when the activists got there, they found local people had beat them to it. The locals were trying to free elks from the compounds where the animals had been lured and trapped, and they were even damaging equipment.

When, in 1996, national codes of agricultural practice were written for raising deer on farms, the recommendations were to cover matters like preventing stress during velvet or new-growth antler removal. The codes didn't even contemplate hunting. The removal of velvet antlers alone was enough to cause controversy. The Canadian Federation of Humane Societies, one of the groups involved in writing the code, insisted on noting its objection to the whole practice, saying not enough was known about pain and stress relief for the animals.

Ian Thorleifson of the Canadian Venison Council said that both chemical and electrical pain relief is used on animals during velvet harvest. He hoped there would be a shift to using the electric, nine-volt battery device exclusively instead of chemicals, because velvet products could then be labelled organic, which made a much better sales pitch. Still, Thorleifson also reported that young animals unused to the annual procedure were so distressed by it that it was hard to measure the differences between removing their velvet using electric or chemical pain relievers or none at all.

With mink and fox fur farms well-established in Canada, elk and deer are seen as valuable newer parts of the industry. Other agricultural efforts to introduce new animals to the food scene seem to come and go as fads. Wild boar was the thing to have in the mid-1990s, but the hoped-for Asian markets for the animal were sewed up by Australian suppliers. The tusked creatures are now the prey in some hunt farms. Emu was another dream animal that had, by the end of the century, failed to deliver the bucks. The big, flightless birds were supposed to be easy to raise, and they provided a source of low-fat meat and oil that was touted for its healing qualities. After the emus failed to live up to their promise, farmers in some parts of the country began slaughtering their flocks. In New Brunswick, for instance, one farmer tried to kill his two hundred emus with the help of a local archery club when his efforts to shoot the five-foot-tall, tame birds ended with only a few wounded. The farmer decided that the archery approach was inhumane, so he had the birds clubbed and their throats cut. Police decided cruelty charges were not warranted because the intentions were good. After all, noted one policeman, a farm nearby was raising turkeys to be shot.[16]

Clearly, humans should simply leave some animals alone, if only for practical reasons. But even when the animals are apparently left alone – out there in the vast wilds that Canadians so pride themselves on – we never really stop meddling with them. We call it *managing* wildlife. For animal activists and many environmentalists this is, to put it politely, an oxymoron.

CHAPTER SIX

Wild Lives

Keeping Humans Happy

This aluminum bird house, so the brochure said, was the best choice for attracting purple martins, those graceful mosquito eaters. Martins would keep coming back for years. And bird lovers could buy an inexpensive little attachment to convert it into a sparrow trap. Better still, the company sold a bait-style trap to put an end to those pesky English house sparrows. Once the sparrows were trapped, it said, "Farmers usually just wring their necks. City folk can place the cage in a garbage bag, tie it to the exhaust pipe of [a] vehicle and the method is fast and humane."[1] Ah, the great Canadian outdoors, full of wildlife, even if it is so darned hard to make it do what it's supposed to.

Majestic scenery and wild animals are two of the things Canadians consider a big part of their world, as much an aspect of their identity, surely, as a public-health insurance system or cold winters. They are also the main images presented to tourists and the world at large. But this picture also has its contradictions – with its wild animals, for instance, that are supposed to stay out of humans' way, from garbage dumps to camp sites, on pain of death or deportation. A town site sits in a national park, Banff, where elk should stay away from the golf course and gardens but not so far away they can't have their pictures taken. In other words, they aren't quite wildlife. They are expected to add to the scenic value, to accommodate what humans have in mind.

Even when animals aren't being raised on farms to feed us or used in research to make us live longer, they are still supposed to be doing something for us – amusing us or inspiring us and maybe earning some money at the same time. Nature, after all, brings in billions of dollars a year when spending for tourism, recreation, hunting, and fishing are counted.[2] Animals, for most of us, aren't fellow inhabitants of this world with their own claim to it and their own lives to get on with. Animals can't just *be*.

Human assumptions about managing the natural world and the animals in it as their personal, ambulatory raw material have seldom worked out well, even from a human perspective. They have most definitely not served animals' interests. Arguments about this idea of management and of animals as resources are at the heart of some of the most enduring and best-known animal issues. If you live in Canada, it's hard not to know at least a little about the battles over the East Coast seal hunt or hunting generally. It is increasingly hard not to notice controversies over whales or other animals being kept in zoos and circuses, about plans to kill geese or deer or bears when their numbers are declared excessive or their presence a nuisance.

Sometimes the animal movement can patch together a shifting alliance with Aboriginal peoples or environmental groups over wildlife, which can make an influential common cause. But united efforts, at least for the law-abiding side of the animal movement, don't hold up well when it comes down to how any one animal is treated. For environmentalists worried about endangered whales, for example, the focus on freeing one such as Keiko, a movie star, can seem a diversion of money and attention from a bigger issue.[3] For them, the important issue is not the fate of this one wild-born killer whale, the star of *Free Willy*, whose plight sparked an international protest. But for a large part of the animal movement, and definitely for the animal rights side of it, Keiko's life must matter or none do. So on many issues, like the use of animals in entertainment, animal activists are on their own.

No one could be more on their own than Trudy Sattler and a handful of thick-skinned, determined Albertan activists. They don't just protest against regular animal entertainment. They protest the Calgary Stampede, the self-declared *Greatest Outdoor Show on Earth*, the multimillion-dollar fair that pulls in more than a million visitors every year. Stampede legend describes it as the World Series of rodeo and "the ultimate celebration of the wild side of the western lifestyle."[4] It doesn't matter that, in real life, no self-respecting rancher would ever let a valuable bull be ridden and kicked around or a young calf be yanked off its feet and slammed to the ground for fun. It doesn't matter that there is more circus stunt than traditional skill involved in milking "wild cows" or chewing on the ear of an unbroken horse to get a saddle on its back in the shortest time possible. This is not a community event that the hometown media or anyone else is going to pan. Not only do most people seem genuinely fond of the Stampede, but it also means big bucks – with sponsors for the chuckwagon races bidding as much as $100,000 to have their names on canvas wagon tops, and winners collecting rodeo prizes worth thousands of dollars.[5]

No one wants to hear about the dozen or more horses dead from the Stampede's chuckwagon races over the years, or the dozen killed or seriously injured in a decade from other events. There are no announcements of the half-dozen calves or two steers killed after they broke their legs during Stampede events from 1986 to 1997. One of the few animals to be eulogized in death was Kodiak Copenhagen, a magnificent 1,600-pound bucking bull who caught his left hind leg between iron gate posts and snapped a bone while he was resisting being ridden. But that story was more about how even cowboys can cry, to show how close the animal-human bond is in the Stampede family. Even the shocking crashes – which have sent several men to hospital and killed seven horses in total – and the three people who have died from injuries only seem to add to the legend of the Stampede's Rangeland Derby, as the chuckwagon race is known. They call it the "half mile of hell" with some pride.

So Sattler and her little band of activists in the cheekily named Animal Agents – CIA (for Compassion in Action) and the older Calgary Animal Rights Coalition were not exactly the toast of the town when they went around handing out leaflets to fairgoers or holding up signs announcing "rodeo kills." Veteran Stampede booster Jack MacDonald, for example, once used a guest column in the *Calgary Herald* to tell the tiny band of protesters that they offended him.[6] They should direct their energies at helping the poor or homeless or children, he wrote, because "chuckwagon stock are extremely well treated." His column appeared in July 1996, just as the first of three horses died within twenty-four hours during the chuckwagon races.

"I tell them I support Amnesty International," Sattler replied cheerfully to the standard why-not-help-people challenge – one that so many animal activists say their critics fling at them. "I sponsor a child. What are they doing?"[7] Though, to be fair, *Calgary Sun* columnist Jack Tennant did call for an end to calf-roping in a 1998 column, arguing that it must hurt the young animal and that it must embarrass people or else the sudden jerk as the calf hits the end of the rope would be shown on television.[8] Tennant did, of course, feel compelled to insist that he is "not an activist of any sort."

Sattler *is* an activist. The sassy, can-do young woman with auburn curls and big glasses said that she figures the best avenue for change is to dog the Stampede using its own rules. Armed with her camera in 1997, she photographed calves at the Stampede just before their release for the roping event, their tails being twisted into a corkscrew by two big hands. She took pictures of them afterward too, as they fell on their heads, face first. She photographed a horse toppled over in a chute before the wild horse race.

She also registered a formal complaint with the Calgary Humane Society, which took the complaint to the Stampede board. As a result, tail-twisting was ruled out and employees assigned to shove on the calves' rear ends instead. It wasn't that the tail-twisting hurt, Stampede public affairs manager Dan Sullivan asserted, but to the public it looked like it did. The Stampede also promised that animals in the wild-horse event would be pulled out of competition if they were too upset or not in top condition. In the uphill world of Stampede protest, these changes represented a considerable victory. "In cowtown, in the thick of the meat, we've done quite well," Michael

Alvarez-Toye, the burly, bushy-haired head of the ten-year-old Calgary Animal Rights Coalition said. "If I were to have talked about animal rights when I came here twelve years ago, I would have got such a shit-kicking."[9]

In Alberta the Calgary Humane Society is one of the groups approved by the province to enforce the Animal Protection Act, which forbids causing distress to an animal. But the law also says that this rule doesn't apply if the distress comes from any activity carried out in accord with normal animal management, husbandry, or slaughter practices. It's the sort of proviso found in many statutes purporting to deal with animal well-being. "That's a huge loophole," Humane Society executive director Cathy Thomas admitted. "As long as people are buying tickets to this, well, you can't argue it isn't normal. In fact, it's better than other rodeos. The Stampede board is concerned about public perception, but if there's no accident, there's no issue to the public and the media. These animals are purpose-bred and maybe it's hypocritical to deal with the Stampede and not with racing."[10]

The public shows "zero interest" in putting a stop to Stampede events and no support for the Society's efforts to intervene with the rodeo, she said. But after one spectacular, multi-horse fatality, the Humane Society was invited to meet regularly with the Stampede board. After that, instead of being harassed when they showed up, Society inspectors were given passes and reports on incidents involving animals. It's true, Thomas grinned ruefully, that "they do pat us on the head sometimes."

One nagging, whispered accusation about the Stampede was that some competitors were drugging their horses in the high-stakes chuckwagon races. There was talk of administering "milk-shakes" (a stimulating combination of brown sugar, baking soda, and water), of injecting enormous overdoses of vitamin-mineral supplements, of abuse of caffeine or even of hard drugs. Although the Stampede had an official drug-testing policy and a list of forbidden substances, two rodeo competitors insisted that the process was far from foolproof and perhaps not intended to be. After all, they implied, this is a family event and neither corporate sponsors nor organizers want the kind of negative image that goes with discovering substance abuse in sports. The two rodeo insiders refused to be identified, saying they believe the sport needs to be cleaned up but they don't want the trouble that would go with speaking out. The rules of the Canadian Professional Rodeo Association – the body that competitors in the professional rodeo circuit have to belong to – say that participants can be fined or suspended for saying things "detrimental to the best interests" of the sport. Insiders say anyone who causes a lot of negative publicity can be forced out of the sport.[11]

Critics say that the drug tests can't find what they don't look for; that because not every horse from each winning team in each race is tested, participants have a chance of getting away with drugging them; that there is no proof that all tests are submitted to the lab hired by the Stampede, or that results are heeded. Drug problems are not welcomed by the organizers of any sporting event, which means there is no real incentive to seek them out in the absence of any publicly criticized problem. Some critics say the Stampede and other chuckwagon racing venues should have an independent drug-testing body, including a local police officer and an animal cruelty inspector. Some argue that the Stampede has become big and lucrative enough to merit an independent panel of judges as well. One of the two anonymous competitors said he had used a banned substance on a horse with an injury, only to have the bad luck that his horse was selected for testing. He said he heard nothing further about it: neither a bad test result nor the expected fine.

On a practical level, there are complaints that a loose system favours the richest competitors in chuckwagon races. Sponsorship is important, because prize money alone won't pay the bills for a good chuckwagon outfit and horses. Winners attract sponsors. They can also afford extra horses. And because the results of drug tests come through after the Stampede is over and are not announced publicly, offenders and their sponsors face no public embarrassment or shame, nor does the Stampede itself.

In 1996, when a number of positive drug tests were reportedly turned in and fines were quietly paid, the Stampede issued a new and more specific drug policy, naming the only medications that would be permitted.[12] Penalties for first offences included forfeiting the prize, a $1,000 fine, and probation for the next Stampede. An offender already on probation would face a $2,500 fine, forfeiting the prize and getting a suspension from the next Stampede. There would be no appeal. The rules state that officials will choose for drug tests any of the four horses from each of the four teams competing in the final heat for the $50,000 prize. (In other nightly races, horses are chosen randomly beforehand for tests, and some horses from the winning teams are tested afterward. Not all horses are tested.)

The Stampede's Dan Sullivan complained that the criticisms from animal activists lump the rodeo in with activities such as medical research, where there might well be animal abuse. The animals' role in this entertainment, he said, is "relatively good for them," and he compared it favourably with any other animal use in the world. According to rodeo supporters, many of the horses in their events didn't make it at the race track and would have been slaughtered if they hadn't been brought into the sport. Sullivan rejected complaints about the flank strap used on bucking horses, saying that the event uses castrated males and mares, so that genitals are not damaged. The competition, he said, is like a cat trying to shake a piece of masking tape off its paw.

Calf-roping is one event that does draw public criticism, and the Stampede has a penalty for cowboys who make the young calf fall by jerking its neck. As for drug testing, Sullivan said the Stampede's policy is a serious, effective one that has inspired imitation by other rodeos. The Stampede reported that "fewer than 20" drivers have been penalized for drug violations since 1982, when the first testing policy was applied to chuckwagon races.[13]

Animal activists argue that horses don't buck for pleasure and would not buck at all without the flank strap circling their abdomen at their tender groin area, which proves their discomfort. Horses, cattle, and calves suffer leg, spine, and neck injuries from the rodeo activities, they say, asking if the same doting crowds would cheer dogs being roped and tied the way steers and calves are. They say that smaller rodeos, the events where competitors aspiring to the Stampede prove themselves, have fewer regulations and worse conditions. A professional rodeo staged in Ottawa in early August 1999, for instance, left one horse dead. The bucking horse died in front of six thousand horrified spectators after crashing head-first into a fence. "It's like selling tickets to traffic accidents," said one sickened critic.[14]

The Stampede was not the only entertainment laying claims to heritage for its animal events. In the summer of 1999, the Montreal-based Global Action Network organized widespread opposition among Canadian animal groups to a bullfight being brought into the city by the Portuguese community. The Portuguese-style fight did not end in death for the half-dozen bulls used. Instead, the animals were jabbed with Velcro-tipped sticks and wrestled by young men trying to immobilize them. The bullfight was presented as part of the community's heritage, and the criticism of cruelty was called an insult. The event, organizers said, was no worse than the Calgary Stampede. The critics had a different point of view. "Any man who pays to see such an event has serious doubts about his own masculinity," Michael O'Sullivan of the Humane Society of Canada told one reporter with characteristic bluntness. "Any woman who goes to a bullfight is either attracted to or dominated by such men."[15] For Andrew Plumbly of the Global Action Network, the event amounted to baiting or tormenting bulls in a way that should be stopped under the Criminal Code of Canada.

The issue caused hard feelings inside the animal movement, as the Montreal branch of the Society for the Prevention of Cruelty to Animals agreed, at one point, to accept money from the organizers for the bulls' later retirement. The Montreal SPCA argued that it was making the best of a bad situation. Other animal groups were outraged at the idea of taking money from a bullfight that they were trying, unsuccessfully, to prevent. When the event began, the Montreal SPCA found itself forced to rush to court for an order to get inside to inspect the bulls. Plumbly videotaped the fights while more than a hundred protesters gathered outside. But the bullfight, the first held in Montreal in more than twenty-five years, seemed to succeed as a community event.

By the turn of the century, protests had become part of the standard welcome when many circuses rolled into town. In Britain in the spring of 1999, the government called for local officials to crack down on circus abuses. An all-party Parliamentary Group for Animal Welfare was harsher. It supported proposals to ban animal acts after a report condemned circus conditions and a high-profile court case found a trainer guilty of cruelty. The court case included a film of the trainer beating a baby chimpanzee and sneering as the chimp whimpered when his orange ball was taken away. In Nova Scotia it wasn't clear if years of work by activists had paid off or been checkmated, but by the summer of 1999 that they had at least caught the attention of the provincial government. The legislature enacted laws requiring permits and regulations for circuses operating in the province, the first jurisdiction to take such a step.

• • •

Dr. Hugh Chisholm is as soft-spoken and polite an activist as you're going to get in the animal movement, a man more easily pictured writing letters to the editor than confronting angry circus hands. An established veterinarian in Halifax, he was drawn into circus protest a few years ago by Angela Miller, a Halifax secretary and animal activist. She urged him to watch *The Plight of Performing Animals*, a video on the circus produced by the Canadian Federation of Humane Societies. He was shocked by the twenty-minute report on the stunted lives of circus animals and the brutality of much of their training.[16] He began going to circuses, investigating for himself, convinced that the facts and common sense could set things right.

Chisholm convinced the Nova Scotia Veterinary Medical Association to oppose travelling animal acts on the grounds that circuses can't adequately meet the needs of wild or exotic animals and that the behaviours demanded of the animals demean them. He founded VOICE, Veterinarians Opposed to Inhumane Circus Environments, and posted the results of his investigations on the Internet with his own photographs taken at circuses in Halifax and Dartmouth. The vet, whose clinic specializes in treating little domestic cats, told of being hosed down by an angry tiger trainer when he was photographing big circus cats in their cages. He reported seeing cages too small for their inhabitants and elephants chained by legs or in "pitifully small electrified enclosures." He saw horses in cramped stalls and bears in the backs of panel trucks. He lodged a complaint with the local Society for the Prevention of Cruelty to Animals after seeing an elephant kicked in the head and hooked in the mouth by her trainer, tigers whipped on the face and dragged by the tail, and one of them forced to continue performing despite having vomited. He was astonished that his orderly, documented report accomplished nothing. The SPCA, he announced on his Web site, reported, "The Crown appeared concerned about the expense of the prosecution and the fact that two days' court time may need to [be] set down to hear the case." There was also the problem that the circus would move on before the court date.

Angela Miller was also surprised that her polite letters made no difference when she first began concerning herself with the circus in the early 1990s. She ended up in TAPA – Taking Action to Protect Animals – an organization that for its first four years focused on the circus. In July 1999 she was dogging a Shriners' circus as it moved around the province. Having a professional like Chisholm supporting the issue gave the activists credibility with the public, Miller said. Opponents couldn't very well dismiss Chisholm as being uninformed about animals the way they do with other protesters, no matter how much time the activists have spent researching issues. Once the circus left the province, she and others sent letters to corporate sponsors, telling them why they shouldn't back this sort of entertainment. She was writing hundreds of letters on animal issues every year. It was a long way down the road she started on as a kid after signing an anti-fur petition.[17]

Gail Zwicker and Beth Mackenzie Kent were also part of the protest and the letter-writing through their Bridgewater-based Nova Scotia Humane Society. They first worked together at an animal shelter, but decided, in 1996, that they needed an animal organization that was separate from the placement agency and could be more outspoken. They had both taken to the streets in front of fur stores, which was not quite what Halifax was used to. Like Miller and Chisholm, they weren't sure where the circus issue would go after the province took action. Chisholm worried that the regulations amounted to an "end run" around critics. Most of the rules, particularly those on training, were unenforceable, he said, and they might amount to no more than a rubber stamp. The rules require circuses to get a government permit. They ban bears, primates, and seals. They declare that "social species" shall not be exhibited alone; that elephants need company, stimulation, and must not be trained by punishments or tethered by their legs; that cages must be big enough to give the cats escape from their feces; that camels and hoofed species must have shade. There is to be no physical punishment, no hoops of fire for the lions to leap through, and no belittling costumes.

The Nova Scotia protesters had already convinced a handful of municipalities to ban animal acts entirely and were working on other towns when the provincial government issued regulations. Zwicker, Kent, and Miller made plans to focus on farm animals while they waited to assess the impact the regulations would have on circuses.

The Shriners, who brought U.S. circus companies to the province for fund-raising, were unimpressed by the critics. They were getting far more attention than their numbers warranted, said Shrine potentate Frank Cordon of Halifax. The new regulations won't be any obstacle for future circus performances, he said. "Those who don't want to go don't have to go. Those who want to protest are free to protest." In Alberta the Calgary Animal Rights Coalition drew a similar response with a 1998 demonstration against a Shrine Circus. There were no plans to change the tradition of more than four decades of using exotic animals, organizers said.[18]

"Animal advocates maintain that the use of animals in these performances is an anachronistic practice which should go the way of the human freak shows that preceded them," Lesli Bisgould wrote. The Toronto lawyer was assessing the possibility of using Nova Scotia's anti-cruelty law to protect circus animals and concluded that it would not work.[19] Animal activists' concerns about the circus, Bisgould said, deal with abusive beatings and training using food deprivation, electric prods, or, in the case of elephants, a hook called an ankus. Travel in transport cages or temporary accommodation on site is often inadequate, and the living conditions and abnormal behavioural demands made on the animals are unacceptable.

On a sizzling June afternoon in suburban east Toronto, I went with Ontario SPCA inspector Debby Hunt when she answered a typical circus complaint.[20] People had been calling the SPCA after driving past a Shrine Circus set up on property at a major intersection. Drivers could see ponies and elephants standing in sun-baked lots, and callers urged the SPCA to do something. A portly, grey-haired man in dress trousers, a short-sleeved white shirt, and a dark red Shriner's fez came to the door of a portable office and sneered at Hunt when she explained the complaints she had come to investigate. "Don't you know where elephants come from?" the man yelled at her. "Don't you know? Africa. Africa, that's where." Having delivered that zoological insight – even in Africa in the heat of the day elephants might head for shade or water or cooling mud to roll in – he went back into the office, leaving a lesser mortal to hastily offer to show Hunt to the animal area.

"Do I look like a pony man?" Mike Donoho snorted when Hunt asked him about the hot-looking little ponies. "I'm an elephant man." His identity established, the elephant man strode ahead of Hunt, assuring her that the elephants, confined to a grassed area behind an electric fence, were fine. They had no shade but there was a water spray and some mud to roll in as the temperatures approached the mid-thirties. Donoho couldn't find anyone who admitted to being in charge of the little herd of black ponies standing behind a low fence in a sun-baked square. Looking nervous, he offered a rushed series of observations. One of the ponies perhaps had an eye infection and was getting antibiotics, and a few looked scruffy "because they're mules." Hunt kept returning to the issue of shade. Donoho assured her that he and a few other men would put up an awning. He went for helpers.

In a breezier, shaded area, a skinny man with a necklace of big teeth was babysitting cages of tigers, leopards, and jaguars. Usually they would take the animals for a walk on a leash, but there were too many people around to do that here, he said. At home, in Florida, the Cat Dancers' animals would swim every day and get exercise. (Fourteen months later one of the Cat Dancers' tigers would also kill another trainer during a walk and be put to death.) The man complained that he had had it with short-term circus gigs, that casino jobs were better because they went on for months and allowed the animals to be settled into more adequate temporary homes. Compared to the elephants and ponies, the big cats at least looked comfortable in the small cages.

There was nothing more for Hunt to do. "You know," she said as she drove away, "it's sad. That jaguar. I looked into his eyes. It's sad."

Rather than try to convince provincial cruelty inspectors to wrestle with existing law, B.C. activists have also tackled local municipalities. By 1999 they too had chalked up a list of towns with bans on animal acts. In presentations to local councils, they didn't debate the ideology of the issue, said Debra Pobert of the Vancouver Humane Society. Instead, they stressed that no elephant or tiger would have any chance for anything remotely like a natural life in a travelling circus.[21]

At Zoocheck Canada's office in Toronto, Rob Laidlaw cautioned that the Nova Scotia regulations might be a useful step, depending upon how they were enforced. After more than two decades in the animal movement, Laidlaw believed in the value of practical, incremental steps. He may also have been cheered by his other conviction, that circuses were living out their last days, that within ten years a combination of protest and competition from exciting, non-animal circuses will have pushed them out of business.[22] If you demand that the world be changed, Laidlaw said, you get laughed at and dismissed. But if you make sensible, specific suggestions armed with facts, you get much farther. For a national organization that prides itself on never dropping an issue until it is settled, it is a realistic approach. Anything more impatient would have driven an animal activist working on zoo issues to distraction, at least in Ontario. Laidlaw had, over the years, become one of the Canadians most familiar with the country's zoos, from roadside petting operations to million-dollar attractions.

While other provinces, particularly in the Maritimes, have made efforts to deal with zoo conditions, Ontario remains the wild frontier. In 1999 the province overhauled its fish and wildlife law and promised that standards would be worked out to go along with the permits required for native wildlife held in captivity. Officials said this work was being done in consultation with the Canadian Association of Zoological Parks and Aquaria (CAZPA), a voluntary association of some 160 members, which was developing standards for care and housing of each species. But for other non-native species, there was still nothing to specify what care they should have. That is a serious omission in a province with perhaps seventy private roadside zoos, maybe two thousand individuals who keep their own non-domestic big cats, thousands who own non-traditional livestock, and hundreds with exotic reptiles. It has been left to municipalities to decide what, if any, bylaws to pass about exotic animal ownership and to humane societies to deal with any complaints that might reach them on the living conditions of the animals, whether at private homes or in zoos. Meanwhile, bureaucrats were reporting that the province had no plan for any further regulation of other species or anything resembling a zoo permit. The province was sticking with the tradition of managing only the native wildlife as a resource under its jurisdiction.

Some fifteen years ago, when Laidlaw, a former Toronto Humane Society inspector, visited a small private zoo near Barrie, Ont., he was shocked to find tiny cages, no drinking water, a bear chained by its neck and crying, and monkeys isolated from any company. He was more surprised at how little Humane Society inspectors felt able to do beyond correcting obvious problems of shade or water. In 1987, after touring the province armed with a notebook and camera, Laidlaw wrote a damning report on the province's zoos and called for a licensing system. Considering that Britain had been licensing zoos since 1981 and the United States had at least set minimum standards of care for captive animal facilities, it was not an outrageous idea. He recommended that the conditions of licences include experience and knowledge in animal care and that facilities meet set standards. He also proposed that no licences be given to animal exhibits that are

essentially public amusements.[23] In September 1998 British veterinarian and animal welfare specialist Samantha Lindley was brought
to Ontario jointly by Zoocheck and the World Society for the
Protection of Animals to check on a selection of Ontario zoos. She
recommended that the province establish an annual licensing system
requiring inspections by experts, keep veterinarian reports on each
animal, require owners to have some training, and give animals
suffering mental disturbances immediate medical attention and that,
if no help can be given, the animal be relocated or killed.

"Most zoos still work on the premise that the public has a right to
see such-and-such a species in downtown wherever, but none can
really answer why," Lindley wrote. "The entrepreneurs of Victorian
England argued much the same when transporting and displaying
savages captured on their travels. . . . Unfortunately, the zoos which
were visited in Ontario were, for the most part, at the bottom of this
evolutionary scale of zoos. Like the basic Victorian menagerie, they
were often impoverished, dirty, misguided and imposed such a degree
of suffering on their animals that many displayed signs of severe mental disturbance."[24]

The same approach in the Maritimes – a British expert brought in
by the two organizations to survey zoos in Nova Scotia and New
Brunswick – produced an equally damning report in 1996 and a call
for licenses.[25] Unlike the Ontario study, this one also got results. New
Brunswick set up a licensing system that required annual renewal, an
inventory of all animals, compliance with CAZPA standards, and a
government permit to own any wildlife. New Brunswick bureaucrats
talk about Ontario in tones of disbelief. It is the province where you
can have a Siberian tiger in your backyard.

"It sets a bad precedent for people to own wildlife," said Gerry
Redmond, New Brunswick's manager of big game and fur-bearers
and the administrator of its zoo permits. "People want them, but to
me it's a wild animal and you should try to ensure that it can exist in a
normal way. Zoos play their part if they're done right. I think society
still accepts zoos and [wildlife] parks. But I think standards are
changing."[26] Redmond said he doesn't necessarily share Zoocheck's

philosophy, but he doesn't dismiss the group's work. Licensing put some of his province's zoos out of business, he said, and probably they should have been closed. Others are being helped along in an effort to reach acceptable standards.

Marineland, in Niagara Falls, Ont., has become the focus of international protest by both animal activists generally opposed to animals being kept in zoos and by those who specifically reject the idea of captive animals performing tricks or being made available for close human scrutiny and handling rather than being observed from a distance in more natural settings. There is a growing sentiment that the justification for keeping animals captive must include research, the conservation of rare species, or educational programs, all with natural settings and a consideration for the animals' behavioural needs, rather than simply showing them off to the curious. That conviction, moving beyond basic sympathy, has motivated demands for government regulation.

When Lindley visited Ontario zoos for Zoocheck and the WSPA, the multimillion-dollar Niagara Falls tourist attraction was on her list. She didn't mince words in her 1998 report. Marineland's attitude to human-animal relationships, she wrote, was medieval in having the animals beg and do tricks for food. Public health and safety were at risk, she said, from children leaning over to be "kissed" by a killer whale or surrounded by aggressive deer seeking food, or by feeding marshmallows to an overcrowded enclosure of bears. She panned the living conditions of the animals, including the whales and dolphins, and noted that in Britain the public no longer regards such marine amusements as acceptable.

In May 1998, Zoocheck focused specifically on Marineland with its report *Distorted Nature: Exposing the Myth of Marineland*, prepared with advice from assorted zoologists and animal specialists. It concluded that the Niagara Falls attraction served no legitimate conservation or educational role, that its safety features were inadequate, and that the total numbers of animals should be controlled. Zoocheck called for Marineland to phase out its marine mammals and improve its land exhibits. It asked the federal government to ban the capture of marine mammals in Canadian waters, it asked the province for laws on zoos, including standards, and it asked humane societies to intervene more aggressively.

Zoocheck's report got media attention. An offended Niagara Falls city council promptly declared its support for one of the town's major employers and corporate taxpayers. At first, council refused to hear a presentation from Zoocheck. Reminded that council never refused to at least hear presentations, it grudgingly allowed Zoocheck to speak to one of its subcommittees, where there would be no television coverage. Marineland owner John Holer, who over four decades had translated $2,000 in savings and a few sea lions into a major amusement park and animal attraction, dismissed the criticisms in local news reports. Who is Zoocheck to say there should be no marine mammals in captivity, Holer told a *Niagara Falls Review* reporter. It was true that a seventh killer whale calf had died the summer before, but, he said, "that's the reality of life." He said he wanted to add more attractions to Marineland, including a shark exhibit.

In late August Zoocheck held a public meeting at the Niagara Falls Public Library to discuss its report. About forty people turned up, and they listened to Laidlaw criticize exhibits as barren and the uncontrolled feeding of deer and bear as antiquated. If the park couldn't meet the animals' needs, he said, it had no business having them. The audience also heard the moderator read a Marineland lawyer's letter warning Zoocheck to stop spreading "misinformation." Mayor Wayne Thompson called the meeting "the kind of thing we've come to expect" from Zoocheck. Only one council member attended. Alderman Kim Craitor said he had heard nothing that would alter council's support for the amusement centre.[27]

Holer accused Zoocheck, "with their so-called experts," of lying about Marineland and of playing on the public's emotions for donations because "it's probably better than working." If his facilities were that bad, he said, the Humane Society would have put him out of business and the public would not have made him such a success. He said he had applied to the Canadian Association of Zoological Parks and Aquaria for accreditation but had been turned down, ostensibly on the grounds that he was selling surplus buffalo, elk, and deer for slaughter to meat packers and because the bears were fed marshmallows. Those treats are only a snack, he said, and the bears love sweets. The real reason for his rejection, he said, was that the industry was very competitive and his success as a private operation had rankled publicly supported institutions like the Toronto Zoo. Toby Styles of the Toronto Zoo was on the panel that inspected Marineland, he noted.[28]

Styles, executive director of marketing and communications at the Toronto Zoo, said later that he was in charge of CAZPA's accreditation program at the time of the Marineland inspection and had spent a day looking at the operation with other panel members. CAZPA's full board rejected Marineland only because of the bear exhibit, he said. The marine exhibits were not considered a problem. Marineland was the only large Canadian zoo or aquarium that was not a member of CAZPA, which was using the standards of its U.S. counterpart while it developed its own. "We'd love to have him in the association," Styles said. Like Holer, Styles is no fan of animal rights advocates. Some of them oppose all zoos, any killing of an animal, and they accord a dog the same importance as a child, he said. The zoo critics among them are not zoologists, have no credentials, and are "just people who care," Styles said.[29]

Holer said he would try again for CAZPA accreditation because he believed it was good for the industry to regulate itself. He defended contact between animals and humans as allowing what the public wants and being a "great educational experience." He hoped to take his one thousand-acre property to a level that would rival Disney. The government's job, he said, is to provide the conditions for people to earn a living and pay taxes. It should pay less attention to the animal rights movement, he said. He blamed animal rights activists for having frightened Ottawa away from allowing whales to be captured in Canadian waters for animal attractions, even if the species is not endangered. "The whole history of man is related, tied in with living off the animals," he said.

Ottawa rejected Holer's 1999 application to capture six beluga whales in waters near Churchill, Man. The town of Churchill, trying to build a whale-tourism industry, objected to the capture on the grounds that the negative publicity would hurt. Vicki Burns of the Winnipeg Humane Society said it was "mind-boggling" that the government would even consider the application, because "these mammals are not suited to captivity."[30] Between 1967 and 1992, Canada allowed sixty-eight belugas to be taken from Hudson Bay. Two of four died shortly after reaching Chicago's Shedd Aquarium, and one fisheries minister, John Crosbie, banned the further capture of belugas for export, though it was still possible to apply for capture of the whales for domestic display. Canadian aquaria are also allowed to trade or sell their whales.[31]

While activists deluged the federal fisheries minister with objections to the capture of the belugas for Marineland, Holer bought three captive male belugas from Russia to join his newly expanded marine show of orcas, dolphins, and sea lions. Both Zoocheck and the Canadian Federation of Humane Societies have urged the government to ban the capture or import of whales and dolphins for display in Canada. Although a specialist's advisory report to the minister was completed, no action on it was expected in the near future, according to department officials. The protests outside Marineland continued, although the most recent ones did not feature the numbers or the arrests of the past. Catherine Ens of Niagara-Brock Action for Animals said her group has encountered repeated resistance from police in their attempts to conduct even legal leafleting or demonstrations. It convinced her that Holer was being given special treatment because of his booming business and the city council's support. (On January 10, 2000, newspapers reported that Holer was the target of arson threats on an Internet chat-line after a beluga whale died.)

· · ·

Smaller organizations have turned to Zoocheck for help on other wildlife issues. In 1995 the Winnipeg Humane Society enlisted Zoocheck's support in a situation regarding polar bears in Churchill. The town had set up a buffer zone and bears repeatedly entering it were being declared nuisances. Nuisance bears were candidates for export to zoos. While the numbers being shipped out were not high, the bears were going to such tropical places as Thailand. Because of the objections raised, by September 1998 the Manitoba government had set conditions that zoos would have to meet if they wanted the province's bears. The province called for periodic reports on the animals' progress and a contract would stipulate appropriate facilities. Only orphaned polar bear cubs unable to survive on their own would be candidates for export.

Bears have featured at the heart of some other much harder battles over animals. One particularly high-profile win for the animal movement – the banning of Ontario's spring bear hunt – thrilled as well as surprised groups that had been working for years with no indication that, suddenly, the government was going to move. When the groups assessed the reason for victory, they drew important lessons.

Robert Schad, a rich Ontario businessman and environmentalist, was not opposed to hunting when he had decided to bankroll a campaign against the spring bear hunt several years earlier. He ended up giving the effort nearly $2 million through the Schad Foundation, a body funded from the profits of his company, Husky Injection Moldings Systems. A member of the World Wildlife Fund Canada's advisory committee, Schad was specifically revolted by the spring hunt. Outfitters had turned it into a business, baiting a spot for weeks in advance to ensure that hungry bears, just emerging from hibernation, could be counted on to frequent that place and then be shot by hidden hunters. Many of the hunters were Americans who were not allowed to hunt bears in the spring back home. Although it was illegal to shoot a female with cubs, that had happened more than once – estimates of how often varied with the source of the estimate.[32]

In the course of the campaign, the International Fund for Animal Welfare Canada made sure that a tough little video against the hunt was delivered to voters in parts of southern Ontario where Conservative members of the provincial government had been elected with narrow margins. "It was a message that politicians understood," said Ainslie Willock, a director of Animal Alliance of Canada who helped put together the Bear Alliance of Canada for the campaign.

The group included not only the big, international IFAW and national groups like Animal Alliance but also environmental organizations.

The Animal Alliance of Canada and like-minded groups had already hatched a plan called Environmental Voters, designed to forge alliances with other social justice groups to deliver a political punch in closely contested ridings during elections. The goal was to prove to government that they should not be ignored. "This is the product of total frustration," Animal Alliance director Liz White said of the Environmental Voters plan. The spring bear hunt victory was taken as proof that raw politicking counted. It was also a sign that environmental and animal groups might make common cause in influential ways. "It's really simple," Willock said. "It's behaviour modification. It's democracy in action, and it's terribly exciting."[33]

The bear hunt decision, announced in January 1999, came as a surprise to activists who had campaigned on the issue for years with little success. While other big game is hunted in the fall, for some thirty years the province had allowed bears to be hunted during both spring and fall. Outraged supporters of the hunt argued that the government had caved in to urban voters, who had supposedly been misled by animal zealots. The motive, the critics of the decision said, was to put a softer face on the government before an election rather than to protect orphaned cubs.

The win inspired other animal groups. In April six organizations, including Bear Watch, advertised in the Vancouver newspapers against the spring bear hunt, particularly for grizzlies, a population estimated at from ten thousand to thirteen thousand in the province. The group, including environmentalists, noted that they were not criticizing hunting in itself, but the hunting of a species at risk. Bear Watch, which had pulled back from the more controversial tactics of past years, was more explicit in its opposition to trophy hunting when it met with the provincial minister to deliver a fifteen-thousand-name petition against grizzly bear hunting. Hunting bears for sport, said Bear Watch's Eric Donnelly, was wrong and repugnant.[34] At the same time in Manitoba, there were also stirrings of opposition to spring bear hunting, with estimates of up to 150 cubs orphaned in 1998.

Angry hunters responded to this issue by complaining that government shouldn't be swayed by big bucks and special interests – an argument that seemed to lack a certain self-awareness – and they underscored their contribution to the economy. In British Columbia hunters were spending an estimated $100 million a year, a figure that suffers by comparison to spending on non-hunting, wildlife-related activities by provincial residents, which a B.C. government survey placed at $622 million in 1996.[35] In Northern Ontario, outfitters said the decision to ban the spring bear hunt would cost the industry $17 million. The Ontario Federation of Anglers and Hunters complained as early as 1996 to the Ontario Ministry of Natural Resources that it was allowing opposing groups too much input for their size.

After Ontario's spring hunting ban, hunters demanded protection for what they called their right to fish and hunt on the grounds of heritage, and they duly found that the provincial government was sympathetic to some form of a heritage hunting and fishing act. Some animal groups looked to Aboriginal communities for allies to oppose such an act. At a meeting on Saturday, July 24, 1999, at the University of Toronto, former provincial resources minister Bud Wildman warned that the hunting lobby had continuous consultation with the government and that the OFAH's Rick Morgan was "the unofficial deputy minister." While he was not opposed to sports hunting or fishing, Wildman said, he rejected the idea of a heritage right to them.

The animal activists, environmentalists, and Native people at the daylong meeting were uniformly opposed as well, though the First Nations representatives were wary of the others. The evening before the meeting, a film event for participants had turned angry as animal activists argued with several First Nations representatives. It was a small reminder of a difficult past. Animal activists have long opposed trapping and the fur industry, activities central to the lives of First Nations people, as well as the whaling conducted by Aboriginal peoples, a limited practice sanctioned by the International Whaling Commission but which many say is manipulated by pro-whaling countries such as Japan and Norway. At the Saturday meeting Eric Johnston and Paul Jones of the Chippewas of Nawash on the Bruce

Peninsula and Rodney Bobiwash of the Anishnabek Nation of Lake Huron made it clear that they needed no guidance on how to view animals or the environment. Still, IFAW Canada's endangered species campaigner Troy Seidle said later that he expected some alliance could be built to oppose the hunting lobby.

Whatever alliance the animal movement forged through its Environmental Voters strategy, it appeared likely that the targets in the next federal election would be keyed to the politics of the seal industry. Ainslie Willock, who came into the animal movement on the seal hunt issue in 1982, described it as bigger, more cruel, and no longer even rhetorically tied to ideas of sustainability. If the government won seven federal ridings by protecting the seal hunt, she said, "Let's cost them seven seats somewhere else."

IFAW Canada's Rick Smith, who has written a doctoral thesis on seals, said the hunt had reached a very different phase from those early protests in the 1960s when it was one of the first such issues to hit television screens with dramatic images of ice and blood. The seal population was so reduced that the hunt from large vessels was discontinued. By 1983 Europe had banned the import of baby whitecoat seal pelts. The Canadian government forbid the whitecoat hunt in 1987 in an attempt to offset the damage of the protest campaign. But from 1982 to 1995, while allowable catches were about 186,000 a year, the actual number of seals landed by hunters only averaged about 55,000.

When the East Coast cod fishery collapsed and was closed in 1992, federal and provincial ministers began linking the seal herd to the loss of fish, despite serious scientific arguments that the connection was inaccurate. That brought proposals for massive kills, although there was no guarantee of markets. After 1996 the allowable kill was boosted to 250,000 and then to 275,000, but governments were subsidizing a weak meat market. Even the prices in Asia for seal penises had fallen from $100 each to about $20. According to Smith, by 1995-96 the hunt had become a "glorified bounty program" that paid for every pound of seal meat landed regardless of the market demand. Rather than take the blame for the collapse of the fishery and their own impossible promises that the cod would quickly come back, politicians were falling back on blaming seals, he said. The extreme political rhetoric was beginning to mobilize opposition, with the support of some Newfoundland academics and scientists.[36]

Canada's seal hunt, one of the last commercial hunts of wild animals in North America and the largest marine mammal hunt in the world, had seemingly become an aberration. Since 1900 most commercial hunts of wild animals on the continent had been ended to prevent populations from being ravaged by greed. But a hundred years later a new rationale had come forward to justify large-scale slaughter. Ironically, this rationale had its beginnings in the environmental movement. It's the idea of "sustainable utilization," which means maintaining a population at the level most convenient to humans. The IFAW, among others, has warned of its impact.

It's a notion that gives a cover story not only to an aggressive push by Japan and Norway to reopen commercial whaling but also to campaigns for a resurrection of an ivory trade that cut in half the population of African elephants in just a decade, until an international trade ban saved them. After that ban was relaxed in 1997 – based on the argument that the trade would allow African countries to sell off stockpiles for enough money to sustain wildlife – ivory poaching once again blossomed.[37]

The "sustainable utilization" argument was also used by the Canadian and U.S. governments jointly in 1998 to justify a massive kill of lesser snow geese, approved on the grounds that they were destroying fragile marshes around James Bay and Hudson Bay. They were, it seemed, to be killed to the tune of a million and a half birds so that they wouldn't die for lack of food. A court challenge by Canadian activists won only some time and a refinement of the plans. Barry Kent MacKay travelled to the region on behalf of the Animal Protection Institute with Canadian zoologist and goose specialist Vernon Thomas. Native elders there told him that the geese levels were not unprecedented. MacKay and Thomas concluded that the region was not being despoiled by the geese but simply being used by them, as was natural. Mackay called the goose kill a "scam" and a "fraud."[38]

The issue of wildlife pits some of the most basic ideas of the animal movement against its critics. Opposition to killing wild animals for their fur strikes at the heart of First Nation legal and treaty claims to manage the natural resources around them. Beyond being insensitive, it is an insult to their heritage. It also offends the traditions and self-image of some rural white Canadians. The injury seems more intolerable because animal activists are viewed as people who live in cities, out of touch with nature and less informed, people who don't care about the humans they wound but only about animals. Their ideas seem to fly in the very face of Canadian history, founded on the fur trade. Equally, the campaign against the seal hunt, devastating in its impact in the 1980s, seemed to deny compassion to hard-working, poor fishermen on the east coast and deny respect for their age-old hunting practices.

But society changes and attitudes change. If furs and trapping were going to be the economic basis of a people, then government assistance wouldn't be such a permanent feature, animal advocates have argued. Continued emphasis on fur only masks the need for a better way to participate in the modern economy. How could animal activists not object to an industry that produces products so unessential to human life and so lethal to animals as fur coats?

Environmentalists and animal rights advocates can travel a fair way down the road together. They jointly want the conservation of natural settings and the animals that live in them. The rub can come when the issues are severed. The whole notion of "sustainable" resources assumes a use that is balanced. If the resource is animal and the use comes after death, the alliance fails. When whales are endangered, for example, there can be a common purpose in attacking the hunting of them. When they aren't, the issue becomes the matter of killing individual, sentient mammals, not whether they might disappear as a group.

Finn Lynge, Greenland's representative to the European Parliament in the 1980s, had little sympathy for animal activists in his 1992 book *Arctic Wars: Animal Rights, Endangered Peoples*, calling them insensitive and destructive to indigenous peoples for their campaigns against seal and whale hunting and against the fur industry generally. He found their whole view of life unacceptable. Only humans have individual interests that should mitigate against a larger group, he wrote. Only they are capable of choosing between good and evil. It is this very innocence that gives the animal world its beauty and that makes animal abuse so awful. This has been the age-old view of human-animal relationships and the basis of human-centred law, he said.[39]

"One basic fact remains: no human group has ever been ready, so far, to sacrifice lives of its own in order to serve the interests of animals in jeopardy," he wrote. "Instead, humans always have been and, presumably, always will be, ready to sacrifice the lives of animals. This is the people-centered reality, and no responsible authority is about to change it. The world is crowded and lives, both animal and human, have to be managed; but the difference is that all agree that policies of containment vis-à-vis human lives should be based upon birth control and family planning, whereas nobody disputes that animal population growth, when it is bothersome to humans, must be regulated through lethal means."

MacKay, by contrast, wrote about the "arrogance that leads humans to assume godly wisdom over nature." He said it reminded him of a family friend, a Mrs. Brown. As a child he had watched her pop starlings into a paper bag and cut off their heads with scissors. There were too many, she said. He remembered the chill he felt when, one day, she remarked on the number of little goldfinches she had seen and wondered if there were too many of them. "In those days, the word 'epiphany' had yet to gain its current popularity, but I think I had one when Mrs. Brown mused about goldfinch numbers," MacKay wrote. "Who are we to decide where there are 'too many' of something?"[40]

CHAPTER SEVEN

Pets

Keeping Humans Company

She was perhaps sixty, on the edge of old age, strolling serenely through a room full of friends. It was hard to imagine the drama that had brought her to Surrey, south of Vancouver: born in the rainforest of Ecuador, taken prisoner, wounded, rescued, and smuggled into Canada. The events would make for a fine movie – for kids. Her life story might be dramatic, but it's not serious, not like it would be if it were about one of us.

Murgatroyd, a yellow-footed box turtle, was captured for food and held in a concrete pen in South America. The sight of her desperately trying to escape, rubbing the flesh from her front legs, moved a missionary to rescue her. A returning student brought her into Canada. She had a series of owners until finally, considered a burden by one of them, she was loaded into a car for the latest turn in the road of her life. She ended up with Christine and Clarence Schramm, in their Rainforest Reptile Refuge.

Now, grown to a stately twenty-seven pounds, she nibbled gently at the pant legs of a man cleaning the glass-fronted room where she lived. She held still when he turned to scratch her head. When Murgatroyd came here, the dozens of iguanas who shared the room, nursing their own pasts, were afraid of her. For a week they stuck to their tree branches, looking down at her, whipping their tails in displeasure. Soon the small iguanas began riding on her back. Once they even napped together – the younger iguanas, a resident cat, a green snake, and Murgatroyd. Christine Schramm talked about this strange combination, almost a scene from Walt Disney, in a defiant tone. But this was a room full of lives too belittled for the Disney treatment. Murgatroyd was a fluke in a world in which happy endings, like serious dramas, are about humans.

Much as we might like to think that life is rosy for pets – those non-humans that half the population of Canada share their homes with and spend some $239 a year per household feeding and caring for – their fortunes rest entirely on the goodwill of humans.[1] If their luck runs out, it's not such a big deal in the human world, where, legally, pets have the standing of private property. It is hard enough to convince the justice system to deal sternly with people who abuse the pets we consider most winsome. Canada, after all, has lagged behind other jurisdictions in moves to bring abuse against animals into the serious world of crime and punishment. What would you expect in the way of justice for most of the residents of this reptile refuge?

In sensible Canadian society, what could be more peculiar than the Schramms' life? They rise at 4:45 a.m., every day, to tend to the castoffs of the human world of pet ownership. They spend every day on lives considered so inconsequential – snakes, turtles, lizards, a few birds, even some exotic insects – that they don't rate a second thought. For these creatures, the Schramms have scrimped and battled and supplemented donations with Clarence's pay cheques from a plant nursery. The Schramms have few holidays and precious little other life. Not that they complain. They love their charges, give them names, and patiently detail their histories to visitors. Christine, a short, sturdy blonde with a booming voice, is a farm girl who does not invite teasing. Clarence is long and lean, with a poker face and cloaked eyes.[2]

Thumper is a greater sulphur-crested cockatoo, a pretty, soft grey bird with a lemon-yellow spray of feathers on his head. For years he lived in a pet store. When the owner sold his mate, Thumper began to pluck out his feathers, methodically and sadly. Finally he was left with the Schramms. Here he eats a lot of different seeds and green peppers.

He starts his day with whole wheat toast. He has toys and a cage he can leave at will. Is this a happy ending? Thumper is quiet, careful as he accepts a peanut. He still plucks feathers from his breast, although most of the plumage is growing back. He still has no mate. Who knows what he feels or thinks as he stares out the window at groups of humans?

In his book *Animal Minds*, behavioural scientist Donald R. Griffin refers to experiments in the late 1960s with pigeons.[3] The pigeons came to distinguish pictures of pigeons from pictures of dogs and other birds. An African grey parrot named Alex learned to distinguish among shapes and colours and to answer in words to questions about numbers of objects.

"Hello," a harsh voice is calling. "Hello hello hello." Maxine is about fifteen years old and as noisy as Thumper, her neighbour, is quiet. Maxine is a macaw, the bird with iridescent blue feathers and striking touches of white and mustard yellow. She had lived in a Vancouver pet store that went into receivership. For a week after the doors were shut, until someone noticed dead fish floating in a tank in the window, no one tended the inhabitants – frogs, fish, a crocodile, birds. Judy Stone, an animal rights activist and one of Christine Schramm's heroes, fetched Maxine from the bailiff. Someone who had been in the shop reported that Maxine would sometimes scream "help!" when she was left alone in a back room. She arrived bald and disturbed. Christine still dreams about a refuge where volunteers could stay overnight, where Maxine would have her own big flight area. The current refuge, in a rented building, is now cramped and filled with more than three hundred creatures. Still, if there were a mate for Maxine, room would be found.

"Hello hello hello," Maxine screams if she is ignored. She still plucks her feathers. Her bare breast looks like a supermarket turkey's. She stares back through the outer window at a visitor, waves a toy, eats a peanut. Is all of this noise and motion a product of anxiety or grief or desperation for company?

"It is customary to assume that mammals and birds are more deserving of sympathetic treatment than fishes or insects," Griffin writes. "And even the most extreme advocate of animal rights is unlikely to mourn the apparent extinction of the smallpox virus.

"But how can we estimate the degree to which various kinds of animals suffer when injured in particular ways? Only as we learn more about their subjective mental experiences will it be possible to do this on an informed basis. This is a tremendous challenge and we are at present so extremely ignorant about the conscious mental experiences of animals that it will be a long time before scientific methods can be developed to measure just how much a given animal suffers under particular conditions. . . . Whatever we learn about the subjective mental experiences of animals has significant potential relevance to ethics of animal utilization by our species."[4]

Someone like Christine Schramm does not need to wait for scientific methods to be developed – for ways to measure animal suffering or their mental experiences – to know what she should do. One day the refuge had a call from a woman who said there was a big bug on her patio, hissing at her children. It was like a June bug, really little more than a few inches long, a species that eats Douglas fir needles and hisses if disturbed. Christine chauffeured the bug out of the flat farm area of the refuge to a park with fir trees and released it. It was one of the refuge's smallest clients.

Terrazo may be the biggest, at least in length. He is a reticulated python, a stacked coil of grey, gold, and black, named for the mosaic floor tiles that his skin resembles. A woman in a North Vancouver apartment found the snake when she went to investigate the sounds of shampoo bottles falling over in her bathroom. The starving Terrazo seemed to have arrived in horror-movie style through the plumbing or walls. Reticulated pythons are probably the world's longest snake, on record at more than thirty-two feet. They are native to Southeast Asia, where they eat mammals and sometimes people.[5] "Reticulated pythons are noted for their nasty dispositions," Christine said. "This one is no exception."

Iguanas simply prefer their own kind once they are grown, some of them to six feet. They will scratch and bite and whip their long tails about when annoyed. At the refuge, they lounge in tree branches in a

glass-fronted room, alone or with their heads resting on other iguanas. "In 1986, it cost about $80 for a baby iguana in a store," Christine
told me in an angry voice. "Now you can get one for $9.99. So it's
worse now. We get kids in here, eight years old, and they say, 'Oh yeah,
I've got an iguana at home.' The parents say, 'Oh, is it cruel to keep
them? Then why do they sell them?' I say, 'To make money.' "

Iguanas started the Schramms down this road. Clarence, then a
volunteer zoo worker, had one when they met. A co-worker gave
him two more. Christine found a caiman – the crocodile most often
sold in pet shops – on sale for $39.99 and looking miserable. She ha-
rangued the merchant until he plunked it into a flea powder box and
told her to take it. Carmen, now five feet long, lounges with a dozen
other big caimans by a water tank.

The creatures just kept coming, and the Schramms' duplex was
increasingly full of aquaria and cages built by Clarence. Relatives were
beginning to make remarks, Christine said. "Lizards, no kids, that
sort of thing." They decided to find a place the reptiles could call
home, somewhere big enough to let the public in to see them and be
told why these creatures shouldn't be considered pets.

The refuge is full of discounted lives. The milk snake, secretive by
nature, was found under a car looking for privacy. What did someone
intend for the anaconda, already more than ten feet long and considered too morose for captivity? Or the African rock python, which can
grow to more than eighteen feet? The rough-necked monitor from
Malaysia can grow to five feet. It holds on with strong jaws when
it bites and needs tropical temperatures to stay alive. Orangina, the
albino Burmese python, did not like going to the beach, draped
around a man, or sitting in the sun or being poked by humans. Three
hedgehogs were cast off by bored children whose mother was proud
to say they would give them only to the refuge. Fran, the tarantula,
was found on a patio by a terrified homeowner.

O.J., the crossbred corn-gopher snake, was another patio find. The
homeowner called the RCMP. Vancouver must have been swept by a
fad for ball pythons, given the number at the refuge. They grow to five
feet in length, sell for about $100, and coil into a ball when handled.

They are cheap, small, and relatively docile as these snakes go, and "You can still brag to your buddies that you have a python," Christine said with profound contempt. Snakes and turtles have arrived at the refuge door in boxes, left by humans who crept quietly away from their pets. Some abandoned this way have frozen on winter days, waiting to be discovered.

"I have the idea now that it's not right to own animals," Christine said. "I used to think zoos were fine. I wanted to be a zookeeper. Now I don't. See how you change?"

But had she turned into a zookeeper after all? After all, the Schramms were keeping creatures in cages, showing them to school groups for a fee. The difference was that this place, however humble, was home. These animals would not be disposed of like property or loaned or traded – not at any price. Christine told a bratty story of how she brushed off a movie company wanting to rent a boa constrictor. "I said, 'I'll ask Jake.' Jake's the boa. So I hauled the phone over and I said, 'Jake wants me to translate. He's better looking than Kevin Costner and he's twice as talented. So he feels he should get twice as much.' The guy hung up."

At closing time at the Rainforest Reptile Refuge, volunteers begin cleaning cages. Clarence has come back from collecting an autograph from a touring *Young and Restless* soap star for a fundraising auction. Orangina, the python who has lived here since November 1993 is mostly folded into a plastic basin of water in his cage. He opens his very pink mouth very wide. Nearby, Terrazo's eyes stare into the distance, perhaps to a remembered past or maybe just to the bite-sized child across the room.

"What do we want?" Christine had a familiar answer ready. "Okay, we want legislation so that pet stores can't sell exotics and reptiles. It should have been stopped ten years ago. Now they have designer snakes, 'snow' boas – they're pure white – and 'albino' this and 'albino' that. Now that it has begun, how can it be stopped? It's such a money-maker."

· · ·

Christine Schramm is not likely to get what she wants anytime soon. Although the pet industry in Canada is working on cleaning up an image it acknowledges is bad, neither the industry nor government shows any interest in banning sales of reptiles or exotic animals for pets. In the summer of 1999 New Brunswick made the first moves of any province to license pet shops, kennels, and other retail animal operations and to begin to impose standards. The lack of control means that local humane societies often struggle with what the Calgary Humane Society's Cathy Thomas calls "the unflushables" – the pythons, iguanas, turtles, and tarantulas that municipalities may ban but more often ignore. Societies may farm them out to foster care or obliging zoos – but many of the rejected pets never make it that far.

The Canadian Federation of Humane Societies and some provincial societies for the prevention of cruelty to animals entertained the idea of developing, in consultation with the industry, a list of animals that could be considered appropriate for pets. That plan is going nowhere, said Louis McCann, spokesman for the Pet Industry Joint Advisory Council of Canada (PIJAC).[6] The organization, based in Orleans, Ont., includes a cross-section of the pet industry – from breeders to retailers to manufacturers. It collects data, provides members with information on animals, and monitors legislative change. McCann complained that the only creatures the Federation would probably consider to be appropriate pets are cats, dogs, hamsters, and maybe rabbits – though, actually, the Federation would add ferrets, birds, chinchillas, gerbils, and mice and rats to that list for pets in the city. In the country the list would expand to horses, donkeys, pigs, sheep, geese, cattle, llamas, turkeys, ducks, and alpacas. The Federation does not suggest exotic snakes or reptiles as pets. The PIJAC disagrees. What the industry wants, McCann said, is to be consulted on any regulatory efforts, as it was in New Brunswick. For its part, PIJAC was developing a national store certification program that would identify pet shops with acceptable standards, trained staff, and information for customers on proper care of each species sold. But that would be several more years in the making; PIJAC represents only a minority of the industry in Canada.

You can hardly expect an interest in the trade in these underrated lives to come from legislators who seem unable to stir themselves even to update criminal law on the most basic of animal cruelty offences. The federal Justice Department issued a discussion paper in the fall of 1998 with hints of fast action once submissions came in from the public on possible changes to the Criminal Code of Canada's treatment of animals. The law, after all, had hardly been touched since 1892.[7] The process only gained momentum in summer 1999, after a string of well-publicized incidents in Ontario in which dogs were dragged behind their owners' cars and suffered terribly. Public outrage grew after it was learned that one of the most badly hurt animals would have had to be returned to its owner pending the court case if the man had been willing to pay the steep veterinary bills. In autumn the government set out its proposed legislation. It would increase the maximum jail term for animal abuse to five years from the existing six months, remove the $2,000 limit on fines, and make it possible for the court to impose a lifetime ban on animal ownership. It would also move the provisions dealing with animals into a section separate from property.

Animal activists had chosen to campaign for changes in the law by stressing that animal cruelty was linked to domestic abuse of humans. This theme – that histories of violent criminals repeatedly showed a background of animal abuse – was credited with pushing the Justice Department into its discussion paper and finally into proposing to change the law. It was as if there had to be something in this for humans.

Meanwhile, in the United States more than twenty-five states were already treating animal abuse as a felony crime. Multi-year prison terms of up to ten years were possible. Fines might range to $100,000, and in some states the laws were as tough as those against human domestic assault. Organized lobbying by animal groups, something that didn't sit well with everyone, was credited for many of the tougher laws. In Arkansas a bid to make animal abuse a felony punishable by up to six years in jail, plus a $1,000 fine, was defeated in part by the lobbying of the Arkansas Farm Bureau. The exemptions for farm practices were considered too vague, and the bureau said it was worried about extremists.[8] In most states it was not the idea of helping animals but the argument that serial killers such as Ted Bundy or David Berkowitz had first practised on animals that seemed to make the most positive impact on rallying support.

Ottawa's discussion paper had asked how the law should draw a line between criminal acts against animals and "justifiable" pain and suffering from activities that are "sufficiently beneficial" to humans to be legal. Existing law bases its anti-cruelty provisions on both the idea that animals are able to suffer as well as their status as private property. Animal activists have seen that property status as a key problem of non-humans being taken seriously before the courts and by society at large. The federal discussion paper asked, delicately, if that principle should change. The government's proposed amendments seemed to avoid a direct answer.

It is not that legislators needed to wrestle with esoteric or groundbreaking ideas. Not only had other jurisdictions dealt with the same issues, but so too had Canadian agencies. The former Law Reform Commission of Canada called for a separate section in the Criminal Code dealing with offences against animals. An unpublished research paper written in 1985 for the Commission made a comprehensive and cogent assessment of existing law, which it said "reflects an inadequate ethical or philosophical position towards animals." Originally, anticruelty law did not rely on the notion of animals as property but simply called it an offence to "wantonly, cruelly or unnecessarily" ill-treat certain domestic animals. It was a 1906 revision of the law that thoroughly mixed property and cruelty offences. The effect, the research paper concluded, was to protect human morals and human interests rather than animal lives. Liberal excuses were included, through words such as "wilful" or "necessary." The reality became that "animals receive very little direct protection of their interests as living, sentient beings."[9]

Debby Hunt struggles daily with the escape hatches provided by definitions in the Criminal Code. Despite being an inspector with the Ontario Society for the Prevention of Cruelty to Animals, she is respected even by those activists who have little time for that institution. "You have to have so much evidence," Hunt complained to me one day when she took me out with her to watch her at work. "They make it so difficult. They have in the code that word 'wilful.' 'Wilful intent.' It makes it so hard."[10]

Hunt also sees a link between animal and human abuse. One caller complained to the OSPCA about a man who was dissecting live animals at his home. When Hunt went there she found live rabbits, rats, a puppy with one eye out, and a weird sort of medical shrine, but no evidence. People said the man had told them that kids were starting to look good to him. Afterwards he left the area, moved somewhere. Another complaint took Hunt to a house where a beagle had reportedly been beaten by a man. A woman answered the door. Does your dog bite? Hunt asked. No, not even when my husband beats me, the woman said. In another case, Hunt wondered what the future held for a twelve-year-old boy, the clear suspect after a neighbour's pet turtle, sunning itself in the yard, had his legs severely burned by someone with a lighter.

In the summer of 1999 mutilated cats were back on Hunt's agenda, just as they had been in an unsolved case several years earlier. Back then it was cats cut in half and gutted, their bodies left in the children's areas of Scarborough parks. The new cases were in the north end of the city, where three cats were found dead. One had been decapitated, another cut in half. A few days earlier five other dead cats, one of them cut in half, had been found in the garbage near a kids' playground. With annual grants eliminated by a provincial government intent on budget-cutting, the OSPCA staff was limited. Hunt and one other inspector covered a huge swath of territory in suburban Toronto with little money to pay for the kind of forensic work that can quickly shed light on harder cases. The majority of cruelty investigations are left to the SPCA, which is authorized by provincial animal welfare laws to enforce the cruelty provisions of the Criminal Code rather than to police. But these agencies are charities, which means their work depends largely on unreliable funding.

In Ontario the OSPCA logged 12,824 complaints of animal cruelty in 1996, with 1,389 animals removed from their owners. In 1998 the totals climbed to 15,884 complaints and 2,247 animals seized. In New Brunswick, reports and criminal charges both grew by 10 per cent in 1998. Saskatchewan had similar increases.[11] Only a small number of abuse complaints – less than one-third of 1 per cent, by one estimate – went to court. It could cost an SPCA thousands of dollars to see a case through the system, including vet and shelter costs for seized animals.

Meanwhile, police and cruelty inspectors have together uncovered a secret world of illegal cockfights and dog fights, and the organized gambling that goes with them. This is a difficult world to infiltrate. Evidence for convictions is tricky. Even the comparatively simple job of closing down a "puppy mill" can be discouraging. These sorts of commercial operations, where dogs are kept almost perpetually pregnant, churning out more litters of puppies for sale than reputable breeders would consider healthy and most often in conditions of serious neglect, are a common feature of Hunt's caseload. The existing law provided a maximum two-year ban on owning animals, which meant that puppy mills could be back in business in three years. Proposed changes could forbid the owners from re-entering the business, if the court chooses to be harsh.

• • •

On one scalding June day, Hunt was battling heavy traffic in suburban Toronto to answer a standard summer call. Someone had left a dog locked in a car, in the sun, with the windows rolled up. It had already been fifteen minutes since the call had come in, the temperature was in the thirties, and the security guard who reported the situation was getting frantic. He could not break the window, legally, but Hunt could. She was still haunted by a case from several days before: a young boxer dog left in the sun behind a house, chained with no water, in even hotter temperatures. The dog was dead by the time she arrived after answering a neighbour's complaint, and his skin peeled off as she tried to put his body into her truck. Only an unconcerned fifteen-year-old was at home.

When Hunt arrived at the parking lot, the car was gone. The owner had come back, brushed off the guard's anger, and left. The rattled security guard told Hunt, more than once, that the dog came to him, not to the owner, when the car door was opened. The guard and some infuriated landscape workers had the licence plate number and they wanted Hunt to promise she would go get the guy, because that was only right.

Most but not all animal groups have supported tougher penalties for animal abuse. According to Michael O'Sullivan of the Humane Society of Canada, the answer rests in more vigorous prosecution of existing laws rather than permitting stiffer penalties in new legislation. Tougher penalties might not be enforced, but they would give the impression that something had been done. To make prosecutions easier, his Toronto-based organization was planning to build data bases of both abuse reports and court rulings that would help prosecutors and also convince the courts of the seriousness of the problem. Lesli Bisgould, a specialist in law regarding animals, was worried that the government could be lobbied during the process of passing its Criminal Code amendments into building in loopholes. Bisgould would welcome a shift of Criminal Code provisions from a property base to a separate category, but suggested that the final impact of any change in the law would depend upon its enforcement.

The government was soon being lobbied. Opponents of the proposed Criminal Code of Canada amendments were clearly concerned about the implications for their businesses, and they wanted specific exemptions. There was unease that the notion of animals as legal property was changing and suspicion at language changes to allow tougher prosecution of cruelty. Wary critics did not want activists to be left with even a toehold from which to press for a more aggressive interpretation of the law. One farm group commissioned a legal opinion warning that everyone from medical researchers to religious slaughterhouses to anglers baiting hooks with worms could risk criminal charges. And there were signs that the complaints were having an effect. Liberal MP Paul Steckle, a key member of the federal government's rural caucus, assured one constituent that he would not vote for the proposed changes without assurances that "traditional activities" such as hunting, fishing, farming, or fur farms would not be harmed. As it stands, he wrote, the proposed changes posed a "serious threat" to these interests.[12]

The Canadian Federation of Humane Societies expressed more enthusiasm for the federal government's planned changes to the law. It called them "a significant advancement." Many of the changes would match what the Federation had been urging for years. But some five months after the government's legislation was tabled, even the Federation's enthusiasm was giving way to frustration. The concerted opposition of farmers, hunters, and the research world seemed to be having the kind of impact that Bisgould had feared. Newspaper reports said the government was considering an amendment to give commercial users of animals an exemption from the country's Criminal Code. Federation program director Shelagh MacDonald said this move would make the new law even weaker than the inadequate one it was to replace.[13]

In fighting for laws at the local level from her West Vancouver house, Judy Stone has been arguing, cajoling, demanding, and yelling about the conduct of official humane societies since 1992, when she gave up her roofing company and turned her attention to animals. By 1998, nine different B.C. municipalities had agreed to write bylaws against dogs being permanently tied or penned without exercise, against inadequate shelter from the weather, and against choke chains as tethers. Stone, an irrepressible, energetic woman, said it was scandalous that charitable groups like her Animal Advocates Society of B.C. must do what a local SPCA had been given public donations and the mandate to do.[14] Her organization had placed more than two hundred dogs in new homes. Considering her views – that SPCA directors do almost nothing, that too few efforts are made to use the laws to help animals, that SPCA shelters would prefer to kill animals rather than spend money on serious veterinary care – it was inevitable that she would clash publicly with the middle-of-the-road animal welfare organization, the provincial SPCA.

In response to Stone, the B.C. SPCA's Stephen Huddart called her "misguided." He suggested that some so-called "rescues" of dogs could amount to theft, and he dismissed her accusations that the SPCA did not try hard enough to place animals or prosecute abusers.[15] Stone slugged back, archly reporting that she was thought to be a "common criminal" thanks to his remarks and that the "common" part offended her. Hundreds of respectable middle-class women have told her that they once stole dogs when they could get no action from authorities, she said. Cases that reached Animal Advocates had always been ignored by other agencies, Stone said, and often she did not know where the dogs had come from. She argued that no one associated with the group had ever been charged with an offence.

Ultimately, her group's clientele speaks for itself. The dog Skyla, a young Blue Heeler, was adopted from a shelter by a family who discovered that her splinted foot had developed gangrene from lack of care. The shelter offered to kill her. Animal Advocates paid for a leg amputation. Judith, a German shepherd, was chained for ten years in a dirty backyard, her hips diseased, her coat matted. No one responded to complaints from the neighbours. She was presented to Animal Advocates, where she was fitted with a cart for her rear legs and adopted by a family.

Once, when a wolf-dog hybrid was running loose in Surrey, Stone was told that an exasperated SPCA employee threatened to shoot the animal if he got one more call about it. The shy but playful young wolf-dog was lured into Stone's car with the enticement of her own dog and was later adopted. Stone had enough pictures and stories of animal rescues to fill a scrapbook. She said she would love to buy a full-page ad in the newspaper to print some of them. The sheer weight of numbers and the photos would prove her argument about the lack of action by authorities to protect animals, she said.

Understanding cruelty to animals requires people to imagine being on the receiving end. For some reason, a *Globe and Mail* editor did not understand the objections – a "veritable fur storm," as an editor's column coyly described them – to the newspaper's publication of a personal essay in which a woman in Nova Scotia described how she tied a hungry, neglected stray cat into a pillow case, attached a stone, and slowly drowned it. If a kid or even a young, macho guy committed such an act, the response would be predictable. In one case, for instance, a young Sudbury man was convicted of cruelty and fined $400 when he tried to dispose of a cat by putting it into a bag and throwing the bag into a creek. The *Globe* article, though, was written by a self-absorbed woman as an exploration of living up to what was called the "interesting metaphorical implications" of women doing their own killing or forgoing the benefits that accrue to them when killing is done by others.[16] *Globe* editor Katherine Ashenburg's subsequent column explained that she found this a thought-provoking, if unpleasant, tale.

In the original article it was not clear if the cat was really sick or just starved. That was irrelevant to the story of philosophic introspection. Whatever the case, its needs would be a burden. As the Nova Scotia SPCA explained when calls in response to the article came in from all over the country, under such circumstances ordinarily a shelter worker would come to get the cat. Ashenburg noted that the people who contacted the *Globe* lived mostly in urban areas and that no one seemed to care about a large cod fish that the writer described killing years earlier, because "apparently the pain of some creatures is more acceptable than that of others." For her own part, Ashenburg sniffed, she was far more distressed about a story of a child who died in an area hospital's emergency room.[17]

Now here was an animal anecdote with trademark ingredients. First came the slights against urban dwellers who don't understand how things are done in these parts (nor, it seemed, did the SPCA, which took the callers seriously). Then came the accusation of hypocrisy – if you don't care about the cod, or at least mention it, you are brushed off about the cat and the casually cruel effort to kill it. For good measure, how can you worry about a cat when there is a dead child in an emergency room to be concerned about? Animal activists have repeatedly complained that they are always asked about why they haven't dealt first with all the human concerns surrounding them. It is as if compassion is a limited commodity rather than the by-product of how a heart works or how someone views the world, and it must not be wasted on lesser beings. Perhaps to offer compassion is to raise other species too high. Perhaps the pain of humans is less acceptable than the pain of other creatures.

Some animal activists even argue that humans shouldn't have pets at all. "We'd like to see a society without them," said James Pearson of the Winnipeg-based People Acting for Animal Liberation. "We prefer voluntary relationships. The majority [of pets] live lives that are quite miserable."[18] According to the Animal Defence League of Canada, animals deliberately bred to be someone's pet are at the mercy of the owner, and this is a vulnerable and often unfortunate position to be in. People should ask themselves if it is right to deliberately breed and socialize animals to be dependent upon our whims, the Ottawa-based animal rights group stated in a position paper on pets. For animals that do need homes with humans, it said, pet shops should be replaced by a humane society or some other such organization that would place homeless or needy animals with humans the way an orphanage does for children.[19]

In the United States, veterinarian Elliot Katz, president of In Defense of Animals, urged the city of San Francisco to amend every bylaw reference to pet owners to include "and/or pet guardians." Katz argued that animals are individual beings, that to refer to them as pieces of property is offensive.

Sometimes, in the draining, difficult world of battling for the animals, legislative or legal victories are won. The Animal Alliance of Canada, for example, convinced the federal government in the early 1990s to crack down on the importation of dogs born in U.S. puppy mills. Sometimes an issue concerning animals engages the public's crucial sympathy without a hint of ridicule. For instance, the Toronto groups ARK II and Freedom for Animals protested in the summer of 1999 against the cruel treatment of dogs in Korea, where some dogs are used for food and some, according to reports, are tortured. The efforts of the activists brought a respectful statement from the Korean Consulate in Toronto. Its spokesperson said that most Koreans did not accept such things as "the beating of dogs as a cooking technique and the consumption of cats as a therapeutic remedy for medical problems." Over time, the candid Korean reply said, cultural practices can change.[20]

Perhaps the consulate was correct that dogs for food is a special interest that could fade away. However, opposition politicians in Seoul continued to press the government to regulate sales of dog meat and to ignore criticisms from abroad. Sales of dog soup or meat in restaurants were banned during the 1988 Olympics in South Korea when the military dictatorship was desperate to have international approval. But more recent years have seen reports of plans for a chain of dog meat restaurants and sales of dog soup in thousands of restaurants. Other reports suggested that thousands of tons of dog meat were being used each year in tonics. Eating dog meat was said to increase virility.

· · ·

Despite the many horror stories, the lives of some animals have gone from desperate to as close to heaven-in-Canada as seemingly possible.

Rachel, for instance, was once a pet, the property of a rich American woman. She wore frilly girl's clothes, had bubble baths, and sat in a high chair to eat cereal with a spoon. Donna Rae played guitar and rode a bicycle to make kids laugh at parties. Then they grew from cute babies into bigger chimpanzees, the kind of pets who could remove the door if someone knocked or bring down the curtains with a casual gesture. At age four in a life that could last for fifty years, Rachel got a limousine ride to a laboratory and a steel cage about double the size of a telephone booth. Donna Rae was fourteen when she left her entertainment job and, holding a human's hand, was walked into a lab. At first she would offer up her arm helpfully for the attempts to infect her with HIV.

These two chimps, and others like them with their own private tragedies, now live just south of Montreal in a chimp sanctuary.[21] They were plucked from the Laboratory for Experimental Medicine and Surgery in Primates at New York University when it was closing. Does that make them lab animals? Does the fact that chimpanzees Yoko and Annie and Billy Jo and Sue Ellen were also used in entertainment mean they are circus animals? Billy Jo and Sue Ellen lived together for fourteen years in New York State, sharing a shed on the grounds of their owner's house. Then, with hugs and waves goodbye, they were off to the lab. What label is there for Tom, a chimp of compelling dignity, most likely born in the wild? Tom is in his thirties, weighs two hundred pounds, and is five feet tall when he stands upright. Like other animals, these chimps are our blood relations. Their particular burden is that they are genetically our closest living kin on the planet.

At the Fauna Foundation's chimp sanctuary – the only one of its kind in Canada – they have also been the source of dispute. Some residents in the rural area responded to them as they would to a load of toxic garbage arriving from out of town. The chimps had been used in hepatitis and HIV research. Of the fifteen who lived there in 1998, eight were infected with HIV, although they might never become ill. They arrived with all the proper permits and approvals from Ottawa and the Quebec government, but the nearby town of Carignan tried repeatedly to get rid of them. The residents were frightened.

These new immigrants, who lived behind special security fences in a special house with a fenced outdoor enclosure, were unaware that they were so unwanted. The sanctuary, established by Gloria Grow and her veterinarian partner, Richard Allan, had been their home since 1997. From their outdoor enclosure the chimps could see a pretty 103-acre farm with a lovely old stone house, a stream, woods, and other rescued farm animals. They would never wander free on this property.

Inside the big chimp house, they could watch through the metal grill on the front of their plank-lined rooms as Grow, the one staff employee, and volunteer workers prepared dinner in a homey kitchen. If there was fruit salad or Jello, there would be a lot of excited screaming. When they first arrived, dinner was difficult because the chimps weren't convinced they would all get some. They soon found out that they would all get the food, that there was enough for everyone. On the soft fall evening I visited them, their dinner was trays full of fruit and vegetables, whole heads of lettuce, and surprise boxes of snacks or grooming aids on the side. Long brown arms waved through the serving slots to get bottled beverages. The noises were getting softer. Some of the chimps were picking a place in the spacious upper levels to sleep for the night, making up a blanket bed or settling into a hammock.

Billy Jo loved to watch the kitchen, and apparently did not like people to stand in front of his spot. If you had been tranquilized by little groups of men with dart guns for liver biopsies every two weeks, you might not either. His thumbs were gone, cut off in the circus, where his teeth were also knocked out. He liked to sit in his plastic chair, sometimes closing off his little room, while he ate his dinner. He liked spaghetti, Pepsi, and painting pictures. He did not like seeing people cry on television. Sue Ellen, like Billy Jo, had her teeth knocked out to keep her from biting in her life before the lab. She liked hot food, bread, broccoli, big hats and long skirts, purses and attention. Annie was born wild and went from a circus to a lab, where she had a baby who was taken away when it was three. She would scrub the walls and floors with soapy water or sweep. She liked to break for coffee, to keep her hair and nails nice, and to make her bed with thick comforters.

Petra was born in a lab. She became disturbed, plucking herself bald and circling the cage endlessly. At the sanctuary she liked onions, pears, coffee, and necklaces of coloured macaroni. She liked to wash her toys and brush herself in front of a mirror. Regis was also born in a lab and had his first blood test at the age of three days. He liked peanut butter and jam sandwiches, wearing scarves, and playing the recorder. He was so mechanically inclined that one evening he opened the inside doors that kept chimps out of the kitchen area. Not much happened. Petra washed some dishes and handed out blankets.

Pablo and Yoko, lab-born but with some circus experience, were the most aloof from humans and had been the longest in a lab. Pablo enjoyed pushing Sue Ellen on the swing. He could put half a dozen tomatoes into his mouth at once and he would never take medication, not even mixed into food or drink. Yoko liked eggs and plums and hid his treasures. Lab-born Pepper worried a lot about being shut inside. She swept, scrubbed the floor, made her bed, and liked to wear socks and sweatshirts and eat watermelon. Tom painted pictures, played chase, and liked a good cup of tea. When he first arrived, he would only accept drinks with unbroken seals. Lab-born Jethro didn't work out well in research because, perhaps wisely, he refused to eat or drink during studies. He liked marshmallows, fruit smoothies, and water games. Little lab-born Chance was quiet. She had spent a year alone in a lab unit without any other chimps. She liked licorice and banana pudding, sunbathing, and games with a water hose. Binky, the other lab-born chimp, liked applesauce and peanut butter sandwiches, cleaning his teeth, and having his feet tickled.

With Jean, the story became less happy. Jean had a breakdown in the lab during HIV studies. She was given to fits and, during them, to biting herself and screaming. After nearly twenty-four years in a research lab, she wasn't able to cope any longer. But Jean was the first chimp who, when Grow went to the New York lab, looked the visitor right in the eye, peering determinedly at the protective goggles lab visitors wear. Grow decided the look meant "get me out of here," and she was determined to include Jean in the group going to the sanctuary. Jean had never had a home or a circus job, like so many of the others. She had to learn how to drink from a bottle and, even now, she had limited chimp relationships. On good days, she liked bananas, a bath with a hose, and a chance to lie outside in the wind. After a year here, she played on a bungee swing and let a special human friend give her a back rub. Now, at nights, she liked to hold Grow's fingers and stare into her eyes while she sipped her evening drink as slowly as she could.

One day Billy Jo had to leave the farm to have x-rays. It was the first time a chimp had left since they all arrived, in September and October of 1997. For hours the other chimps waited. "It was like a morgue in here," Grow said. "They didn't know if he was coming back. The chimps were very angry."

Richard Allan said he was not an animal rights activist. He just believed some things needed to be changed. When Grow came back from an animal rights demonstration in the United States in 1996 with her heart set on this project, they poured their own money into it, plus some from the Jane Goodall Institute. The sanctuary was structured to ensure that the animals would be provided for if they outlived Grow and Allan. There are perhaps a dozen such sanctuaries in the United States and about two thousand chimps in that country alone awaiting retirement homes. The local opposition to the Quebec sanctuary meant that regional health officials spelled out a list of safety requirements, including an on-site vet clinic so that the chimps would never again need to leave their home to receive health care. At least the dispute may have produced a model for retiring chimps around the world.

"I find it harder and harder being with everyone. I see how smart they are. At the end of the day, I'm locking them up. It's just a better jail," Grow said, giving in periodically to the guilt that Goodall, the famous primatologist, warned her against.

If these chimps had been lucky enough to live wild and undisturbed lives from birth, perhaps Grow's bouts of gloom about being a jailer would be realistic. But this was as good as life was going to get – ever – for these chimps, whose only other option would have been more years as raw material for experiments. Their lab pasts couldn't be erased by Grow's love and care. Even the uninformed could see that their behaviour was at times odd, a product of their traumas, as they flicked repeatedly at non-existent things on their arms or bit at themselves. Jean might still have closed her eyes and pretended you were gone. But she would also sit outside to feel the sun on her skin. And Rachel, the betrayed pet, looked peaceful sitting by herself at a picnic table in the fall sunshine, daintily, one at a time, eating the Smarties she had lined up with her long dark fingers.

"They are so, so forgiving," said foundation worker Arryn Ketter. "I can't imagine any human, who has been through what they have, being forgiving."

Ketter's point – that the chimps seemed able to forgive treatment at the hands of humans that humans themselves would rarely forgive – echoes the words of other activists. The animals they help so often seem willing and able to make another start, in life and with humans, if the chance is given to them. In a cause that has so much pain and so few victories, knowing that offers at least some moments of joy.

CHAPTER EIGHT

Parallel Worlds

This can be exasperating. It would seem logical that any movement that has, on one edge, a sort of nascent domestic revolutionary wing with the country's police forces sniffing its tracks, and even has the civilian CSIS lurking around, might for that reason alone draw serious public attention. After all, the public pays the bills for these efforts and, as the 1970s showed, the public often takes a great interest in how its police force and spy agencies define which groups are threats to society and need to be monitored. Added to that, U.S. congressional hearings dealt with the illegal side of the animal movement and heard expressions of concern from the FBI, providing the sort of American stamp of official importance that usually announces something of world class significance. But when it comes to the animal movement in Canada, even with the official scrutiny attracted by its illegal side, even with its serious set of moral and political issues, public attention is almost resolutely denied.

The official scrutiny is undeniably there. The 1998 report from CSIS counterterrorism specialist G. Davidson (Tim) Smith complained that the cell structure in the Animal Liberation Front was making it hard to infiltrate and that a pattern of sound planning and security measures made the illegalities themselves hard to solve.[1] Smith noted that most animal rights activists were not advocating the use of violence. But, he added: "Terror itself is the chief tactic of the animal rights activists. They use violence with the expressed intent of coercing government to act in a certain manner, to enact particular legislation. Their terrorist methodology is to engender fear by threats of poisoned candy or other consumer goods, by obnoxious graffiti, by abusive and threatening telephone calls, by the mailing of letter bombs and by the destruction of property."

What Smith meant when he referred to poisoned candy or other consumer goods was the sort of thing that the Animal Rights Militia did both in England and in Canada. The ARM started in England in the early 1980s on the premise that the ALF did not go far enough in direct action. The ARM saw poisoning hoaxes as an effective form of economic sabotage. One of ARM's most celebrated actions was its media announcement in England in 1984 that it had poisoned Mars candy bars because the company used animals in tooth-decay experiments. The poisoning scare was later acknowledged as a hoax.

In January 1992 the ARM decided to take similar action in Canada against the Cold Buster bars invented by a University of Alberta scientist. The group announced that it had poisoned some eighty-seven of the bars with oven cleaner and returned them to a number of store shelves. It sent samples of the poisoned bars to the media. The reason, the ARM said in letters to the Edmonton media, was that for years rats had been frozen, starved, and killed in the development of the anti-hypothermia product. Again, the poison warning was later revealed as a hoax.[2] In December 1994, just days before Christmas, the ARM also claimed to have injected rat poison into turkeys in the Vancouver area in Safeway and Save-On-Foods outlets.

According to Smith, the animal movement's extremists had used economic sabotage with some success, sending insurance rates soaring, increasing security costs in industries, and causing expensive damage and loss of revenue as well as negative publicity and the destruction of records. These tactics, he said, had forced the closure of many small businesses as well as scientific and commercial research facilities.

FBI director Louis J. Freeh noted in early 1999 that while the incidence of attacks by animal rights extremists had dropped in the United States, the potential for destruction had increased with the ease of getting explosives and recipes to make them. "Animal rights extremists," he told the U.S. Senate Committee on Appropriations, "continue to post significant challenges for law enforcement as well. Various arsons and other incidents of property damage have been claimed by the Animal Liberation Front (ALF) and the Earth Liberation Front (ELF)."[3]

John Thompson's anti-terrorist Mackenzie Institute had warned in a 1993 report that for three years there had been a new militancy in the animal rights movement, with the ALF as the main player.[4] In 1990, the report said, ALF was into its third year on the FBI list of active domestic terrorist groups and had committed two "violent" terrorist acts plus eighteen other different criminal actions, mostly trespass and vandalism. In Canada, the report said, ALF had a record of forty-eight incidents of vandalism, sabotage, and other illegalities between 1981 and 1992. In Britain, the report said, ALF had raided a police headquarters and taken hundreds of documents on both itself and the Provisional Wing of the Irish Republican Army. "Clearly, in the U.K., the ALF can no longer be regarded merely as a collection of crackpots," the Mackenzie advisory concluded.

Animal rights extremists may not have a record to date of physical harm to people, Thompson said, but they are particularly dangerous when it comes to property damage.[5] The Animal Liberation Frontline Information Service made much the same point in its report on the ALF in Canada. "Canada has been a leader for Animal Liberation Front actions since 1979," it proudly stated. "The first primate liberation in the world by the ALF happened in Ontario, which set a precedent for future primate liberations."[6]

The Information Service recounted highlights from the ALF record. Canada is home to the legal North American ALF Supporters Group, which gives legal support to ALF activists and prisoners across North America. An April 25, 1989, fire in Vancouver meat markets put two of the stores out of business and caused a total of $10,000 damage. The greatest monetary damage in Canada occurred in the $100,000 loss to an Edmonton fish company, when three delivery trucks were torched and its building vandalized, and the $100,000 damage to the University of Alberta research laboratory. Among the many mink raids in Canada, one of the biggest was the release of six thousand minks at a B.C. farm in 1998. On New Year's Day, January 1, 1985, at the University of Western Ontario, ALF raiders took three cats, subjects of stroke research, and a rhesus monkey with the herpes B virus. There had been a break-in at the same university building in August, but the raiders only photographed a yellow baboon, which had been immobilized non-stop for months in a restraining chair, also for stroke research.[7] An early Canadian laboratory liberation came, on June 15, 1981, at Toronto's Hospital for Sick Children. Raiders that night took rabbits, guinea pigs, a rat, and a cat – one of eighteen cats at the lab with its ears cut off. The mutilated cat made the front page of *The Toronto Star* after a reporter met secretly with two unnamed men and a woman responsible for the break-in.[8]

• • •

To really find out about the animal movement in Canada – legal or otherwise – you have to turn to the Internet, where a rich and busy world carries on, unbeknownst to most of us.

The legal side of the animal movement has its own vibrant life on the Internet. The tidbits flooding in daily to *AR-News*, for example, range from letter campaigns to protest announcements to media reports from around the globe. One posting offers the names and addresses of bounty hunters paid by the U.S. state of New Mexico to kill mountain lions. Another says that a town in northwestern Spain has abandoned the tradition of tossing a goat off a bell tower every year, marking a small success for protesters. If protest is your thing, one site provides the dates and times to picket the annual International Mink Show in Milwaukee. In a movement with scarce resources and a need to rally widespread troops, e-mail is a blessing. Free newsletters deliver the latest in a country's legislation, news, and campaigns. There are vegan recipes, Web sites for Canadian groups dedicated to finding homes for the hunting dogs abandoned each year at the end of the season, and calls to sign e-mail petitions to governments, businesses, and organizations around the world.

There are even places to trade poems, songs, and fiction. Animal Rights Counterculture, a U.S. group based in Wisconsin, maintains one Web site that offers alternatives to "Little Red Riding Hood." One tale was about splendid greyhound dogs, rescued from terrible lives on race tracks. The contents, group president Mohan Embar notes, "may be used in unchanged form by avowed animal rightists." The style may be a little unpolished, but the message of the stories and lyrics is clear. "You complain about your rights," says "The New Martyrs," a poem, "but what about theirs?"

The International Wildlife Coalition Web site offers a gripping diary from Pat Gray, president of the Canadian Animal Distress Network and the PEI Marine Mammal Stranding Network, as she makes daily observations about the Canadian seal hunt. "I was surprised to see the remains of a seal hunt off the shore . . . carcasses of seal pups," Gray reports from Prince Edward Island. She says she was followed and watched by an angry-looking man as she observed a boat near shore. She watched several persons jumping on and off the boat's deck, dragging carcasses on board.

The Animal Alliance of Canada and Zoocheck Canada post regular briefings on issues and the latest news developments involving animals on their sites. An activist with few colleagues in the immediate area can draw on a wider community to help out. If someone needs facts about elephants to bolster a public plea against circuses or help to write a statement to the media, it can be found on-line. If it's not readily available, a plea on *AR-News* will bring a flood of e-mails offering help. Tactics can be shared – from Canada, for example, to Animals Australia, an umbrella organization for groups in Australia and New Zealand.

For the outlaw side of the movement, where anonymity is crucial, the Internet has become a sort of history-on-the-run that exists almost nowhere else.

Illegal actions from all over the world are recorded on the Internet, including some so recent or so small in scope that they have scarcely made it on to police blotters. The Animal Liberation Frontline Information Service, the North American Animal Liberation Front

Supporters Group newsletter *Underground, No Compromise* magazine, and a host of British organizations with on-line newsletters or Web sites are all easy to find. The North American ALF Supporters Group replaced a purely Canadian support group in the early 1990s, at a time when the animal rights movement in the United States was feeling the heat of a crackdown and Canada provided a safer base of operations. Articles posted with the Frontline Information Service from California said such repression had not been seen since the 1960s and 1970s. At least half a dozen U.S. grand juries were calling environmental and animal rights activists to testify, and jail terms were being handed out to some of them who refused to do so.

The Internet, or publications available through it, tell the story of Native American Rodney Coronado, who pleaded guilty on March 3, 1995, to aiding and abetting a fire at Michigan State University. The fire destroyed years of research for the fur-farm industry. It was the seventh in a series of ALF raids called Operation Bite Back, targeting fur farms and fur-related university research operations. Coronado's arrest on an Arizona reservation on Sept. 28, 1994, was a breakthrough that police and the FBI believed would bring under control a long string of ALF actions. He had a record of illegal activity dating back to the 1980s, from attacks on Icelandic whaling ships to sabotaged hunts in Britain and the United States and charges of destruction of fur-shop property in Canada. In California, Coronado and Jonathan Paul had been investigating the fur-farm industry. Coronado even spent time studying the best way to release animals from fur farms. When Paul refused to testify before a grand jury, he was sent to jail. Author Rik Scarce, who had interviewed Coronado and other ALF activists, was also jailed when he refused to answer questions about the ALF and Coronado.[9] Coronado ended up with a sentence of fifty-seven months, breaking Darren Thurston's record for the longest sentence received by an animal liberationist in North America.

Coronado's beliefs and record were covered at length by *The Globe and Mail* in a two-page spread that gave a small speaking part to David Barbarash.[10] In thirteen paragraphs in a sidebar the paper summed up Barbarash's history and quoted him as saying that just because something is illegal, it is not necessarily immoral. This slight coverage was more than most mainstream media reporting had offered the Canadian activist to that point.

As a morale booster, the Internet diaries allow the illegals to keep track of how they are doing and celebrate successes. It also ensures wide distribution for reports of incidents that would never make the national or international media. The Animal Liberation Frontline news service reported in July 1998, for example, that a University of Guelph researcher had his car tires slashed and car windshield smashed and that "ALF" was spray-painted on the road near his home. The service described the university as one of the largest "users and abusers" of animals in the country. The Guelph incident, once recorded, was filed into the on-line archives, which go back into the 1980s, and where you can find details of a huge arson in the United States next to news of the release of a few mink or nine hens in some Scandinavian country.

The Internet also doubles as a fast, anonymous way of sharing information. Message boards allow activists to ask, anonymously, if anyone knows where to locate chinchilla farmers in Utah or how to find a good e-mail bomb for a "hactivism" campaign. The archives of events provided a warning, for example, that Finnish mink farmers had taken to shooting at animal liberationists.

The Internet also provides access to the sort of how-to material that raises the hackles of the authorities. You can read a careful explanation of how to pick locks or how to plan and execute sabotage on machinery and what tools you will need. You can find the addresses of those who offer publications by mail if they aren't on-line. You can, for instance, get the mailing address for the North American ALF Supporters Group to buy a copy of *The Power Is Ours*, an update of an English manual on tactics and incendiaries, or *Arson around with Aunti ALF*, which focuses on making simple incendiary devices. You can learn that napalm can apparently be made from equal parts of soap chips and a fuel like gasoline or turpentine, stirred over hot water (not over an open flame) until it is paste-like. Or you could learn to whip up the more portable combination of melted wax and sawdust, cooled and cut into chunks. One site offers a sketch and instruction for the simple incendiary favoured by the European ALF activists – matchsticks tied around an incense stick and fastened to the inside wall of a paper tube, with lots of match heads on the tube bottom.

Clearly this is provocative stuff. But if you don't want it, you don't have to look for it. If you did, you might also find it in old CIA or U.S. military manuals that are for sale in used or specialty bookstores as well as on-line, along with books on how to make illicit or duplicate identification papers. A CIA sabotage manual published in the early 1980s for anti-Sandinista activity in Nicaragua is still making the rounds, complete with instructions on how to make that old standby, Molotov cocktails – narrow-neck bottle filled with gas or kerosene, even better with shredded soap or sawdust added, rag in the neck down far enough to touch the liquid, and a sealed top.

As authorities take increasing exception to the kind of material being made available on-line, there is talk of finding a way to ban the use of encryption, coded messages that make e-mail meaningless to anyone but the intended recipient. Several of the animal liberation Web sites offer codes and explanations of how encryption works to anyone planning to contact them. An FBI document explains that readily available encryption allows "a vast array" of criminals and terrorists to hide their communications, even from legally authorized interceptions.[11] But, it notes, the encryption codes are used by more than criminals and are considered useful for ensuring that the claimed sender of an electronic message is really the sender, for protecting privacy, and for preventing tampering with the message. But the FBI said that some investigations, involving child pornography, illegal hacking, and terrorists in Northern Ireland, have been hampered by messages that could be legally intercepted but not read. The agency noted that the mood of Congress had, so far, not matched its own concerns. A number of bills had been introduced, but not passed, that would prevent state or federal governments from requiring plain text access to coded messages for law officers.

Nothing contributes more to the culture and legend of the illegals than the "prisoner of war" listings, which give the names and mailing addresses of those who have been charged and convicted and jailed for their crimes in the name of animals. To feel a part of the struggle, you needn't have some suspect publication coming to your door with rude drawings or inflammatory rhetoric. You can send e-mail letters to be passed on to prisoners without any fuss and stay current on the latest developments even if you never attend a protest. Jailed activists receive a flood of letters to assure them that their sacrifices are honoured.

The case of Barry Horne was a classic example. Sentenced in December 1997 to eighteen years in jail for arson that caused millions of dollars in damages to stores on the Isle of Wight, Horne (denying most of the charges) went on a hunger strike to back demands that the new Labour government appoint a royal commission on vivisection, as one of its spokesmen had once promised. The Animal Liberation Frontline Information Service quickly sent out backgrounders, detailing how the promise was made by Labour's animal welfare spokesman, who had said there would be a commission on the necessity of animal experiments. A week of action – protests against the party and the industry – was scheduled with times, places, and nearest rail and subway stations detailed. Police and the courts might have called Horne dangerous, ruthless, and a terrorist, but to many in the animal movement around the world he was a hero. He got the longest jail sentence ever given to an animal rights activist – longer even than some sentences for murder or rape – and his risky hunger strike lasted sixty-eight days and put him at death's door. As his health failed, almost hourly alerts flashed around the world along with details of more protests and exhortations to join letter campaigns. The middle-aged son of a mailman only gave up his strike when the government indicated it would do an independent analysis of vivisection, which would be given to an all-party group on animal welfare.[12]

The Internet and the alternative press also describe a diversity among the illegals. Canada has ALF, but it also has ARM and the Justice Department, not to be confused with the federal government department of the same name. The Justice Department was initiated on the conviction that "animal abusers had been warned long enough."[13] In England the Justice Department was the source of letter bombs sent in

1994 to companies exporting live animals for slaughter across the Channel. The group's first effort, apparently, was in October 1993, when a parcel exploded in a postal sorting office. By November 1993 the ALF press office in England had received a statement from the new group and a video of a bomb, to add weight to its claim of responsibility. By then, parcel bombs had already exploded at the homes of two research industry employees, who were reported unharmed. The group's statement made it clear that this was a group not unwilling to do violence. It said: "We've sat back for years and watched the AR (animal rights) activists ask nicely for all the abuse to stop – the more daring risk their lives and liberty but still the unacceptable number of tortured animals keeps rising. The torturers become more extreme. . . . All this without fear of retribution from the authorities and at worse damaged property c/o the ALF, which we wholeheartedly encourage. . . . We won't be asking anyone to stop messing with animals and will make no excuses for our violent intervention."

The list of animal liberation organizations runs to dozens and changes over time, from Animal Avengers to Farm Animal Revenge Militia to the Vegan Revolution, according to the Internet postings. In Canada, aside from ALF, the most active groups seem to be ARM, the Justice Department, and a group called the Provisional ALF. This last group reportedly sent hoax bombs to animal industry representatives in February 1998. Canadian activist Thurston said that the groups that did not renounce violence against people "make the ALF look nice." Barbarash told a television interviewer that he hoped violence would not become a regular feature of the illegal movement.[14]

• • •

The on-line world has another side – the opposition is fighting back. Some Web sites aim at legal and illegal animal activists with little distinction. They promote medical research using animals or defend the fur and agricultural industries. Americans for Medical Progress, a group dedicated to maintaining public support for the use of animals in medical research, is one of these. With a board largely representing drug companies and research institutes and advisors, including a former U.S president and a senator, the AMP passes on quotes from the FBI about the threat of radical animal rights organizations, reproduces favourable news and feature articles, praises medical developments, and keeps track of activist crimes and criminals.[15]

Other sites are more directly aimed at the illegals. The EcoTerror Response Network offers a mirror image of its foes, promising to pass on anonymous information about crimes to police, an echo of how the animal rights service catalogues ALF attacks. The site is reached through the American Center for the Defense of Free Enterprise, "advocates for industrial civilization, technological progress and productive harmony between man and nature."[16] It lists criminal incidents, convictions, and indictments, adding its own assessments. The ALF, it says, is a "violent animal-rights terrorist group." Canadians Thurston, Barbarash, and Rebecca Rubin have made its lists. Barbarash complained that it took a threat of legal action for the U.S. organization to drop its unfounded suggestions that he was connected to attempted murder in Canada. The Center's Web site directs visitors as well to other "dangers" posed by legal groups. There are, for example, environmentalists who are lobbying to "stop all economic activity" in areas such as northwestern British Columbia, where an access road to allow the reopening of an old mine was being protested.

The Wise Use movement, which is promoted on the Center's Web site, is a corporate answer to environmentalism and casts itself as a group dedicated to balancing the needs of man and nature. It proposes such reforms as logging old-growth forests, opening more public lands to resource exploration, allowing development in national parks, and helping industries to sue environmentalists. Private investigator Barry Clausen has been linked to the Wise Use movement, but he is more familiar in Canadian news reports dealing with animal rights and environmental extremists.[17] In one report Clausen, described as a specialist in environmental terrorism, drew comparisons between the pipe bombs used by the Anti-Fascist Militia and the methods of animal liberationists.[18]

Critics see Wise Use as an example of concerted efforts to marginalize even legal groups involved in animal or environmental movements by painting them as too extreme to deserve a hearing. When the Center's vice-president Ron Arnold appeared before the U.S. House of Representatives crime subcommittee, chairman Bill McCollum said his testimony would help to educate Congress.[19] "Human beings have an obligation to be good stewards of our environment," McCollum said. "Yet the very fact that we are already taking these important strides underscores how inexcusable and unnecessary violence and destructive behavior in the name of this cause really is." Arnold's message to the subcommittee was that politicians should not be fooled by the alleged differences among activists. "I'm stating that there is no difference between eco-terrorism and animal rights terrorism," he said. "Generally there are another bunch of groups who either ignore [terror] or don't denounce it publicly. We have asked all environmental groups to issue denouncements of this kind of crime. We have not been very successful. We don't really know what that means."

In a newspaper interview Arnold was even more specific. There is very little distance between the ALF and People for the Ethical Treatment of Animals, he said, referring to the biggest legal animal rights organization in North America and perhaps the world.[20] Arnold argued that PETA knew about some of ALF's Operation Bite Back actions ahead of time and that one of PETA's key people was "in complicity." PETA often defends ALF actions, which outrages the other side. Clausen was quoted in the same newspaper article with Arnold, insisting that the same people can be found in the ALF as in the Earth Liberation Front (an environmental direct action group) and PETA.

One form of Internet electronic warfare that members of the animal movement share with some other political causes is the emerging use of "hactivism." Described as a sort of electronic civil disobedience, it manages to apply the trespass and blockade or sit-down tactics of earlier generations to the Internet.[21] One strategy is a special program to overwhelm servers with repeated requests so that other users or customers are blocked out or the computer system crashes. In fall 1998, for instance, a Chinese government Web site was hacked and "Boycott China" was scrawled in an on-line graffiti message with links to such sites as Amnesty International.[22] The animal movement used the tactic against such targets as U.S. fur markets and big private research facilities. The Karolinska Institutet in Stockholm, Sweden, for example, complained of an "e-mail bombing" in October 1998.[23] The Institute said several attempts had been made to overload its computer system, and it linked this to its work on HIV and Aids. "The animal liberation group Djurens Befrielsefront has claimed responsibility for the attacks which are an attempt to compel Karolinska Institutet to cease co-operation with the Swedish Institute for Infectious Disease Control, SMI," a press release said.

Such attacks on computer systems have been co-ordinated on-line by animal activists with open invitations for supporters to follow a detailed country-based timetable. While some critics condemned such actions – professor Reg Whitaker of York University told *The Ottawa Citizen* they were "infantile and annoying" and potentially a "serious menace" – it was the process rather than the content that drew attention.

But, again, little of all this turbulent on-line animal world has registered with the public. For the most part the mainstream media do not cover the animal rights movement even in its extreme form in the way they cover, say, the anti-abortion movement. Some specialty publications, like the farm press, are more careful to record such news items as raids on mink farms. *Ontario Farmer* editor Paul Mahon observed during the Chatham, Ontario, mink trial in April 1999 that the "animal rights terrorists" were clearly staging a public relations event. He was convinced that, without media coverage, they wouldn't have done the deed. He wondered if it wouldn't be better to downplay such "calculated" crimes. That didn't stop *Ontario Farmer* from publishing a two-page spread on the crime the following week.

The Ottawa Citizen, as an exception to the general rule, has made consistent efforts to look seriously at the animal movement. In following the illegal side, the newspaper went after CSIS files through the Access to Information Act. The files it managed to obtain showed, despite heavy editing, that the spy agency saw the potential for "serious violence" by animal rights extremists and considered this a possible "threat to the security of Canada." A CSIS memo of July 1997, about the time that Thurston and Barbarash were coming under heavy scrutiny on the west coast, set down in writing that the service considered this kind of potential threat to security to fall within its mandate. The CSIS act defines terrorism as the threat or use of violence – against either people or property – to accomplish political goals. That would include illegal animal rights actions. Since CSIS has the official task of warning the government in advance of such dangers, the whole issue of what the spy agency has decided to do in Canada to track Canadians deemed to be terrorists, in advance of any illegal actions, would probably be of wide public interest. The RCMP, after all, has its own unit dealing with environmental and animal groups.[24]

Mainstream Canadian television programs rarely deal with animal rights and animal activists, but Barbarash did almost make a prime-time television network appearance on the highly rated CBC-TV program *the fifth estate*. The program decided to air a made-in-Britain documentary on "the British animal liberation movement." The documentary, originally aired in Britain in December 1998 on the Channel 4 program *Dispatches,* was broadcast in Canada on January 26, 1999, with the title "All in the Name of Love." Francine Pelletier, who narrated sections of the show for the Canadian audience, is a well-respected and experienced Canadian journalist. She introduced the film as "a shocking report about a love that goes beyond all reason. Most of us take it for granted that, when it comes to living things, humans are tops and animals, love them though we might, are a distant second. But for some people, animals hold a far higher place in the scheme of things and must be protected from any and all harm."[25]

Usually, Canadian journalists do not like to be seen as being too cosy with police, politicians, or other authority figures. They pride themselves on being willing to call to account even the most powerful. That made *the fifth estate*'s closing an especially strong statement of censure when Pelletier announced, "After the [British] broadcast, the program's producers handed their information over to the police. An investigation is under way."

A journalist clearly more suspicious than *the fifth estate*'s producers might be forgiven for wondering if the report was less about love-crazed animal activists who break the law than about police who have taken a very active interest in the British animal movement, both legal and illegal. The star of the show, Graham Hall, could have easily been mistaken for an undercover police agent bent upon infiltrating and discrediting animal activists. But the British narrator specifically pointed out that Hall was an animal rights campaigner himself with a reputation built on infiltrating and exposing groups of people involved in illegal animal blood sports. Apparently, in a pivotal encounter the previous summer, Hall had met an activist who so shocked him with her support for violence that he set aside his work against animal abusers and vowed to expose activist lawbreakers.

As its goals became more focused his undercover work took him into interesting territory. The real target became Animal Liberation Front spokesman Robin Webb, who with the editors of *Green Anarchist* magazine and the British *ALF Supporters Group Newsletter*, was also of great interest to police.[26] They had been charged in 1997 in England with inciting unknown persons to commit various illegal acts at unspecified times – that, in essence, through their publications and announcements of illegal actions, they had incited people to copy them. The content of their work is similar to much that is available on Web sites today. Several of the editors were found guilty and given jail terms. Simon Russell, a former editor of the *ALF Supporters Group Newsletter*, was found not guilty. Thurston had been scheduled to testify at Russell's trial – to tell the court that it was he, Thurston, and not the Brit who had put a report on the Internet about some actions – when he was turned back at Heathrow airport. At that point, Webb was still to be tried. Britain's alternative press, protesting that the charges against Webb and the editors constituted an attack on freedom of expression, campaigned for public support.

Graham Hall persevered for seven months, keeping his hidden camera running to reveal one woman activist as the "secret publisher" of an underground newspaper for fellow liberationists. This might have been an opportune moment to put the documentary in context for a

Canadian audience. British law is not the same as Canadian law, and much of what Hall was secretly recording about the behaviour of activists would not be considered illegal in Canada. The British government had been embroiled in controversy for some time about its sweeping plans for a loosely worded Terrorism Bill, the details of which were set out first in a December 1998 public consultation paper and then approved as law by the House of Commons and sent to the House of Lords by the spring of 2000.[27] The law is unusual by Canadian standards. It allows the government to ban groups it labels terrorist and to jail anyone who possesses information that might be "useful" to terrorists, who fails to inform police if they suspect other people, who invites support for a banned organization, who is in the same place as an article connected to an act of terrorism, or who even wears clothes or items that suggest support for a banned group. It might also have been a useful time to explore the notion of property damage as "violence" and, as in the case of the British law, of property damage as "terrorism." Critics of this definition of terrorism note that you can use it as a legal tool to crush civil disobedience and fairly routine political protest. Hall's documentary might have provoked a skeptical response from a Canadian audience if it had been set in the context of Britain's existing and future security laws, which were then being debated in the form of the discussion paper, or of the ongoing police pursuit of Webb. In that context, the idea of being accused of being a "secret publisher" or the timing of Hall's documentary might even seem sinister.

The documentary interviewed a British medical researcher, Colin Blakemore, who said he had been attacked, been sent razor blades in the mail, and received death threats for his work, which used animals. It did not explain that Blakemore was no ordinary scientist. He was one of the most vocal defenders of the use of animals in medical research. His work – dedicated to treating the vision problems of infants and youngsters – sometimes involved sewing shut the eyes of kittens.[28] "There was an ALF death list and he was on it," Pelletier pointed out.

The publication of a death list is shocking news, but the list was apparently prepared not by the ALF but by the Animal Rights Militia, a group that has said there is a need to go further than ALF policy would allow. According to Webb, the ALF has used firebombs for more than twenty years in Britain without harming anyone. But Hall was determined to nail Webb, telling him he wanted to give the ALF money, reporting that Webb had suggested a way to "launder" it to groups more violent than the ALF, although there is no on-camera statement confirming this. What the camera does show is Webb handing Hall an animal liberation magazine that features detailed bomb-making instructions. Webb clearly takes care not to get his fingerprints on the magazine. Off-camera Hall's voice says, "Robin Webb has just supplied me a bomb-making manual. Unbelievable!"

The documentary ends in a rush and with confusion. The narrator says that Webb is telling Hall how to make an explosive that can be detonated with a device used in the theatre. Hall asks Webb to get him such a device. Webb says it could take a month to do that. Then, obviously becoming suspicious about being recorded, he wants to look inside Hall's jacket. In any case, the ALF spokesman with the alleged taste for violence apparently let the spy escape with his films and his person intact.

To add Canadian content to the program, Pelletier travelled from Toronto to Vancouver. She set up an interview with Barbarash, she said later, because she was at a loss to understand why, on behalf of animals, people would go to the lengths depicted in the British documentary.[29] She said she did not grasp why anyone would lead a life of self-denial, as many of these activists seemed to do, simply in the cause of animals. How did they think that this would change the world? For her generation, she said, political action was admirable and the notion of changing the world for the better was a real incentive. "But it was power to the people – not to *animals*," she said.

In the end, Pelletier said, the interview with Barbarash did not turn out well and was not used. Moreover, she said, it seemed potentially too damaging for a person facing criminal charges to be connected with the British documentary by an interview on camera explaining why some people involved in animal activism broke the law. As for the documentary itself, Pelletier agreed that "there was something fishy" about it.

But it was good television – it was heavy on dramatic film footage shot in undercover style – even though it was utterly lacking in explanations or a context that would make the accusations seem one-sided (and slow down the pace). These days there are few social or political movements about which journalists would air a damning TV documentary without including a response from the other side. They would only do that when they are dealing with a truth that is patently obvious – to themselves and, presumably, to their audience – and when they are confident they won't be sued. There are only a few subjects or people they can treat in that way. Journalists don't need to ask the Mafia for its side of the story. They don't need to go to extreme efforts to record the comments of white supremacists or murderers. Now, apparently, they can add animal liberationists and their law-abiding supporters to that short, unsavoury list. Indeed, in the United States, where opponents tend to paint all animal rights activists with the same, broad brush, the law-abiding supporters of animal liberationists say they are being targeted in ways that most legal protest organizations – like groups supporting convicted criminals, for example – are not.

· · ·

In spring 1999 a Democratic Senator, Diane Feinstein of California, and a Republican Senator, Orrin Hatch of the mink-farming state of Utah, successfully tacked an amendment onto a juvenile justice bill in the wake of shootings in a high school in Colorado. The amendment would make it a federal crime to distribute information on how to make bombs or weapons of mass destruction if the person doing the explaining or teaching knew or intended that the information would be used to commit a federal, violent crime. It would also create a national clearinghouse to be used by all police forces dealing with incidents of animal terrorism and eco-terrorism. Senator Hatch singled out the ALF Web site and the *Final Nail* publication available on it as the sort of things he wanted to outlaw. The Web site "is a detailed guide to terrorist activities," Hatch told the Senate.[30]

The efforts of Hatch and Feinstein followed a bid by the Minnesota Senate to silence the public supporters of ALF actions. On the heels of an April 1999 ALF raid on the University of Minnesota, one of the most costly raids ever in terms of damages, the state Senate approved an omnibus crime and judiciary financing bill with two extra bits tacked on at the last minute. The first, later scrapped, would have made it a crime to promote, advocate, or take responsibility for a criminal act with the intent to instigate lawbreaking or obstruct criminal investigation. The second, which passed both houses of the state legislature, would entitle the victims of any unauthorized release of animals (from labs or commercial establishments, for example) to damages if they sued. The award would be at least $5,000 or three times the actual damages, and third parties would also be liable, so that anyone who planned, took responsibility for, and otherwise helped or encouraged such activity would also be liable for similar damage claims.

The University of Minnesota lab raid was a shocking event in the state and a major one for the illegal world. Local press reports described the theft of more than one hundred lab animals – pigeons, rats, mice, and salamanders – as a serious setback for research into Alzheimer's and other diseases. It could, they said, take several years and more than $100,000 to reproduce that research. Damages to the lab were estimated in the hundreds of thousands of dollars. The North American press office for ALF was also located in Minnesota at that time. Its spokespersons explained that ALF targeted this university because it was large and did some of the most painful of medical procedures. Press officers told reporters that the ALF goals were to liberate animals, inflict economic damage on those who use them, and reveal to the public what it considered research "atrocities" against animals.[31]

For its part, ALF assembled a video of the Minnesota lab raid and contested the reports that the raids had set back valuable research by years. Its press office distributed releases quoting doctors who challenged the university's claims. One said that the key knowledge of Alzheimer's disease comes from non-animal research. Another said that mouse and human physiologies and metabolisms are so different that results from research on mice amount to speculation. Another argued that memory loss, a trait of some specialized mice used in research, was common to hundreds of diseases, which undermined the research into Alzheimer's. All of this testimony gave the unknown raiders a legal solace in the debate in just the way that infuriated the politicians and the research community. To them, it was about criminals breaking the law, not about the ethics of their research.

An angry senator named Kevin Kjonass, then an ALF press spokesperson, as someone he would like to see in jail. Kjonass's apartment was searched by the FBI and files were seized. In May 1999 Kjonass was handed a subpoena to appear before a state grand jury investigating the lab raid. His appearance before the grand jury lasted about an hour, he later reported. He said he refused to talk about ALF or how he got information about ALF actions, claiming a right to freedom of association and to freedom from compelled testimony.

Meanwhile, the North American ALF Supporters Group, with its Willowdale, Ont., postal address, was leaving it to the ALF press office to deal with the public. The Supporters Group is anonymous and intends to stay that way, although it is a legal operation. In an e-mail exchange of questions and answers in March 1999, a group member identified only by an initial explained, "Despite the wide support within the A/R (animal rights) movement for the ALF, there are many who might decide not to work with us on unrelated campaigns had they any idea we were doing SG [Supporters Group] work as well." Members of the group are volunteers. They deal with up to 250 pieces of mail a month – requests for basic information, publications, or subscriptions to *Underground*, letters from other groups, and regular correspondence with prisoners. Letters and e-mail come from around the world. Finland, Sweden, England, and Germany are the most frequent sources of mail, after the United States. "Certainly nothing we've ever published is illegal in North America," the group member said, "although the laws are different in the U.K. and much of what we distribute freely here cannot be distributed by our counterparts in the U.K. ALF SG. Even our magazine, *Underground*, can often contain information that would get any activists trying to distribute it in the U.K. into trouble."

Money from sales went towards telephone bills or vegan supplies for jailed activists, publishing *Underground,* and ALF-related campaigns. Although the group said it had no way of contacting the ALF, did not know the identity of ALF activists, and had no advance notice of illegal actions, ALF cells could contact the group to pass on information about what they had done. There had been no official run-in with police, the group's representative said, although, "We can say with fair certainty that our e-mail and home phones are monitored. One of the reasons why we've chosen to keep a low profile is to avoid any overt trouble with the police who may mistakenly believe that the SG is somehow involved with running the ALF itself." The Supporters Group exists "because these people [ALF activists] have put their freedom and sometimes their lives on the line because they couldn't sit by and watch animals die needlessly."

As the group suggested, legal animal groups, with a few exceptions, had not been publicly supportive of ALF or other lawbreaking activists. The argument was made, not without reason, that the outlaws made the others look less radical, that their threat created an opportunity for other animal rights activists to be dealt with by people who would otherwise have never given them the time of day. For their part, the legal activists argued that the illegals made them look bad. Because of that, the legal activists said, they are not considered polite company. Their efforts were undermined by illegal actions that their foes held up to the public.

These conclusions were, to some extent, justified, but there is also merit to the argument that the legal activists were not getting very far anyway, that they were jousting with industries that would only respond to the bottom line and to economic pain and, in some cases, with companies that were dealing respectfully even with dictators and undemocratic police states when they had to. In late 1999, for example, after a sustained campaign of illegal attacks – and legal lobbying – the British government produced a bill that would put an end to fur farms in England and Wales by the end of 2002. That only a small bit of the fur-farm industry remained by the time the bill was introduced – making it a step the government could easily contemplate – was as much due to the cost and trouble caused by illegal actions as by public protest.

Directors of the Animal Alliance of Canada routinely distance themselves from the illegals. Animal Alliance is non-violent and passivist, director Liz White said. She believes that illegal activity does not help the animal movement's cause. The Alliance does not even conduct or join legal protests. It lobbies and campaigns to influence the public. "It's hard enough to get in and to have any credibility," White said.[32] Her voice is the one that is most often heard in Canada when the media need comments on news events involving animals. But most often what she is invited to supply is a reaction. Media attention focusing on issues that White and other legal animal advocates try to raise is much harder to get.

The Western Wildlife Unit of the Animal Liberation Front in the United States offers this reply to critics in its *Memories of Freedom* booklet:

> Some people within the animal rights and environmental movements believe that to achieve our goals we must present our ideas in such a way as to appeal to mainstream society, that with public support we can legislate change and influence our political representatives to see us not as a threat, but as harbingers of a new age. . . . So to the apologists of the animal rights and environmental organizations who are quick to denounce the defense of earth and animals to preserve their position and favour by our enemies we say, we are warriors, nothing more, nothing less. The ALF leaves the path of moderation to those who sincerely believe that that is the road to victory. . . . Without illegal action on the path in pursuit of liberty and justice, many of this century's greatest social changes would never have been achieved.

People for the Ethical Treatment of Animals has described ALF as an important part of the animal movement, like the French Resistance in the Second World War or the Underground Railway during slavery. The Army of the Kind, PETA has tagged the ALF in some literature. It was ALF action that brought out the evidence that made some progress possible, PETA has argued. ALF activists broke into University of Pennsylvania labs that had for years denied access to humane society officers. They stole records of research work that government officials had allowed to be carried on for years. When the gruesome, callous videotapes were made public, the lab was finally cut off from its generous government funding. Sometimes this is the only way people find out what is happening, and that is why PETA has acted as spokesperson without condemning the ALF, the organization has stated.

In the United States, Ingrid Newkirk, national director of PETA, wrote a dramatic story of the founding of the ALF there, describing how it was modelled on the British organization of that name.[33] It is a book full of admiration, written by a woman who is one of the most high-profile legal animal rights campaigners in North America. But in Canada the response to ALF actions by the animal rights movement has been either silence or sometimes condemnation.

Barry Kent MacKay, who has spent much of his working lifetime in the animal movement in Canada, is firmly opposed to illegal action. In an essay, "The Violent Underside of a Just Cause," he argues that illegal activities make the animal movement no better than those it attacks and that they help to create a myth of terrorists that turns the public away. While illegal actions may be planned as non-violent, he says, it is too easy for something to go wrong. "Direct action has become more than a mantra, to a vocal minority, it is virtually a religion or cult complete with dogma and a demand for total support." If you don't give that support, you are ostracized, which is a painful price to pay for a dedicated person who "has the intelligence to realize that . . . public support is needed and at least some tactics damage that support."[34]

MacKay sums up the basic criticisms most law-abiding members of the animal movement make of the outlaw fringe. He explains in his essay that he was surprised to find the instructions for making an incendiary device so easily available on the Internet through animal liberation links. This, he says, is "antisocial behavior." If people who believe in the cause didn't have to be intimidated into joining it, he asks, why should it be necessary to intimidate others? "Perhaps there should be a word to distinguish people who seek to destroy livelihoods but in a way they sincerely think won't put anyone, animal or human, at risk of death or injury from those terrorists who plant bombs in marketplaces, on airplanes or other places where there is certainty of injuring and killing people, such mayhem being the objective. However, even if the English language contained such a word, I suspect that the distinction would still be false."[35]

Peter Singer, whose 1975 book *Animal Liberation* inspired a generation of activists and helped to launch the animal rights movement in the United States, drew a different sort of line after watching the laboratory raids that made up the first phase of the movement in North America. In the 1990 edition, he warned: "It would be a tragic mistake if even a small section of the Animal Liberation movement were to attempt to achieve its objectives by hurting people. . . . The strength of the case for Animal Liberation is its ethical commitment."[36] A warning against physical violence it might be, but it does not contradict the basic ALF credo of direct, illegal actions that do no harm to living creatures.

The original British ALF traces its roots back to the early 1970s, when some members of the Hunt Saboteurs Association decided to move from legal protest against hunting to direct action against the property of hunters. They called themselves the Band of Mercy, resurrecting a name that young members of the Royal Society for the Prevention of Cruelty to Animals had used in the early nineteenth century. At first the group conducted raids on kennels and vandalized fox hunters' vehicles by putting water in fuel tanks and tacks in locks and slashing tires. By 1973 their actions had expanded to other targets, including several costly arson attacks on a drug company laboratory. Ronald Lee, one of the Band's founders, and other key activists were arrested during a lab raid, and their time in prison coincided with the retirement of the Band name.[37] Lee emerged from prison as the ALF began a string of raids on labs and on companies supplying them with

animals. The startup of the U.S. ALF included boot-camp-style training in England. By the late 1970s the U.S. version of the ALF was in
action, as was the Dutch ALF. According to some activists, the 1979
release of porpoises from a Hawaii research lab and the 1979 liberation
of five animals from a New York medical centre were among the first
North American ALF operations.[38]

As the illegal, direct-action side of the animal movement aged in
Britain and the United States and an assortment of organizations
developed, internal frictions grew over the directions taken. The outside debates about violence, about what constitutes violence, and
about running risks or threatening risk to human life were nowhere as
serious as the debates within the movement itself. In Britain, by the
late 1980s, the movement was already debating whether the poison
hoax or letter-threat style of action – the sort of thing identified with
the ARM rather than with the ALF – should be denounced by other
parts of the liberation movement. It was not an argument against illegal action or against economic sabotage but about the value of non-
violence in the conduct of such actions. It was this quality, the Robin
Hood image of activists risking only their own freedoms and lives for
animals, that had given earlier illegal actions against laboratories in a
number of countries a sympathetic reception even among people who
would never normally countenance breaking the law.

In the United States *The Animals' Agenda*, a must-read magazine
for the animal rights movement, published a provocative article in its
July-August 1998 edition. Editor-in-chief Kim Stallwood, a veteran
of British animal rights organizations and a former PETA executive
director, suggested in an editorial that the future of legitimate illegal
direct action was in question and needed serious evaluation.

"There can be no denying the unbelievable challenges of liberating
animals from vivisection laboratories and factory farms without being
caught," he wrote. "It is also a great challenge to contain our anger
when we see people abusing animals under any circumstances. But
should the challenge of liberating animals and the legitimate anger
we feel give license to illegal activities that do not have a reverence for
life and an adherence to nonviolence? . . . The original ALF heroes –

for that was what they really were – have been replaced in part by a generation of activists who are not grounded in a reverence for life and the principles of nonviolence."[39]

In the magazine's feature article, Freeman Wicklund, a long-time activist and founder of the magazine *No Compromise*, said the current direct-action strategy was counterproductive. Attacks on businesses make the animal users look like victims and do not win public support, he wrote. He recanted earlier support of ALF actions and now advocated a non-threatening, Gandhian style of non-violence that would not likely even have the same short-term benefits of immediately freeing animals. His piece drew a strong reaction, much of it anguished.

When about one hundred activists gathered at the farmhouse of the United Poultry Concerns organization on Chesapeake Bay in Virginia at the end of June 1999, Katie Fedor, then press officer for the ALF in North America, came to argue the issue. Outside the windows, battered-looking chickens rescued from intensive farms found shady spots to sleep away the hot afternoon at UPC's chicken sanctuary. Inside, Fedor, a poised young woman, defended the use of direct action to free animals and economic sabotage to drive businesses under.[40] ALF actions today are not all so different from the old days, she argued to the applause of most of the audience. She had recently been struggling to explain to the public the major ALF raid on the university lab in Minnesota, and now she was appealing for less public criticism of direct action by animal rights groups. That criticism only allowed the enemy to claim that the attacks on their animal use were not shared by all animal rights people and to deflect the issue away from the animals, she said.

If these animals in labs or corporate farms were people, asked PETA's Bruce Friedrich, would animal advocates still suggest waiting for the seeds of change to be sown and to produce results? Would they worry about the suffering of those who lost jobs or livelihood? The audience members seemed more in fear of the unplanned results of some tactics, like arson, or negative publicity from major property damage than opposed to breaking the law.

When featured guest Patty Mark took the floor to explain her intrusions into Australian chicken farms to rescue birds from filthy, harsh conditions, she won a standing ovation. Mark, editor of *Action Magazine* and co-ordinator of Action Animal Rescue Team, brought shocking video footage shot during rescues of farm animals, the stuff of vintage ALF action. The Australian activist, who looked more like a nursery school teacher than the veteran of courts and jail that she was, clearly spoke to their hearts.

In the animal movement, not even all the law-abiding activists believe that there are many genuinely effective legal alternatives to breaking the law. If you break the law, said Lesli Bisgould, who has defended fur-farm raiders in court, they tell you to use the political system, because "That's the way our democracy works." Animal activists are told they must convince the public to give their concerns a hearing, she said, but they are greeted with anger when they stage protests. There seems to be almost nowhere for these issues to get a hearing and no way for that public to be lobbied. Sometimes, she said, people break the law out of sheer frustration or based on the conviction that things will never change.[41]

Bisgould specializes in legal cases that involve animals. For that, she had to follow a course in the United States, because the subject doesn't rate as a specialty in Canadian law schools. The cases usually take lots of time, cost a lot, and don't often win. "I always tell people, 'We're going to lose and lose and lose. And then one day we'll win," she said.

Vancouver Sun columnist Nicholas Read writes a regular, serious column about animal issues for his newspaper, a unique journalistic assignment, but one that he said seems constantly in danger of being cancelled in favour of more traditional content. One attempt to kill it was reportedly beaten off by complaints from devoted fans, many of them activists. "In some way, it legitimizes what they do," said Read, who has contrasted Canada with Britain, where animal issues figure into mainstream politics. "I think this is sad. I wish I didn't have to do it at all. I wish it was a respectable area of interest."[42]

Darren Thurston looked momentarily blank when asked about whether some room on the political agenda for animal rights issues would give activists an alternative to breaking the law. Certainly it would be good to see more debate and action in the political arena, he said politely, but he didn't expect any such thing because corporate interests control the agenda.[43]

"I have got boxes of letters," convicted mink-farm raider Hilma Ruby said of her efforts to make legal change. "I get the same silly responses. It's essentially a form letter. 'Thank you for your concern.'" Ruby said that much of what happened in the Ontario mink raid she helped carry out "was almost a last resort. . . . I'm really sad we're called terrorists."[44]

Frustration with making progress in any reasonable time frame does give some Canadian activists an empathy for the illegals. Beth MacKenzie Kent, the middle-aged, respectable head of the Nova Scotia Humane Society, does not take part in illegal activity, but she said she can understand why some activists are driven to that action out of frustration. In Toronto, Danielle Divincenzo of ARK II stressed that ALF actions were non-violent. "I'm very proud of what they do," she said. Michael Alvarez-Toye of the Calgary Animal Rights Coalition has protested and lectured in schools on a whole range of animal issues. He said he had never taken part in illegal activity but, when progress seems so elusive, "Sometimes I wish I had the balls – and was twenty years younger and was able." In Vancouver, Judy Stone of the Animal Advocates Society said she disapproved of food-poisoning hoaxes and violence. But as for other, non-violent illegalities, "There's a place for all of it," she said. "We're many oars all pulling in the same direction."

Here we come full circle. There are concerns that law-abiding activists try to raise publicly, real moral and ethical issues that go unaddressed on the political agenda even while decisions affecting them are being made. Public acknowledgement that the animal movement exists is found mainly in pockets of special interest that focus more on reasons to reject the movement than on responding to its message. There is no reason to suppose that people who champion issues involving animals will fade away if they are ignored. That isn't the history of the movement here or in other countries. After all, they have been ignored for years and little by little they have chipped away at the wall of silence that seems to surround them. They have taken to the courts and to the streets.

Now what is more likely is that both the legal and illegal sides will grow. If the political agenda cannot finally make room for them, the rationale of the law-abiding activists for withholding at least morale support from the outlaws may slowly crumble.

CHAPTER NINE

Back to the Future

It was a chilly, misty night in a quiet corner of rural Ontario when Robyn Weiner and her friends stole through the pitch dark towards the rows of sheds where the mink lived. Weiner was elated and nervous, sneaking through the night to save little creatures from death. She was also on the brink of what she would later consider the most traumatic event of her life, little more than an hour from disaster. As the furtive band of animal liberationists dispersed throughout the farm to accomplish their assigned tasks, the noise of the mink could not drown out a different noise. Human voices, yelling and coming closer: the farmers.

"All I remember is being grabbed and put in a headlock," Weiner later said as she probed recollections she had been trying to push away. "At one point, he was dragging me, yelling at me, 'I'm going to fucking kill you.' "[1]

The Animal Liberation Front raid had gone about as wrong as it possibly could. This was a five-person band that spanned generations and ideologies. One was a diehard but ailing activist, ready to bow out and leave the field to younger colleagues. Another two were younger and exuberant, at an age when changing the world can seem not only a possibility but also a duty. Another was a confused hanger-on who later seemed unsure about what he was doing there or why. Him aside, these were people who lived noisily open, above-ground lives of mostly legal activism. They were not trying to confine their animal work into discreet corners of their lives. If there are harbingers of a new attitude towards life in the ranks of the animal movement, then these are the faces of the messengers. They look and sound like the people next door.

People who lived in the little southwestern Ontario town of Blenheim, population 4,600, sixty miles from Windsor, woke up on April 1, 1997, to shocking news. Five Americans from suburban Detroit were appearing in court there after 1,500 mink had been released from cages at a fur farm on the edge of town. The three women and two men had been arrested in the wee hours of Easter Sunday, one of them inside Ebert's fur farm, the others outside. It was the second time in two weeks that the farm had been raided by animal liberationists, said William McLellan, one of two owners of the farm. The culprits of the first raid remained unknown. The second raid was much bigger and more devastating. It put part of his family's fur business out of operation. Provincial police from nearby Chatham announced that morning that the five people arrested appeared to be linked to the Animal Liberation Front, a clandestine organization unfamiliar to most people in the area. But the fur farmers among them knew about the ALF – they had been following its infuriating rhetoric and anonymous warnings on the Internet.

The Ebert raid was a "cowardly act of violence and vandalism," Fur Institute of Canada chairman Bruce Williams announced. The Fur Institute and the Canada Mink Breeders Association urged authorities to crack down.[2] It would be two years before the courts finally finished dealing with the last of the five Americans, with two women and one man jailed and two other people fined, two years before the angry McLellan family was able to put the ordeal behind them. The last American to be jailed as a result of the raid was twenty-nine-year-old Gary Yourofsky, a supply teacher and journalism graduate. He went defiant and in handcuffs – and without admitting guilt – to his sentence of six months in jail. His not guilty plea had led to a full trial and was intended to make clear his uncompromising attitude towards the authorities.

Still, despite the ongoing worry in the fur industry about this and other, even bigger attacks on other Canadian fur farms by animal liberationists, most of the mainstream media paid scant attention to the events or the issues.

Even if attacks on mink farms were not a North American phenomenon of growing importance, the Ebert farm raid offered a prime opportunity to get an inside glimpse of the illegal side of the animal movement, the object of considerable police scrutiny across North American and Europe. In 1991 ALF had declared war on the North American fur industry with the first stage of its Operation Bite Back campaign. After a series of sometimes spectacular attacks, police in the United States believed they were getting a grip on the movement. Then ALF struck four fur farms in British Columbia, actions that included one of the first mink raids in Canada. It had continued its work ever since.

The episode in Blenheim on an Easter morning was newsworthy. It was a made-for-media tale of a doomed adventure with an offbeat mixture of characters, plot, and mishap. It was a good story on a traditionally slow news weekend, and the resulting trials offered a close account of an ALF raid.

The main event was a four-hour drama played out on the unlit gravel roads of one of the quietest parts of Ontario, a Keystone Kops series of cars following cars following a van with various characters passing each other in darkness and, at times, encountering each other face to face. The occasion would be followed by two years of court appearances and peculiar deals that left some of the activists lightly punished, others in jail, and a crusty veteran of Ontario's judiciary sounding alternately amused and outraged.

• • •

A few weeks before the raid, in mid-March 1997, an Internet message carried a report with a chippy, triumphant tone:

> On March 15, our band of eco-anarchists paid a visit to the Ebert's fur farm in Blenheim, Ontario, on Mink Lane Road.

We were amazed at the openness of the operation. The sheds were practically next to the main road, with no attempts being made to hide the farm from the public. . . . Once we figured out the latches, we started opening the cages and collecting the breeding cards. When possible, we damaged the cages. The mink were ready to party, rushing past us to the nearby safety of wooded farmland. . . . One of our group left a spray can autograph on the feed shed, just to let them know that we care. When we had released about 240 of our captive comrades, a truck pulled up to the front gate that we had already pried open. Saddened to leave without finishing our intended business, we managed to escape detection by hopping through the back fence and meeting our driver up the road. Though it is maddening to have been so close to freeing so many, we are somewhat comforted by Mother Jones' words: "Mourn the dead and work like hell for the living."[3]

The way farmer William McLellan would tell it in court two years later, that first raid had left him worried and tossing in his bed at nights. That first time, he was phoned at home by a hired man who had arrived at the farm to find some two hundred mink running loose and about $500 damage to cages. McLellan wasn't sure if it was some kind of one-off prank, but he had a feeling something else might happen. So he and his son Tom decided to keep watch.

After all, the Internet had also made it clear that something called Earth Week was coming up at the end of the month. There were defiant warnings that fur farmers should beware. The Canada Mink Breeders Association warned McLellan that his operation might be attacked in the last week of March.[4] The seventy-four-year-old farmer and his son, co-owners of this farm site that had been in the family for eighteen years, made a plan to drive past the Mink Line operation every hour or so. There was no house on that property and no one to sound the alarm if intruders returned.

Things were quiet when they drove by the operation one Saturday evening at nine o'clock. But McLellan felt "kind of worked up." He drove miles around the countryside looking for signs of trouble, but all was still quiet close to midnight when he turned the watch over to friends and employees to get some sleep. He had church in the morning to think about.

David Cameron, another mink farmer and an occasional worker during pelt season at the McLellans' farm, had been at a hockey game that evening. It was sometime after midnight and before one o'clock when he drove towards the fur farm to check for trouble. In the distance Cameron saw a vehicle driving slowly past the fur farm, too far away for him to make out its shape. Already, he was suspicious. Not many cars travel the back roads of southwestern Ontario after 10:30 p.m., and those that do go straight to their destinations. He caught up with it, a green van bearing Michigan plates, and to avoid being spotted stayed close only long enough to jot down the numbers on a cigarette package.[5]

As one of the accused, Alan Hoffman, told it, the five Americans had gathered at Hilma Ruby's mobile home near Detroit some ten days earlier to talk about freeing mink from a fur farm. All but Hoffman were dedicated members of animal rights organizations, legal groups that protested and lobbied on behalf of animals. But the idea had taken hold to make something happen. Nothing came of that initial meeting because a date couldn't be found that would suit everyone. Then, on Saturday, March 29, 1997, Hoffman joined the others in a volunteer work session at a pig sanctuary to help muck out. Everyone came dressed for the job and brought extra boots and clothes. After several hours of work, he and his four comrades piled into the van, dirty and smelling of hog manure, and began to drive. The idea, he told the court, was to go to Ohio and liberate some mink. When they couldn't find the Ohio farms, they took a vote in the van about going to Canada to a farm that Ruby knew how to find.[6]

Hoffman insisted that he had been the lone dissenting vote and that, by the time they decided to go to Canada, he simply wanted out of the whole adventure. The short, forty-nine-year-old truck driver with thinning hair, dark-rimmed glasses, and a hesitant, soft voice offered a lame excuse for himself. He was only there, he said, because he had been talked into it by his young nephew, Gary Yourofsky, "a passionate advocate of animal rights." For a year or two Yourofsky had been telling him about animal abuse, showing him videos and urging him to join one of two Detroit-area animal rights groups. That night Hoffman wanted to get out of the van when they reached the Windsor border crossing, he explained, but he didn't have much money with him and he was afraid it was not a safe neighbourhood to be left on his own. So he carried on, assured by his nephew that the only penalty if he were caught would be a $25 fine. He said they made plans for the roles they would all play once they got to the mink farm. At one point during the drive police came along, got the van to pull over, and checked it out, apparently because it was going so slowly. The liberators, it seems, were trying to read maps and instructions on where fur farms were located.

Robyn Weiner, a petite twenty-eight-year-old child welfare worker with deep blue eyes and long, curly dark hair, found it hard two years later to replay the evening clearly in her mind. It was a nightmare that still brought tears to her eyes. What she recalled of the outset of that evening was that, "It all sounded wonderful. I was just going to release mink, save mink." A dedicated defender of animal rights, she had successfully challenged the mandatory dissection of animals in biology class as a student at Eastern Michigan University. Weiner did not believe it was morally wrong to raid a mink farm. She headed off to help animals that night buoyed by the feeling that she was going to do good, without any real thought for the consequences.

No matter how personally the McLellans might have taken their worries about an attack that night as they kept watch, their farm seemed a randomly chosen target. It was, Hilma Ruby recalled later, simply the closest one they could find. There wasn't a lot of planning ahead of time, she said. "We weren't pros."[7] Patricia Dodson, a forty-nine-year-old secretary, drove the van. Ruby, a retired registered nurse, was by her side giving directions. By Hoffman's version of it, Dodson was to drop them off at the farm and come back in an hour. They drove by the mink farm two or three times before Dodson left them at the gate in the dark. It was about then, as the Americans scaled the farm gate and headed for the rows of mink cages in the pitch dark, that Cameron spotted and followed Dodson's van.

After noting the van's plates, Cameron decided he had better check in with William McLellan. The nearest roadside phone was broken so he headed into Blenheim, just minutes away, to the 7-Eleven variety store, the only place open at nearly 1:45 a.m. When he contacted McLellan, the farmer told him just to keep an eye on things, that it was likely nothing. But as Cameron hung up he saw an Ontario Provincial Police cruiser on the street. He flagged it down, reminded the police of the raid two weeks before, and told them about the van. Almost immediately they saw the van driving right by them, there on Talbot Street in downtown Blenheim. OPP Constable Douglas Knight followed it and stopped the vehicle, finding only Dodson inside. He said he had no reason to disbelieve her when she held up her map and said she was lost. He gave her directions to Chatham. But his partner, Constable Stuart Bertram, was far from satisfied as Dodson drove off. While she had been talking to Knight, he had peered in through the van's passenger window and sighted a crowbar, walkie-talkies, binoculars, extra clothes, and a second purse.[8]

"I got very suspicious immediately," he told the court. "It's not normally what I see in a vehicle. They ring out to me as materials used in burglaries." So the police watched Dodson's van as it turned off the road to Chatham and onto a gravel road that would take her nowhere. They stopped her again, told her they had doubts about her and invited her to the cruiser's back seat while they checked her licence. With growing suspicion about Dodson's story and the earlier mink raid on their minds, the officers called in another officer from Chatham for a consultation. Within minutes of his arrival, the excited voice of the OPP dispatcher called out on the cruiser radio, "The mink farm just got hit." Patricia Dodson was placed under arrest.

Bertram had already found Ruby's identification in her purse, Yourofsky's in the cup holder between the two front seats, and Weiner's in a beaded purse. Hoffman's wallet and driver's license were in a duffel bag. They found a blue address book with a membership list for Humanitarians for Animal Rights Education (HARE), a Detroit-based animal rights group, and Yourofsky's membership card for Animals Deserve Adequate Protection Today and Tomorrow (ADAPTT), a Michigan animal rights group. Filling in the picture, they found copies of something titled *The Final Nail: Destroying the Fur Industry* and a yellow paper with addresses, including the Ebert's farm. They found a photocopy of a map of the area with highlighting on Blenheim and three other small towns. With Dodson on board they headed back to the farm.

By 2:00 a.m., some twenty minutes before Dodson was placed under arrest, Cameron had called back to tell McLellan and farm manager Michael Davey to rendezvous at a nearby cemetery. Together they rushed to the farm. McLellan had already seen mink running beside the fence along the road, so he knew there was trouble. He left the younger men to bolt over the gate while he tried to position his vehicle's headlights to pierce the gloom. The farm lights, used to trick the pregnant mink into faster gestation, weren't due to come on until four o'clock, almost two hours away.

Davey could see mink racing in the darkness and ran to the feed shed, where he used a telephone to call the Chatham police. Then he charged off down one of the alleys between mink sheds, searching for intruders. Someone was running at him in the dark. "Who are you?" he yelled. The dark figure turned and bolted in the opposite direction, followed by someone else. That person – Robyn Weiner – he managed to grab. "She went down on her knees," Davey said. "I thought she might try crawling under the pens. I called out for Dave. We asked her a few questions and then we locked her in the cooler." David Cameron, a burly six-footer, helped Davey take Weiner to the feed room. Cameron had also given chase to two other intruders, but had lost them.

"I started to run but it was muddy," Weiner remembered later of the jumble of events that began with men yelling in the dark not long after they had arrived at the farm and ended with her being grabbed. "I was locked in a freezer room, a room with a steel door, and people kept coming by and opening and closing the door," she said. "They would yell 'Who are you with? Come on, you weren't here alone.' I said I was alone. Then I told them 'There may be other people but I don't know.' I felt like I was in there forever, but I don't know how long it was. They kept threatening to do things to me, not let me out. You know, [saying] 'You're going to die.'"

When the police arrived, there was a conversation with the farmers about who would stay with her while they searched for others. Weiner remembered being handcuffed, crying and pleading, frightened at being left in the hands of the farmers. "I think she can be quite thankful we put her in the cooler," McLellan told the court, much to the apparent amusement of Mr. Justice Anthony E. Cusinato.

By that time Hoffman was hiding in a muddy field near the farm. He told the court that he had started removing breeding records from the tops of cages, as did Weiner, while Yourofsky was helping Ruby to open cages. By the time they heard the farmers coming Weiner had moved into a different shed and, Hoffman said, he had lost track of her, Yourofsky, and Ruby. He fled on the farmers' arrival. As he ran, he tossed away a pouch with the breeding cards. When he reached a muddy field just outside the farm he heard a noise and found Yourofsky. Together they watched as, some fifty yards away, Ruby stood still, giving herself up to the police.

"I laid in a muddy ditch," Ruby recalled. "I could hear animals scrambling away. It was just such a sense of joy. I ended up surrendering, more or less. I walked down a road, knowing the police would come, and I thought, 'It's worth this, to hear those little animals out there running around.' I was just caught up in the heat of the moment."

Dodson, Weiner, and now Ruby had been arrested. By about 3:30 a.m., Yourofsky and Hoffman had made their way on foot to Blenheim. The bars were closed and the 7-Eleven store was the only sign of life in town. Back in the field, OPP canine handler Wade Jacklin and his dog Bandit were already slowly tracking their way towards town and the store, finding Hoffman's pouch in an orchard on the way, following the scent.

Daniel Hux was working alone in the little convenience store that night with not much to do at that hour but put in time. He watched two strangers at the phone booth outside. Later, when he identified Yourofsky as one of the two men who came in that night to ask him where they might get a taxi, he would remember Yourofsky's distinctive shaved head. The two said they had been dropped off in Canada as a college prank and had to get a ride to Detroit, but they didn't have any money. Yourofsky showed Hux a necklace, a link chain that he offered to sell. "I didn't have the money to put into a necklace," Hux said in court. "I told them they could talk to the cab driver." He called the town's one and only taxi for them and saw them wave as they drove off about a half an hour later.

But before they left, Hux had more company. Joseph Hebert, one of McLellan's farm workers, had been called out of bed to help with the chaos. McLellan had asked him to pick up some coffees for all of them on his way over and that meant a stop at the 7-Eleven. There are conflicting versions of this, but Hebert said that when he arrived he saw two men outside, with their jeans and running shoes covered with mud. Inside, the clerk told him the story about the prank. After seeing Yourofsky and Hoffman drive away in the cab, Hebert took the coffees and went back to his employer's farm to help in the search for the raiders.

Tim Abrams, who was driving Blenheim's only cab that night, agreed to take the necklace as collateral. The two men, he said, "looked like they had been through a creek. They were covered with mud." He set out down Highway 401 and, little more than ten minutes later, the police contacted him on his cell phone. Constables Knight and Bertram had also arrived at the 7-Eleven store, hard on the heels of the two Americans. The officer with the dog would soon be there too. Armed with the identifications from the van and the description from Hux, they called the taxi driver on his cell phone and warned him they were on their way to meet up with his grey Oldsmobile. He was to play along and stay on the phone. His passengers, Abrams said, seemed to think he was being stopped for a speeding offence when the police pulled him over. But they were there to arrest Hoffman and Yourofsky. Abrams never did get his $35 fare or the necklace.

In a span of just hours, five Americans were in jail in Canada facing charges of break and enter, mischief, possession of stolen property, and possession of burglary tools. This was not your regular burglary. There was, after all, no loot. The stolen property was the breeding cards, carried away to damage the business by the loss of important genetic records. Even if the raid had been successful, the intruders would have left empty-handed, and their exploits – succeed or fail – would have been proudly recorded on the Net in the easily accessible, diligently maintained archives of liberation activity from around the world. The immediate damage included repairs to the farm fence and cages estimated at a cost of $4,000 to $5,000 and the loss of some 1,500 mink worth about $163,800 in pelts. The McLellans were later awarded more than $770,000 for lost business and damages in a civil suit against several of the Americans. The farmers seemed unlikely ever to collect that sum.[9]

In the Blenheim case, the arrests were followed by statements to police from both Alan Hoffman and Robyn Weiner. Hoffman might be considered a lost cause, a man who simple happened to be in the wrong place at the wrong time. But Weiner was a follower, a believer, and her statement was considered a betrayal not only by her close friend Gary Yourofsky, but by activists elsewhere. "We were like brother and sister," Yourofsky said of Weiner. "She had a key to my house. Neither of us would go away to school because of our dogs. . . . I want her away from here. I don't want her hurt, I want her shunned. It was more than me she sold out. It was the animals."[10]

But far more damaging to Yourofsky, in immediate terms, was his uncle's conduct. Hoffman's statement to police was read out in court, and it was a jumble of desperate pleadings that "this is the first and last" such thing he would ever do, that he had only been there because of his nephew. "I didn't know the three ladies at all," he said. When they were together later in a cell, Yourofsky expressed his disgust. "Haven't you seen enough movies to know you don't have to say anything?" he asked his uncle in exasperation. (Later, as his son was led away to jail, Gary's father, Ronald Yourofsky, would correct a reporter's reference to Gary's uncle. "He *was* his uncle," he said.)

Hoffman was fined \$5,000 and spared a jail term. Like the others, he was also ordered to pay a \$34,298 share in restitution to the McLellans.

Weiner's statement to the police about her own activities seemed to link Hilma Ruby to the first, earlier raid on the fur farm, though Ruby denied any involvement in that event. "These 'activists' have turned against their own and expressed their willingness to work with the authorities against their fellow defendants," an Animal Liberation Frontline news bulletin commented.[11] "This is NOT OK and must not be tolerated within a direct action movement. Once activists make statements which incriminate others or compromise the defense of others, they are excluded from support."

Underground warned that there were too many willing informers. The raid in Blenheim "should stand as a good example to others to pick your cell-members carefully," the magazine advised.

> Already we have seen one participant make statements to the police that were read in court, including a blow by blow account of everyone's alleged activities that night. A second participant, under pressure by family and police also appears to have made statements, and even implicated the other defendants in a previous raid.
>
> So what's to be done? One step may be to pick up the latest *No Compromise* (Issue No. 6) and read the article, *Creating a Security Culture*, for basic tips on how to prevent your activities from becoming known by everyone from your landlord to the local P.C. Plod walking the beat. It's also time that people stopped trying to earn "scene points" by bragging about what they've done or what they know. . . . Far from being "cool" or "admirable," this kind of boasting and rumour-milling is a sign of weakness and these folk should be avoided at all cost, especially if you plan to break the law in any way. As activists face daily police harassment and surveillance and animal abusers vow revenge, it's about time people realized that illegal direct action is not a game. The lives of animals and the freedom of ALF warriors are at

stake, and we all play a part in making sure the liberations safely continue.[12]

For Weiner, the arrest that followed the ill-starred raid began a numbing series of days when all of the five Americans remained in jail until bail was set. She was repeatedly questioned and then left alone.[13] The first night she contacted her brother, not willing to confront her parents with what had happened. Finally her father called the jail. The strip search, the arraignment on charges – none of it yet seemed real. For a week before her release, she was under intense pressure from her parents and lawyer to co-operate with police. She said she was advised that because she was the only one caught on the farm itself, she stood to face the worst penalty. That meant nothing worse would happen to the others than happened to her – which didn't turn out to be true. Help yourself, help the others, was the message. She was told that no one would feed her cats back home in her apartment, that Yourofsky's beloved dog Brandy was sick, that he didn't know it was going to be put down and that he would be grateful to get out before it died. She remembered it as the most traumatic experience of her life. "I was genuinely torn," she said. "I had people that I cared about on both ends."

For a few months afterward, freed (with a fine, a conditional sentence, and community service) Weiner stayed out of sight at home. She was upset and unhappy, and the people she had worked with as comrades were not speaking to her. The newsletter from ADAPTT, the group she belonged to and for which Yourofsky served as president, referred to her in updates about the case as "seditious."

"I understand the anger," she said. "What I don't understand is the treatment from so-called compassionate people. We're talking two years, now, down the line. This is intentional. This crap, maybe it's not crap, but it's two years now and it needs to be put aside. We have work to do. We don't have the luxury to be picking and choosing who's going to work for these animals."

Weiner didn't want to be seen as self-pitying. She said she would not be forced out, nor would she give up her activism. She denied she had done anything that would hurt animals. She remained in the

close confines of the Detroit-area animal rights movement, determined to put the whole episode behind her. "It just happened," she
said. "I try not to keep going back and ripping it to pieces. It's what
happened." She continued to maintain that the raid as a whole was
not wrong. "To let those animals free? No. For those that lived."

Almost two years after she walked out of the Ontario jail, Weiner
refused to come back to the Chatham court to testify against
Yourofsky. Her deal with the courts in return for her pre-trial co-
operation later angered another judge, who concluded that he was
being asked to make up for that deal in sentencing others of the five.

Farmers across the country closely followed the sentencings.
Even those whose livestock did not include mink wanted to know
what would happen to the animal rights people. Farmers, after all,
have heard about animal rights actions that never made the press.
They wanted to see how seriously the courts would view these people. Some complained that changes the federal government was considering to animal cruelty sections of the Criminal Code of Canada,
would make cruelty convictions carry a harsher penalty than those
imposed on animal rights extremists. For mink farmers, the court
process was intensely personal, which became abundantly clear the
day that Patricia Dodson and Hilma Ruby appeared in provincial
court in Chatham after pleading guilty to charges of break, enter and
theft, and mischief and, in Dodson's case, to possession of house-
breaking tools.

On that Monday morning, January 18, 1999, for some reason court
was being held in a hopelessly inadequate room with seats for only
two dozen spectators. The crowd of farmers and their wives, neighbours, friends, and family monopolized all but a couple of seats inside
the courtroom and much of the hallway outside. As a result, for the
afternoon session, while her mother's immediate future was being
debated, Ruby's daughter was unable to listen. One reporter had to
wheedle a spare seat usually used by court staff.

As each public seat was vacated, it was carefully handed over from
one farmer-friendly spectator to another. People who couldn't
squeeze inside took turns looking through the small window in the

courtroom door, staring in at Dodson and Ruby. Local lawyers who wanted to peek in the window to see the famous visiting lawyer, Clayton Ruby (no relation), seated at the defendants' table, had to give up any hope of making a casual pass by the door. They had to shoulder their way through like any witness or spectator. "Pay-back time," one short brunette woman said with a grin, smacking one fist into her palm, as she greeted her friends in the upstairs court hallway.

Usually, the legal proceedings in a provincial court have a numbing formality and ritual. The process is designed with a concept of justice that sees crime as an affront to the community, not to an individual alone. The neutrality of the judge and the rules combine to create an environment in which personal feelings stand aside and the judge and the court govern. That January day in Chatham was different. For an observer, it was like elbowing your way uninvited into a crowded party at someone's home. People stared coldly at anyone thought to be from the animal activists' side or simply an outsider. It was impossible to avoid their hostility. The crowd, mostly women, whispered together at the sight of any strange face and made contemptuous remarks about the big-city lawyer who, it was said, was having the whole day scheduled to accommodate his desire to make a final, late-afternoon train back to Toronto. ("Absolutely," lawyer Ruby later confirmed cheerfully about the priority of his travel plans. "I made it quite clear to the judge.")[14] The bulk of the crowd outside the courtroom shared an angry, respectful silence when they heard that one of the McLellan family was speaking to the court, explaining tearfully what the raid had cost the business.

The prevailing mood was not lost on the judge. "I'm not pandering to the lowest common denominator," Judge John Desotti told the courtroom. "No matter what we think down at the coffee counter . . . 'Yeah, send 'em away'. . . . We'd like to do what is appropriate. That's our job." He was blunt and sounded fed up with Crown Attorney Susan Cote, who had urged him to put the women in jail for eighteen months, followed by probation with money to be paid in restitution.

These were Americans, Cote said, and in Utah the courts had just handed out a jail term to a mink raider. The judge waved off the photocopy of a news report on the Utah case that she offered. You cannot demand jail "because they're Yankees," he told her.

The judge said it was not his fault that the Crown had given Weiner a fine and some community service she couldn't serve, as it turned out, because she couldn't cross the border after her conviction.[15] A fine is pointless for defendants with no income. (Ruby was ill, unemployed, and poor. Dodson would be out of a job if she were jailed.) These were also first-time offenders, like Weiner, and the sentences had to be balanced. "I'm on the horns of a heck of a dilemma," the judge complained, saying he would need some time to consider the sentencing, which he would announce on February 22, 1999.

Those remarks gave Ruby, who had a heart condition, arthritis, and other ailments, some hope that she might avoid jail, although only a faint one. On the weekend before the sentencing she closed up her mobile home, made arrangements for her three dogs to be cared for, and made a last-minute check on a stray she had driven to the Humane Society. And she contemplated a second stint in jail. After her arrest, it had been ten days before she had been released on bail. She had listened to Clayton Ruby's advice that she would do better if she made a statement to court expressing her regrets for the hardships of the McLellans. "I declined," she said later. "I wouldn't be able to lie and say I feel remorseful."[16]

Just before she went back to Chatham for sentencing, Ruby took her eighty-five-year-old mother out to lunch. "She doesn't understand any of this," Ruby said. "I told her, if you don't hear from me Monday night, I'll be in jail. She has to accept it. She begged me to just flee. I said, 'Ma, I can't do that. It's a principle.' I don't intend to live on the lam. I did this because I believe in something. Why would I flee the consequences? I wanted to stand up and accept it. It was a calculated risk and we got caught."

It was bitterly cold on February 22, and this time the sentencing had been scheduled for the largest courtroom in the courthouse in Chatham. But for half an hour before court began, the doors were left locked and everyone milled about the cold parking lot. Patricia Dodson wore a smart pant suit and a trench coat. She might have been a lawyer in from out of town. Hilma Ruby wore a graceful mid-calf skirt, long rose sweater, and wine-coloured tights. This was not what women here would wear downtown on a frigid Monday morning, and certainly not to court.

But the style was not just in clothes. These women had an air of confidence about themselves that, as much as anything they had done, seemed to infuriate the audience. They were so clearly unapologetic and unashamed. Ruby's daughter Meriam Alkadimi was offering videos of conditions on mink farms to show that the whole business was cruel and bad. To the crowd, these were animal fanatics and Americans and not sorry – you could feel the resentment. But the larger courtroom, crowded by lawyers awaiting scheduling for other cases, made the atmosphere much more ordinary and neutral than it had been in January.

Lawyer Lesli Bisgould pleaded for an intermittent sentence, arguing that the women had shown up for countless court appearances and that a certificate to allow a border crossing should be possible to obtain. That would let Dodson keep her job and fit the attitude towards first offenders, Bisgould argued. Her argument was turned down. The judge ordered the two offenders to jail on a ninety-day sentence, which would mean serving sixty days. As soon as the sentence was delivered, Ruby turned, looking radiant at the news whispered by her daughter Meriam. Her first great-grandchild, a seven-pound thirteen-ounce boy, had been born sometime after she had left home for court at 7:00 a.m. She handed her belongings to her daughter and followed the guards, looking content and calm.

She knew what the drill would be from her time served in London's jail after her arrest – shower, strip search, and distribution of sweat suits, running shoes, one set of underwear, a toothbrush with a cut-off, two-inch handle, one sheet of paper, and a stamped envelope. After a few days she and Dodson were moved to the Vanier Centre for Women in Brampton, just outside Toronto. She missed her three dogs, but Ruby seemed well able to handle the two months in jail. It was an attitude that ALF literature tried to encourage.

"After all the historical social movements for change – civil rights, women's rights, gay-lesbian rights – you'd think people would understand that social change has its casualties," she wrote in one letter from prison. "The yoke of oppression and greed isn't relinquished easily. Some of our people are in prisons around the world for up to 18 years! Some have been beaten and some have been killed. But we're not going to stop."[17]

Ruby's daughter was tired and angry as her mother was led away to jail, bitterly contrasting her jail term with the comparatively lighter treatment accorded Weiner and Hoffman. The mood, Alkadimi said, was that of a "lynch mob." But if this was meant as a message to others, she said, it would fail. "They're the voices for the animals."

In court Alkadimi had praised her mother, telling proudly how a younger, U.S.-born Ruby had brought her children home from Iraq to the United States with an outraged Iraqi husband on their heels. Her father felt his honour was offended by the deserting Ruby, who had often been punished by her in-laws in Baghdad by being locked away from her children, Alkadimi told the court. Her father chased them around their house with a sword, trying to kill them. He was arrested and deported back to Iraq. Her mother, on welfare with five children, worked her way through college to become a registered nurse.

Ruby had a more modest way of describing herself and her animal rights dedication: "I look at myself as a soldier. I'm not a general. I'm not a major. I'm a soldier. . . . I'll be 62 in August (1999). I won't see results, not in my lifetime. That's not going to stop me from trying. It's a social movement."

It was one in a list of social causes she had supported before she found the animal movement about eight years earlier. Married young to an Iraqi student in the United States, she moved to Baghdad in 1958 for ten years, filling her time there by teaching English to diplomats and the blind. She designed a program to teach student nurses enough English to allow them to take further training in the United States. A United Nations agency consulted her about the use of aid money for the blind in Iraq – she recommended a Braille printing press – but war broke out and she left without learning the results of the plan. Now, in another turn in a life that could make a movie, Ruby was going to jail. She said she knew that some people would think her conduct outrageous. "At one time, it was legal to hold slaves," she said. "What the McLellans do for a living is wronger than the law is right. . . . I'm a big believer in fate and destiny. This is where I'm supposed to be right now."

• • •

If Ruby believed that this mink raid was a kind of last hurrah for her, Yourofsky clearly saw himself as just getting started. He found animal rights in 1996 the way some people find religion, as a touchstone that gave his life purpose. He called it "my life's work." After his arrest and jailing something happened to the gregarious, energetic young man. He discovered in a real and personal way that he could go to jail and survive it. Like other activists who have made that journey, he came out of it all with what he saw as a liberating insight. If you don't fear jail, you break a system that relies largely on fear as a deterrent. If you go to jail, at least it brings home to the public that this is serious stuff, and, as an extra, you get a small taste of what animals experience. It is, all in all, "like you were reborn."[18] What good will it do the courts to warn that jail awaits lawbreaking activists if that warning doesn't scare them?

After the Ontario arrest, Yourofsky was on a roll. Back home in Detroit before his trial in Chatham, he was arrested and arrested again, all of the incidents minor protest situations in which charges could have been avoided – a disorderly conduct charge for swearing at a Detroit police officer, for example. When he spoke, at the invitation of teachers, to an audience of affluent, middle-class kids at a suburban Detroit high school before his trial in Chatham, Yourofsky was introduced as president of Michigan's most powerful animal rights group and a man who had been arrested six times, once in connection with the "release of over 1,500 mink in Canada." The students, more than one hundred of them, applauded and cheered. Aside from a queasy few who fled holding their mouths, they watched his grisly video of slaughterhouses, burn tests on live pigs, and monkeys with their eyes sewn shut for research, and they heard his call to revolution.

"I have come here today to ask you to join me in a remarkable crusade against the heartless forces of oppression," his voiced boomed through the auditorium. It was an appeal that few ordinary teenagers would not find attractive. "The animal rights movement is not necessarily polite, safe or popular. But it is right."[19]

The students listened while he condemned major charities for the animal-based research they funded, researchers for their hot pursuit of grants, famous circuses as slave holders. He gave a heady, charismatic performance that won wholehearted thanks from the teachers who organized it. He had helped the school program in its efforts to make students active, involved, and responsible citizens and had won "100 instant converts to vegetarianism," they wrote. They invited him to speak again in the following year's schedule of speakers on political issues.[20] Clearly, a chasm yawns between the legal system's view of what decent folk think and what teachers figure are the views of a younger generation.

The day that Gary Yourofsky was sentenced, he had copies on hand of the statement he planned to make in court. He was clearly going to jail and, although the attitude of the judge was hardly sympathetic, Yourofsky made no attempt to soften the blow. In his presentencing statement in court he went out of his way to announce that he would observe a symbolic hunger strike in jail, "for every mink that ever languished in a tiny cage and was savagely murdered at the Ebert's Fur Farm . . . and for the 40 million other animals worldwide that have the skins ripped off their backs in a disgusting display of barbarity in the name of vanity."

In a voice that gained in volume as he addressed the court, he said: "One day every enslaved animal will obtain his or her freedom. . . . The true, devoted humanitarians who are working towards the magnanimous goal of achieving freedom for animals cannot be stopped by unjust laws. As long as humans are placed on a pedestal above non-humans, injustice to animals will fester. . . . Enslaving and killing animals for human satisfaction can never be justified. And the fur industry must understand that the millions of manual neck-breakings, anal and genital electrocutions, mass gassings, drowning and toxic chemical injections are completely unjustifiable."

Tom McLellan told the court that the "brutal" attack on his family's fur operation made it almost impossible to recover after missing the peak prices of the season and losing their breeding records. Two years after, some of the mink recaptured on the night of the raid were still hanging as pelts in storage, awaiting some future improvement in prices. In November 1998 the McLellans closed down the Mink Line part of the farm. A Canadian farm family shouldn't have to lay awake nights, living in fear from threats on the Internet to fur farmers, he said. "These people place no value on the rights of humans," McLellan said. "Is this what animal rights is about? . . . This kind of criminal destruction must come to an end."

Throughout the trial, Mr. Justice Anthony Cusinato had seemed at ease with the farm witnesses, but his gaze kept returning to Yourofsky, the young man with the shaved head, glasses, and an unrepentant air. When Yourofsky read his statement to court, the judge gave him his undivided attention. When Yourofsky interrupted him on the issue of the number of mink left dead after the raid – "Even if sixty escaped, they got to freedom," he interjected from his seat – the judge made no attempt to cut him off. When the judge addressed the court to pronounce a sentence, he took time to talk about the animal liberation publication *The Final Nail*, a copy of which had been found in the van. Clearly, the contents had made a big impact on the judge.

The pamphlet "raises tremendous concerns in the eyes of the court," Judge Cusinato said, noting that it gave addresses and told how to build electrically timed devices and held out hope that the fur businesses would close down. "You may not necessarily have been the owner of the pamphlet," he said to Yourofsky. "You were aware of this pamphlet." The attack was intended to put a fur farm out of business, he said, and that was exactly what happened.[21]

By the time the judge was pronouncing his sentence, an updated version of *The Final Nail* was available on the Internet. "It's been great to see fur farms across the U.S. and even Canada getting raided, fur stores getting smashed up every week – fur stores have even been burned to the ground," the latest issue exclaimed. In a two-year interval, thirty-four fur farms in North America had been raided and about fifty thousand "fur farm prisoners" released. The total number of farms raided in the eight or nine years since Operation Bite Back, phases one and two, was much higher. More than forty-three were attacked in the United States in phase two alone. *The Final Nail* described what mink farms looked like, warned about security, and advised that mink should be freed after weaning time but before winter so they can learn to hunt. It noted that, in Finland and Sweden, some activists were using henna-based dyes to ruin the pelts. They carried the dyes in squeeze bottles and squirted them onto the mink. The publication described the making of an incendiary device that could be fitted inside a cigarette package, its workings fashioned of a battery, little light bulbs, match heads, and watches. The devices could be tucked into combustible materials somewhere in stores that sold furs, put in place between 3:00 p.m. and closing time, so they would be out of sight and not go off until everyone had left the stores. The idea was to trigger the sprinkler systems of large department stores. The result would be water damage rather than a runaway fire, with expensive damage to retailers who sold furs.

It is unlikely that Judge Cusinato would have been reassured by the publication's disclaimer that it was "NOT intended to encourage anyone to do anything illegal." The judge said he had no illusions that any amount of jail time would change Yourofsky's views. But he wanted "to send a message to those that would do likewise that a jail sentence will be awaiting them. . . . There's a legitimate means in which to make change," he told Yourofsky. "To take the law into your own hands does nothing more than create anarchy. . . . In your zeal to accomplish your goal you have shown a complete indifference and a disregard for the rule of law."

William McLellan had arrived at the sentencing of the last of the Americans who raided his farm convinced that putting up with this sort of attack and constant stress was not how farmers should have to live. "These people believe in doing violence to make their point," he said. "In Canada, we sit around a table and talk."[22] He left the court-room declaring himself satisfied with the jail term. It might discourage others, he said. As for the attitude of those like Yourofsky, McLellan said he had heard and read enough that, "I understand where he's coming from. But I don't know where he's going."

Just yards away, Hanna Gibson, the rescue and cruelty investigator for ADAPTT, Yourofsky's group, was talking to reporters about the McLellans' business. It was, she said, "evil. It needs to stop and it has." As for the jail term, "This isn't going to stop anything."

As promised, Yourofsky did begin a hunger strike in jail and was sent to solitary confinement for that misconduct, giving up his pillow, Bible, toothbrush, reading material, and soap. Days later, when authorities threatened to add an additional month to his sentence, Yourofsky ended his hunger strike at ADAPTT's urging. It was more important to get him out and back in action, ADAPTT executive director Lana Mini said in the Internet postings that kept activists informed about this celebrated prisoner.

The jail time did not tame Yourofsky's exuberant, boyish style. In a letter from inside the London detention centre in June 1999, he answered detailed questions about jail life. His food was sometimes good (best dishes were a stir fry, bean cakes, and a spinach-carrot pie) and always vegan. The routine was a dreary round of eating and watching television with a twenty-minute afternoon outing. His shared cell was twelve feet by eight feet, with inmates locked in at meals and nine o'clock in the evening. He was already planning his arrival home and the "10,000 kisses" he would give his collie-shepherd dog, Rex. He was busy answering a stack of letters from supporters. He had found a friend in another inmate who had listened to Yourofsky long enough to have decided he wanted to start his own ADAPTT office in Windsor. Yourofsky's letter, like several messages he would soon be posting to a growing e-mail list from home, was signed cockily, "Abolition. Liberation. Freedom."

He was barely home in his spartan apartment in suburban Detroit when he began a fierce on-line argument with a medical researcher who seemed almost to be baiting him. Both of them were sending their cutting exchanges to Yourofsky's e-mail list. Furious at this approach to his supporters, Yourofsky ordered the researcher to back off or be made to do it. Gleefully, the researcher announced he had informed authorities of the "death threat." That aside, Yourofsky plunged into a non-stop round of protests – against the circus, against fur, against medical research on primates – as a high-profile campaign by another organization, leaving arrests in its wake, orchestrated nationwide demonstrations. As the summer of 1999 wore on, it was unclear how long the clean slate of the irrepressible, unrepentant Yourofsky would last. He told one reporter that he had poured all of his own resources into his organization and had no intention of paying the court-ordered fine to "mink murderers."[23] After one of many demonstrations, he was charged with disorderly conduct for barricading the front of a Detroit animal-control office in which dogs had been killed despite offers of homes for them.

• • •

The Hilma Rubys and Gary Yourofskys will undoubtedly remain a mystery to people like the McLellans. There is not likely to be any time soon when people with such different views sit down at a table to talk about fur farms. If they did, it is unlikely that the premise that the industry is evil would be on the table. The mink industry firmly welcomed the jail sentences delivered by the courts.

The difference between animal rights outlaws and other criminals, lawyer Clayton Ruby said, is that, unlike the animal people, "most criminals aren't trying to do good." It is not a distinction that would cut any ice with the judiciary or mink farmers. For both of these parties, the aspiring mink liberators are not idealists. They are serious criminals and, possibly, terrorists – international terrorists, in this case, which is an impressive label. Possibly, too, they would just be dismissed as fanatics who just don't want people to use animals for anything.

If these were people out on a spree, say, to rob convenience stores as an alternative to regular jobs, those descriptions might be adequate. But they are not getting anything out of their supposed wrongdoing, except perhaps a jail term. And given the few activists who have been caught raiding fur farms, a jail term is not going to make the issues they are concerned about or their actions go away. Surely, if, as the president of the Canada Mink Breeders Association said when the Blenheim raid happened, there had been twenty-seven such attacks on North American mink farms in the previous twelve months, a little more discussion of those issues is merited.

The direct action of the Blenheim raiders was a definite step up from the activities of someone like Sandra the pet thief. The raiders were attempting to free animals destined to die so that humans could wear a luxury coat made from their skins – but their action was also aimed at putting an end to that sort of business. It was a kind of economic sabotage – and of a quintessentially Canadian industry.

In the mid-1990s Canada produced about 4 per cent of the world's mink. At that point, there were 1,200 mink and fox farmers in North America. By one tally, sixty liberations of tens of thousands of animals occurred on North American fur farms in the four years ending in August 1999. Sure, the perpetrators of those deeds don't want animals to be exploited – period. But they could have done any number of things to act on that desire. Instead, a lot of them chose to focus on fur farms. These activists don't believe that it is right to pen up animals that are wild by nature, just so their skins can be sold to produce a non-essential consumer good. They believe that the living conditions on fur farms are so unnatural and distressing that it is better to give the animals a chance to run for freedom, even if a lot of them are not going to make good their escape during a raid on a fur farm. If the animals die, at least it won't be at human hands, suffocated or electrocuted, for the sake of a fur coat. At least they will get a moment of running free. Even the British government was, by 1999, committed to a ban on fur farms, although it had not yet set a timetable.

In the wild, mink are solitary. They swim and range over square kilometres. In Canada, the voluntary guidelines on ranched mink recommend that a single male mink or a female mink with a litter should have a pen with a floor area of at least 325 square inches with a minimum height of 13 inches. Other mink, with one to a pen, should get a floor area of at least 186 square inches. One recommended way to kill them is using carbon monoxide. The guidelines say one mink should be allowed to collapse in the gas chamber before another one is put in. Another method of euthanasia is electrical stunning followed by neck-breaking.[24] But these are only guidelines. In Canada, pens are often a bit bigger, but they can also be smaller, since the conditions are all voluntary.

Industry spokesmen often dismiss critics by saying that these mink are not wild animals, that they are twice the size of the three-pound wild version, and much quieter, that they are quite healthy living permanently in the pens and that most of them wouldn't survive in the wild. Reports on their living conditions on fur farms vary. Critics say the genetic manipulations to produce some white mink or pastel varieties or blue have brought deformities – deafness for some, a twisted neck for others, a weak immune system in some cases – that make life that much more of a misery for the animal.

In Norway, where there is more fox-farming than mink-farming, the Department of Agriculture expressed concerns in 1994 that these animals, with limited domestication, were living in small cages with little stimulus and no outlet for their natural behaviour, no matter how healthy they might seem physically. As several European countries tightened the regulations on fox and mink farms, the European demand for mink coats dwindled. For major producing countries, like Finland, the primary export market is Hong Kong and South Korea, where animal welfare and animal rights groups make no trouble. In Finland, there was controversy over the use of hormones to create so-called super-foxes, animals with luxurious coats but debilitating health problems.

In 1998 the anti-fur crusade in Britain revved up once again, although there were only some fourteen mink farms left. The customers of a major furrier with an aristocratic clientele received hoax letters warning them that the shop had gone into bankruptcy and they had better remove their furs if they didn't want to see them destroyed. The fact that the customers' names were known seemed as upsetting as any danger to their furs. British activists dedicated themselves to filming the gassing of mink and capturing examples of cruelty that went to the courts. At the same time, raids and mink liberations continued, as did controversy about whether other wild animals were being hurt when swarms of hungry mink were let loose.

In the United States, ALF fur-farm raiders accusing farmers of keeping animals in filthy conditions, released thousands of mink in Wisconsin and burned a regional mink feed mill in that top mink state in August 1999. An ALF communiqué, relayed through the Canadian press office for the ALF, promised that "1999 will be a crippling year for this blood-soaked industry." In Finland in January 1999, a farmer shot and injured fleeing raiders. U.S. mink farmers had been adding guards, dogs, heavier fencing, and, in some states, even handier weapons to their operations since the 1991 burning of an Oregon State University mink research lab and mink food co-op.

On August 26, 1999, the *Chronicle-Herald* in Halifax reported that the RCMP and FBI were investigating reports that Nova Scotia fur farmers and a fur trader had received razor blades and veiled death threats in the mail. They got letters with warnings to get out of the business, the newspaper said. It quoted an unnamed mink farmer who said others in the business had agreed not to talk about the threats. It was a first for Atlantic Canada. In September the underground Justice Department issued a statement on the Internet about some one hundred razor-blade letters it said had been sent to fur farmers and others in the fur industry across North America during August. The letters carried a warning, according to the Internet statement, that the recipients had until autumn 2000 to get out of the business and release their animals. Attached was a long list of recipients, including seven "informers." Robyn Weiner's name was on that list, although she said no razor-blade letter had arrived in her mail.

The outlaws of the animal movement say they are convinced that nothing will change without illegal actions. In earlier years they hoped that the public would come to agree with them if they released information about the animals and the conditions they lived in. But, increasingly, activists argue that the people who profit from using animals are not open to persuasion, that their customers are increasingly in distant countries where animals have few champions to lobby for them, and that only an economic penalty will make a difference. Activists who have turned to illegal acts had no confidence that public support could be won and then translated into action that would help animals, except perhaps in the very long term.

Freeing animals from cages is one thing. Trying to put the cage owners out of business is another, as Judge Cusinato's worrying over the *Final Nail* publication illustrated. It is one thing to chide or even punish what you think are misguided idealists. But the protection of private property is a serious issue, and talk of economic sabotage smacks of revolution. The judge insisted that there are legal means to achieve change.

Will there be discussions of animal issues around a table, as the farmers suggest is the Canadian way? Will there be a legal means to achieve change, as the judge says? Consider the response of the research community to questions about how many animals they use and why. Think of the reaction in agriculture when one of the most conservative of animal groups in the country balked at endorsing how green antlers were to be sawed off the heads of deer and elk. Look at the reaction to criticisms of circuses or hunting practices, or at the timidity of the government's response to toughening up laws about cruelty to animals. The prospects seem slight.

Surely, if there is little real opening for significant changes on these issues there will no doubt be more activists like Gary Yourofsky – indeed, a generation of activists prepared to use legal routes if they are open, but not unwilling to take illegal detours around the barricades.

Postscript

Chic died on Good Friday, April 2, 1999.

She wasn't the only non-human friend of mine who ever died. Just a little more than a year before, beautiful Boots didn't survive a highway accident in Tennessee. But somehow, Chic's death was even sadder. At five, she was young to die. But the main problem was how little could be said about it.

Chic and her mate Leftie were from a pet store. For nearly five years, every morning had begun with a noisy routine of bread and games. Unlike their distant relatives, neither parakeet was ever going to be free in the hot wilds of Australia, nor could they have stayed alive there if they did have the chance.

Chic made much of the small life she had been allotted. She hatched eggs, and she and Leftie and their daughter Juni worked out a life for themselves. They spent certain parts of the day in flight around their room and on patrol along an indoor window ledge. They spent certain parts of the day on top of curtains, murmuring and dozing. They bathed and played and tossed vegetables around. When there were new slices of cucumber or green beans or bits of orange, Chic was first to investigate. Leftie had eyes only for her, following her lead even when he clearly wasn't sure he should.

Chic radiated her personality clearly, if differently than humans. She could convey anger or a desire to play. She did some things –

turning somersaults and swinging from ropes – just for the hell of it. And she chose, despite her companions, to pay attention to the humans around her. She wasn't merely reconciled to life among these aliens. She explored her world and accepted it. Chic would park on the monsters' glasses to smooth their eyebrows. She bopped noses, but not hard. She nibbled human lips gently with a beak that could shred wood. That humans were huge, potentially dangerous, and couldn't make bird sounds was simply how it was. After Chic died, Leftie nudged her side and tried to ruffle her neck feathers. Over time, he gamely took on the humans, edging himself closer to the big faces, hopping on and off the arms, buzzing the huge heads when they came into the room. He carried on with the odd human and budgie flock that was his life.

When Boots died, people understood the sadness in the death of a dog. Chic's death would mean little to them. Why? Birds aren't serious pets, for most people. They are less familiar, which distances them. Physically they are less like humans than cats or dogs are. They don't relate to humans in the same way. They don't show affectionate or loyal behaviour in the way that endears dogs or cats or horses to humans. Instead, their behaviour suggests that, however limited it might be, their life is something they own and their actions theirs to decide. Without the signs of a clear and beneficial relationship to humans, how is the loss of a bird's life to be felt?

Chic lived a circumscribed life. She was a house guest at a cottage one warm summer night and rode in a motor boat to get there. She often travelled by car. Even so, her life was nothing like the adventure such a bird would live naturally. Yet with only this limited life experience, Chic did something too few humans do. She crossed the species barrier, casually and voluntarily. So on that Easter weekend, what was gone was an open heart and a kindred spirit, a loss humans can understand once they recognize it.

Most humans are determined to believe that, after all, they are only human. *Only* can mean different things. When it means that we are able to recognize only ourselves and not ourselves in other species, it causes trouble – not for us humans, perhaps, but for everyone else, because humans rule the planet. Is it asking too much for humans to accept, instead, a different kind of *only* – that they are only one version of life on Earth?

Across the country a loosely knit political movement concerns itself with the relations between animals and humans. Some parts of the movement are odd, some parts irritating, and many parts visionary. To try to shut it out of the mainstream is a singular failure of the human heart. It is also futile.

This movement draws its adherents increasingly from the young, from a new generation of activists. The animal rights activists want people to look beyond the differences among species and see sentient, fellow creatures. In that, they want a revolution. But unlike their predecessors in the mythic Sixties, these activists are working in ungenerous times. While they believe humans are entirely capable of making that leap beyond themselves, the younger activists, at least, don't really expect that most people will. They expect to have to use the courts and to force politicians to change laws by showing they can cost them votes. Some of them believe they might have to go to jail. But they also believe that what they are after is as much an issue of social justice as were earlier fights for civil rights or women's rights.

They are people who are trying to make a difference, which is what everyone is told to do. They are young, like Troy Seidle of Waterloo, Ont., a recent science graduate, endangered species campaigner for the International Fund for Animal Welfare Canada, a director of the Canadian Federation of Humane Societies, and chair of its experimental animals committee. He was refusing to dissect frogs by Grade 7 and, in Grade 10, wanted to take up the issue with his astonished teacher. Or James Pearson, co-ordinator of People Acting for Animal Liberation, in Winnipeg, who looks like an academic and speaks in the full, grammatical sentences of a former English honours student. He decided to leave academia for the animal movement, "a social justice issue like any other, an oppressed or exploited group." That has meant working at whatever will pay the bills and accumulating a record with police for protest activities. It is, he says, "sometimes a bit difficult being me."

Their ranks include people who fit society's usual definition of respectable, like Barry Crozier, teacher at Parkview Education Centre in Bridgewater, N.S., and advisor to his school's animal rights group, Students for the Ethical Treatment of Animals. Members study issues, attend demonstrations, and take their convictions with them when they graduate. Bridgewater's Beth Mackenzie Kent, a middle-aged woman, can remember her first protest. It was in front of a fur shop. Her husband thought she was shopping, and, she says, "I was scared to death. I shook the entire way into Halifax and the entire way back." Ingrid Pollack, founder of the Vancouver Humane Society, battled to save turtles from being beheaded and sliced up, still alive, in local food markets. She talks about what happens if you behead cold-blooded creatures like turtles or snakes, tells how the head "lies there and feels the pain for about an hour. The eyes follow you around." She used to talk about different things, before 1979, when she was working for an airline. Then a flight attendant invited her to watch a film about testing cosmetics on animals, at a gathering rather like a Tupperware party. "For me, it was just like an evening at the Frankenstein Society," she says. "It changed my life."

The animal movement has in its ranks people with enough experience to make detailed proposals for what should change, for what governments and business and society could do. Their ideas vary from the more minor proposals that the animal welfare side would make to the more sweeping changes sought by the animal rights world, but they offer the makings of serious public policy. At the least, the self-policing approach to the use of animals would end.

There are some steps that could be taken. In agriculture, voluntary guidelines for the treatment of animals raised for food must be rewritten by people independent from the industry; then they should be turned into law, with real penalties and provision for on-farm inspections. The lead of other countries in outlawing unnatural confinement of animals – the radical development that has masqueraded as "normal practice" – could be followed. Conditions need to be policed throughout the system, from farm to abattoir. The pathetically lax approach to millions of deaths and injuries of animals in transport each year should not continue. As a start, an automatic inquiry system for unusually high death and injury rates among all transported animals – a system already worked out in theory – should be applied. The provision for buying your way out of charges should end, and the cases should be pursued as serious.

Canada is one of the few Western countries without national legislation to regulate the use of animals in research, where industry has been allowed to bully any critics. In its draft for a national standard and set of rules to guide xenotransplantation, the federal government has included the concept of a National Review Board. There is no reason why such a body should not assess and rule on the ethics of any use of animals in all research, rather than simply in clinical xenotransplant trials. It is not a radical step, compared to other countries, like Britain. In other countries, serious efforts are made to devise alternatives to the use of animals in research. In Britain the government made £259,000 (or more than half a million dollars) directly available for research into alternatives in 1998-99. If Canada were to ban the routine use of animals in research (and ban it outright in testing products), with an effective future date, there would be an incentive for alternatives to be found. The National Review Board could eventually review research proposals with the assumption that any use of animals would have to be justified as a special case. Medical research would not grind to a halt. It might cost more, but the pharmaceutical industry is among the most profitable on Earth. In the meantime, the excessive secrecy that the research world uses to shield itself from public view must be ended.

Given that Canadians clearly have ethical qualms about the dazzling new fields of research – genetic modification and xenotransplantation – the government should put definite legislative limits around what can be done to animals, even in small numbers and on an experimental level, until these concerns are translated into policy. The research world should be made to assume responsibility for the lives of animals it uses so that there is money provided to retire them. That could start with the monkeys the federal government houses in inadequate facilities in Ottawa.

Changes proposed in late 1999 to the Criminal Code of Canada to toughen penalties for cruelty to animals were far from radical. Politicians were simply following their interpretation of public attitudes. This part of Canadian law should not be left to the uneven enforcement and unpredictable funding of charities. At the least, the law should be enforced uniformly by special officers within police forces, where authority already exists. Many Humane Society investigators could easily make the switch to local police ranks. The move would show the courts that abuse of animals is taken seriously in more than the letter of the law. The message would be even less ambiguous if all treatment of animals, whether in agriculture or business or research, was specifically included. The trade in exotic animals – whose lives as pets are so often a misery – might be curbed by saying that, barring evidence to the contrary, keeping animals in conditions unsuitable for their natures amounts to cruelty. Since the premise of a law against cruelty is that the victim has feelings, the law should be made to clearly recognize the sentient, living status of animals and that they have interests apart from humans that must be considered.

The animal movement could provide any number of ideas for consideration. But first there has to be a recognition that these are matters of public policy – part of the political agenda – that deserve serious and continuing attention. An existing parliamentary committee could easily be given a mandate for regular examination of issues involving animals, as could standing committees of every provincial legislature. Failing that, there should at least be politicians who are willing to form the kind of non-partisan caucus that exists in Britain to provide an ongoing hearing to these issues. It is supposed to be the Canadian way, to sit around a table and talk things out.

● ● ●

Those are a few of the things that *could* happen. What are some of the things that are happening?

The Grey-Bruce Humane Society in Ontario did drop a reference to "stray" animals from its official mandate just before New Year's Day 2000. Gerry Weinberg continued his lawsuit against the Society.

On January 5, 2000, the first North American Animal Liberation Front raid of the year happened in the U.S. state of Washington, where twenty-three rabbits were taken from a breeding facility that supplied researchers. The ALF issued a communiqué announcing: "Lab raids are back, slaughterhouses are being firebombed, mink are running free. . . . A vegan insurrection is underway." ALF spokesperson David Barbarash issued a press statement from British Columbia, noting that, in twenty years of activities in North America, ALF has "remained completely non-violent, in that no humans or animals have been injured or killed."

Over the Christmas and New Year holidays, Gary Yourofsky placed a series of thirty-second commercials on television in Detroit. The ads showed animals dying in traps, being electrocuted, and suffering, with a voice-over message denouncing the fur industry. The ads were sponsored jointly by ADAPTT and the California-based In Defense of Animals. Yourofsky, who had been advised by a judge to find legal ways to achieve his goals, was ecstatic. Television stations had never before accepted such ads, he told his e-mail audience. "It was revolutionary." In early January he explained bitterly that the station, after receiving criticism from the fur industry, had decided it would never again run such commercials.

In January *the fifth estate* followed up on the British documentary it had carried in 1999. Filmmaker Graham Hall said that, after making the film attacking the ALF in Britain as violent, he was lured into an ambush, hooded, abducted, and painfully branded across his back with the letters ALF. Robin Webb, the ALF spokesperson in London who had borne the brunt of Hall's accusations in the documentary, told the BBC that the attack on Hall had nothing to do with the ALF. Webb suggested that many people might have a grudge against Hall and repeated his assertion that Hall had taken his words out of context in the film. That, said Webb, is why he had no fear of prosecution after the film was aired.

Francine Pelletier, host of *the fifth estate* segment, noted that no charges had been laid by British police after Hall turned in his documentary tapes to them. "The British police have refused to offer further explanation," she told the TV audience in what seemed a dark hint at police failure rather than any questioning of Hall's work. She linked the British event to the attack on Tom McLellan's mink farm in Chatham, making no mention of the arrests in the Ontario case. She quoted the mink farmer as saying there was a "lack of legal restraints on animal extremists" that will lead to more violence.

From Britain also came news reports suggesting that the government would ban the puppy farms that provided animals to research labs, a prospect that left animal rights activists dissatisfied. They wanted the government to live up to a campaign pledge to institute more sweeping limits to animal testing.

Just before New Year's Day, the Japanese Diet made laws providing new fines and possible jail terms for cruelty to pets. The Korean government abandoned a bill that would have legalized dog meat sales. Acting Russian President Vladimir Putin vetoed a bill on cruelty to pets that would have banned eating them, saying other laws already dealt with cruelty.

In the United States, President Bill Clinton approved the use of a new "dolphin-safe" label for tuna that would apply even to fish caught by using the big, encircling nets blamed in the past for killing some hundred thousand dolphins a year. This weakening of standards for the use of the label followed a World Trade Organization ruling against U.S. law. WTO rulings or even the prospect of negative rulings are being used to challenge laws that protect animals, Cathy Liss of the Animal Welfare Institute wrote in a letter to the *New Scientist*'s Internet Web site in late December. Animal activists are worried that similar challenges could be brought against European laws against battery cages for hens or crates for veal calves, she said.

In early January 2000, primate experts issued a warning that twenty-five species of monkeys, apes, gibbons, lemurs, and other primates could soon be extinct. "As we enter the new millennium, we risk losing our closest living relatives in the animal kingdom," Russell Mittermeier, president of Conservation International, said in Washington, D.C.

In Ottawa the federal government gathered input to its draft for rules on xenotransplantation, the science expected to solve the shortage of organs for transplant. The draft struggled, posing questions that were supposed to be up for debate with assertions that seemed to close off debate. The benefit to humans of using animals in this way, the draft said, must be weighed against the ethics of using any animal species for the benefit of another species. But, it said of the pig, "There is no evidence that it shares capacities with human beings to the extent that primates do. As such the adverse effects suffered by the pigs used to supply organs for xenotransplantation would not outweigh the potential benefits to human beings." Having neatly disposed of the whole issue, it then pretended those questions were still open: "This transfer between species still raises fundamental issues of who we are and where we are on the evolutionary scale."

This, surely, is an acknowledgement that issues involving animals are both important and political. The problem doesn't seem to be in asking who we are in relation to other species. Rather, it is in allowing answers to be heard.

Notes

INTRODUCTION

1. Jeremy Rifkin, *The Biotech Century* (New York: Penguin Putnam, 1998), p.103.
2. Ibid., pp.198-202.
3. Amy Blount Achor, *Animal Rights – A Beginner's Guide: A Handbook of Issues, Organizations, Actions and Resources* (Yellow Springs, Ohio: WriteWare, 1996), pp.96, 97.
4. Corbin Andrews, "Message to Alien Life Contains Errors," *National Post* (Toronto), June 23, 1999.
5. Interview with Lesli Bisgould, Toronto, Feb. 18, 1999.
6. Interview with Clayton Ruby, Toronto, May 12, 1999.
7. Alan Herscovici, "The Rise and Fall of Animal Rights: Holding Activists Accountable," an essay available on the Fur Council of Canada's Web site <www.furcouncil.ca>. Herscovici is the author of *Second Nature: The Animal-Rights Controversy* (Toronto: Stoddart Publishing, 1991).
8. Karen Davis, of United Poultry Concerns, speech to the Seventh Annual International Animal Rights Symposium, Washington, D.C., July 10, 1994.
9. David Selby, *EARTHKIND: A Teachers' Handbook on Humane Education* (Staffordshire, Eng.: Trentham Books, 1995). Selby is also an editor of a new book, *Weaving Connections: Educating for Peace, Social and Environmental Justice* (Toronto: Sumach Press, 2000). In a conversation, Aug. 6, 1999, Selby discussed the reaction to the magazine article based on his humane education handbook.
10. Peter Singer, *Animal Liberation* (New York: New York Review/Random House, 1990), pp.6, 224. The point about "portraying animal advocates as

sentimental animal-lovers" is from the 1975 edition, p.1. In 1999 Singer was still controversial. He was appointed to a chair in bioethics at Princeton University. In the uproar that followed – largely because of Singer's views on euthanasia – Princeton trustee and former Republican presidential candidate Steve Forbes wanted him fired. For a good account of this, see James Bandler, "Furor Follows Princeton Philosopher," *The Boston Globe*, July 27, 1999.

11. Peter Singer and Paola Cavalieri, eds., *The Great Ape Project: Equality beyond Humanity* (London: Fourth Estate, 1993). Details on this book and others on the subject as well as more information on the international efforts to enshrine rights for apes can be found at the Great Ape Project's Web site <www.greatapeproject.org>.

12. Dr. Bernard E. Rollin, professor of philosophy (and physiology and bio-physics), Colorado State University, "Ethical Use of Animals: Law and Morality," speech to the Canadian Association for Laboratory Animal Science (CALAS) Ethics Forum, Montreal, June 9, 1997; and Ruth Harrison, *Animal Machines* (London: Vincent Stuart Publishing, 1964).

13. Gary L. Francione, *Animals, Property and the Law* (Philadelphia: Temple University Press, 1995), p.29.

14. Jeremy Bentham, *Introduction to the Principles of Morals and Legislation* (1789), quoted in Rod Preece and Lorna Chamberlain, *Animal Welfare and Human Values* (Waterloo, Ont.: Wilfrid Laurier University Press, 1995), pp.30-31. The Preece and Chamberlain study is one of the few Canadian books on animal rights and animal welfare, and it provides a historical look at some issues from a deliberately middle-of-the-road view.

CHAPTER ONE. THE OUTLAWS

1. Rick Ouston, "Activists' 'Secret' Lives Probed," *The Vancouver Sun*, March 30, 1998.

2. Thomas Claridge, "Judge Rejects Prison for Animal Rightists Who Broke Windows," *The Globe and Mail* (Toronto), Dec. 23, 1988.

3. Interview with David Barbarash, Vancouver, Nov. 14, 1998.

4. Interview with Darren Thurston, Vancouver, April 16, 1999.

5. Dr. David Neil, quoted in Randy Boswell, "Expect Animal-Rights Terrorism, Activist Says," *The Ottawa Citizen*, Nov. 27, 1997. The article also quotes Neil as saying that Canada needs strict safeguards to prevent abuses of animals in testing, or radical animal rights activists will "blow things up." He called for legislation and monitoring of labs, adding: "If the average civilized Canadian realized that we are one of the few countries in the developed world where the animals outside the university setting have

no protection and if they realized what can potentially happen to those animals, they would not be happy."

6. Canadian Press, "Terrorists Blamed for Theft of 29 Cats, Kennel Damage," *The Vancouver Sun*, June 3, 1992. The following point about the criticism of the Alberta Society for the Prevention of Cruelty to Animals is from the same source.

7. Telephone interview with Eric Donnelly of Bear Watch, Vancouver, June 4, 1999.

8. Robert Matas, "RCMP Probe Animal-Rights Vandals in B.C.," *The Globe and Mail*, July 12, 1995.

9. Kim Bolan, "Bomb Links Target to Nazi Experiments," *The Vancouver Sun*, July 27, 1995.

10. Diane Rinehart, "2 Activists from B.C. Sought in Death Plots," *The Vancouver Sun*, June 6, 1992.

11. Interview with John Thompson, Toronto, Dec. 8, 1998.

12. Rinehart, "2 Activists from B.C. Sought."

13. Interview with David Barbarash on CBC-Newsworld, *Big Life*, April 28, 1999.

14. G. Davidson (Tim) Smith, "Commentary No. 21," April 1992, CSIS Web site.

15. G. Davidson (Tim) Smith, "Commentary No. 74," Winter 1998, CSIS Web site.

16. Jim Bronskill, "Spy Agency Watching Anti-racists," *National Post*. June 9, 1999.

17. *Animal Liberation Front Primer*, 2nd ed., undated.

CHAPTER TWO. POLITE COMPANY

1. "B.C. SPCA History Book," draft, Vancouver, April 1998, a centennial project provided by the SPCA. I am indebted to this lively little book for historical references.

2. Toronto Humane Society, brochure; also, John Kelso, *Early History of the Humane and Children's Aid Movement in Ontario*, (Toronto: William Briggs, 1911). The history of the battles over vivisection in both England and the United States are recounted in engrossing detail in Susan Sperling, *Animal Liberators: Research and Morality* (Berkeley: University of California Press, 1988).

3. Provincial court proceedings, Owen Sound, Ont., Dec. 14, 1998.

4. Interviews with Alison Folkes, late 1998 and early 1999. Other Humane Society members were also helpful.

5. Interview with Frank Green, Chesley, Ont., March 31, 1999.

6. One of a series of conversation with Gerry Weinberg, Meaford, Ont., Feb. 1, 1999.

7. Interview with Victoria Earle, Newmarket, Ont., June 1, 1999.

8. *Sun Times* (Owen Sound), April 5, 1999.

9. Letter from Nick Hedley, legal counsel, Charitable Property Division, Office of the Public Guardian and Trustee, to David Lovell, Grey-Bruce Humane Society lawyer, Owen Sound, July 19, 1999.

10. Letter from Hedley to Lovell, July 19, 1999; and Don Crosby, "Weinbergs, Humane Society Hearing Stalls," *Sun Times*, July 21, 1999.

11. Interview with Judy Stone, Vancouver, Nov. 13, 1998.

12. Interview with Tom Hughes, Jan. 19, 1999.

13. Donn Downey, "Humane Society President to Retire in Wake of Criticism," *The Globe and Mail*, Oct. 23, 1987.

14. Joseph Hall, "Humane Society Attempts to Block New Animal Group", *The Toronto Star*, Dec. 2, 1988; Mark Bourrie, "Shelter Wants Curbs on Powers of Ontario Humane Society," *The Globe and Mail*, Dec. 23, 1988.

15. Letter from Tom Hughes to a Beeton, Ont., woman on Dec. 29, 1988.

16. Interview with Barry Kent MacKay, Richmond Hill, Ont., Aug. 18, 1998.

17. Danielle Crittenden, "Agony before Death," *The Toronto Sun*, Oct. 17, 1982.

18. Kathryn May, "Chief Vet Attacks Humane Society," *The Toronto Star*, Sept. 17, 1983.

19. Memo from Holly Flegg to the Toronto Humane Society Board, March 19, 1984.

20. Interview with Barry Kent MacKay, Aug. 18, 1998.

21. Interview with Stephanie Brown, Toronto, Sept. 10, 1998.

22. Ian Harvey, "Activists Leash THS," *The Toronto Sun*, Nov. 13, 1986.

23. Interview with Vicky Miller, Toronto, Sept. 28, 1998.

24. James Gray, "Strikers End Fast but Baboon Still Caged," *The Toronto Star*, Nov. 18, 1984.

25. Lynne Thomas, "The Plight of B43," *The Globe and Mail*, Nov. 10, 1984.

26. Toronto Humane Society, *Our First Concern: The Animals*, March 1986.

27. Letter from Robert Hambley to Ontario Attorney General Ian Scott, Nov. 11, 1986.

28. Interview with Holly Penfound, Toronto, Nov. 25, 1998.

29. "THS Fires 4 Activist Staffers," *The Toronto Sun*, June 1, 1990; and "Humane Society Fires Four after Board Fight," *The Toronto Star*, June 1, 1990.

30. Letter from Howard Levitt to Barry Kent MacKay, March 27, 1991.

31. Barry Kent MacKay letter to Barb Caplan, Toronto City Council Clerk, Feb. 9, 1996.

32. Interview with Jack Slibar, Toronto, Oct. 5, 1998.

33. Reports in *Kitchener–Waterloo Record*, September 1991.

34. Interview with Victoria Earle, Newmarket, Ont., June 1, 1999.

35. Interview with Catherine Ens, St. Catharines, Ont., Feb. 10, 1999.

36. *The Standard* (St. Catharines, Ont.), March 10, 1989, plus other reports in the same paper.
37. "Land Deal Threatens HS Grants," *The Standard*, Jan. 10, 1990.
38. Lee Hewitt, Not Just a Dog Catcher," *The Standard*, Aug. 31, 1996.
39. Interview with Michael O'Sullivan, August 1999.
40. Interview with Danielle Divincenzo, ARK 11, Toronto, April 22, 1996.
41. Interview with Frances Rodenburg, Ottawa, Oct. 19, 1998. She later resigned from her job as executive director of the Canadian Federation of Humane Societies.
42. Interview with Retired Brig.-Gen. Chris Snider, Ottawa, Oct. 16, 1998.
43. Interview with Stephanie Brown, Toronto, Oct. 5, 1998.
44. Interview with Stephen Huddart, Vancouver, June 2, 1998.
45. Interview with Cathy Thomas, Calgary, Nov. 9, 1998.
46. Interviews with James Pearson and Vicky Burns, Winnipeg, June 8, 1998.
47. See Sperling, *Animal Liberators*.

CHAPTER THREE. RESEARCH: KEEPING HUMANS ALIVE
1. Interview with Pat Milke, during visit to Health Science Laboratory Animal Services, University of Alberta, Edmonton, Nov. 12, 1998.
2. John McArdle (AVVS science advisor, American Anti-vivisection Society), "Rodent Research: Relevant or Ridiculous," *AV Magazine*, Spring 1998.
3. Canadian Council on Animal Care (CCAC), *Trends in Experimental Use of Common Laboratory Species in Canada*, Annual Utilization Survey, Table III, Ottawa, 1996.
4. News briefs, *New Scientist Magazine*, on-line edition, July 31, 1999.
5. "More Tests on Animals Despite Labour's Poll Pledge," *The Electronic Telegraph* 1059 (April 19, 1998); see also "GM Mammals Used by Researchers Rise to 95,000," *The Electronic Telegraph* 1520 (July 24, 1999).
6. Hank Daniszewski, "UWO Pioneers Animal Transplant," *The London Free Press*, July 8, 1998.
7. Margaret Munro, "Cultivating Body Parts," *National Post*, April 6, 1999; and Stephanie Brown, "Why Animal Organ Transplants Hold Catastrophic Health Risks," *The Ottawa Citizen*, Nov. 13, 1999.
8. Martha Groves, "Transgenic Livestock May Become Biotech's Cash Cow," *Los Angeles Times*, May 1, 1997.
9. Massachusetts SPCA/American Humane Education Society, "Genetic Engineering: A Look at the Welfare of Animals in Biotechnology Research," paper, Boston Center for Laboratory Animal Welfare, undated.
10. Reports on biotech profits, Reuters, March 3, 1998.
11. Groves, "Transgenic Livestock."
12. CBC-TV, "Willow the Goat," *Country Canada*, Jan. 27, 1999.

13. Jill Howard Church, "The Business of Animal Research," *The Animals' Agenda*, July/August 1997, pp.30-32.

14. Interview with Denna Benn, Guelph, Ont., Oct. 27, 1998.

15. Gary Francione, *Rain without Thunder: The Ideology of the Animal Rights Movement* (Philadelphia: Temple University Press, 1996), p.21.

16. Obituary for Henry Spira, *The New York Times*, Sept. 15, 1998.

17. Francione, *Rain without Thunder*, pp.22, 23; also, Achor, *Animal Rights*, pp.96, 97. See also Ingrid Newkirk, *Free the Animals!* (Chicago: Noble Press, 1992), pp.12-34.

18. Francione, *Rain without Thunder*, p.24.

19. Mark Nusca, "Stolen Monkey Carries Deadly Virus," *The London Free Press*, Jan. 2, 1985.

20. Telephone interview with George Harapa, Toronto, March 12, 1999.

21. Interview with professors David Fraser and Dan Weary, Vancouver, June 4, 1998.

22. Rollin, "Ethical Use of Animals: Law and Morality."

23. CCAC, *Trends in Experimental Use of Common Laboratory Species in Canada*.

24. CCAC, *Guidelines on Animal Use Protocol*, Ottawa, 1992. The CCAC's Web site offers information about its role and procedures.

25. Interview with Brig.- Gen. (retired) Chris Snider, Ottawa, Oct. 16, 1998.

26. Interview with Stephanie Brown, Toronto, Oct. 5, 1998.

27. Telephone interview with Dr. Bill Holley, Peterborough, Ont., Aug. 3, 1999.

28. Stephanie Brown, "How the Public Views the Effectiveness of the Canadian System," speech to the Canadian Association for Laboratory Animal Science (CALAS) Ethics Forum, Montreal, June 9, 1997.

29. Interview with Gilly Griffin, Ottawa, Oct. 15, 1998.

30. David H. Neil, "Surveillance of the Use of Animals in Research, Testing and Teaching: The Effectiveness of the Canadian System," speech to the Canadian Association for Laboratory Animal Science (CALAS) Ethics Forum, Montreal, June 9, 1997.

31. "Creature Comfort in the Lab," *University Affairs* (Association of Universities and Colleges of Canada), February 1999. The CCAC also has many descriptions of its role and mandate on its Web site.

32. "Monkey Housing Inhumane at PHB," *Caring for Animals* (Canadian Federation of Humane Societies newsletter) 4, 2 (Fall 1987), p.1.

33. *Resource* (CCAC newsletter) 14, 1 (Fall-Winter 1989), pp.1, 4.

34. Health Canada information officers, answers relayed from bureaucrats to questions.

35. "Allan Rock Comments on the Monkey Colony," *Caring for Animals* 15,1 (Summer 1999).

36. Interview with James Wong, Ottawa, Oct. 15, 1998.

37. Cheryl Harris, "Coultson Readies Response to NIH Probe," *Daily News* (Alamagordo, New Mexico), on-line edition, March 17, 1999. In Defense of Animals' Web site posted information as of July 1999 at <www.idausa.org/spinal>.

38. John Barnes, "Offences against Animals," unpublished paper, Substantive Criminal Law Project, Law Reform Commission of Canada, Ottawa, October 1985, p.36. A good guide to the Animals (Scientific Procedures) Act 1986 is provided on the British government's Web site at <www.homeoffice.gov.uk/ccpd/dguide.htm>. The law also allows for unannounced inspections.

39. Abi Berger, science editor, "Animal Tests Rise in Great Britain," *British Medical Journal*, Aug. 14, 1999, pp.319-402. The *Bulletin of the European Union* reported on the European Parliament's regret at the lack of progress in finding alternatives to animal tests on its Web site <europa.eu.int/abc/doc/off/bull/en>.

40. Britain, Secretary of State, *1997 Report of the Animal Procedures Committee*, presented to the British Parliament in November 1998 (London: The Stationery Office, 1998).

41. Letter from Dr. Miles Johnston, Toronto, Jan. 4, 1999.

42. Resumé of CCAC Activities, April 1980-81, presented by CCAC to the Association of Universities and Colleges of Canada.

43. Annual Report of the CCAC, 1986.

44. Sam Revusky, *Battles with the Canadian Council on Animal Care: A Memoir* (St. John's, Nfld.: Yksuver Publishing, 1997).

45. Ontario Ministry of Agriculture, Food and Rural Affairs, Toronto, data provided Jan. 27, 1999.

46. Information and Privacy Commissioner of Ontario, Order P-1537, March 4, 1998, p.4.

47. Information and Privacy Commissioner of Ontario, Order P-557, Oct. 20, 1993, p.6.

48. Interview with Dr. George Harapa, Toronto, March 12, 1999.

49. *Caring for Animals* 15,1 (Summer 1999), p.7.

50. Thomas Walkom, "NDP in No Rush to Ban Animal Testing for Cosmetics, *The Toronto Star*, Feb. 28, 1995.

51. Philip Johnston, "Britain Ends Animals Cosmetics Tests," *The Electronic Telegraph* 1271 (Nov. 17, 1998).

52. Letter from Cy Wilding, Vice-president of Government Relations of the Cosmetics, Toiletry and Fragrance Association, to an Ontario MPP, July 12, 1994.

53. Derek Baldwin, "Ontario Set to Prohibit Animal Tests for Cosmetics," *The Toronto Star*, March 29, 1993.

54. Letter from Premier Bob Rae to Andrea Maenza, May 9, 1994; and letter from Agriculture Minister Elmer Buchanan to Andrea Maenza, June 27, 1994.

55. Paul Recer, "Saccharin No Longer Considered Carcinogenic," Associated Press, May 15, 2000. Britain, like the Netherlands, disallows the general use of animals in the production of antibodies, with some exceptions, because alternatives are widely available. Producing antibodies in the bodies of animals is a common procedure in lab work, and it causes pain. Even the non-binding guidelines of Canada's CCAC do not urge such restrictions. While the CCAC was able to spring into action when it received a handful of letters urging it to insist on alternatives – staff were called in to deal with the crisis of criticism – the agency has taken a more unhurried approach to the content of the issue. A committee is to consider it.

56. Lois Rogers, "Cloning Research Hits Setback," *The Toronto Star*, May, 15, 2000; reprinted from *The London Sunday Times*.

57. Carolyn Abraham, "Donor Organ Pigs Not Inspected by Health Canada," *The Globe and Mail*, Feb. 13, 1999.

58. Margaret Somerville, "Care and Caution towards Pharming Animals" (op-ed article), *The Globe and Mail*, March 1, 1999.

59. Health Canada's Web site provided access to the "Proposed Canadian Standard for Xenotransplantation," at <www.hc-sc.gc.ca/hpb-dgps/therapeut/zfiles/btox/standards/xeno>.

60. Brown, "Why Animal Organ Transplants Hold Catastrophic Health Risks."

CHAPTER FOUR. AGRICULTURE: KEEPING HUMANS FED

1. Interview with Ian Duncan, Guelph, Ont., June 7, 1999.

2. A.M. Phipps, L.R. Matthews, and G.A. Verker, "Tail Docked Dairy Cattle: Fly Induced Behaviour and Adrenal Responsiveness to ACTH," paper presented to the New Zealand Society of Animal Production, 1995; and Lindsay Matthews et al., "The Effects of Taildocking and Trimming on Milker Comfort and Dairy Cattle Health, Welfare and Production," executive summary of a report, August 1995. Both were kindly supplied by AgResearch, Ruakura Research Centre, New Zealand Pastoral Agricultural Research Institute Ltd., Hamilton, New Zealand. Skepticism about the value of tail-docking had been raised in Canada as well at the Western College of Veterinarian Medicine, University of Saskatchewan, in 1994. In a paper delivered to a dairy seminar, research professor and herd medicine specialist Joseph M. Stookey said it was hard to believe that tail-docking was necessary, given that everyone had got on without it for so long. In

New Zealand there was no proof that the spread of leptospirosis, a disease that could be passed from urine-soaked tails, had been affected by tail-docking. The United Kingdom, Germany, Sweden, and Norway had all decided to prohibit tail-docking of cattle as a general rule, Stookey said. Clean barns, cleaner tails, or more adequate bedding were all sensible alternatives and "less invasive than renovating the cow!" Stookey said. "The dairy industry cannot expect to improve its image in the eyes of the general public by engaging in such a procedure." Joseph M. Stookey, "Is Intensive Dairy Production Compatible with Animal Welfare?" in *Advances in Dairy Technology: Proceedings of the 1994 Western Dairy Canadian Dairy Seminar*, vol. 6, pp.209-19.

3. This involved an experiment that made it necessary for hens to take deliberate action to get out to dust-bathe, raising a little weighted door. That part was working. But as if to confound Duncan, the hens wouldn't necessarily dust-bathe once they went to the trouble of getting to the nice little dusty spot, even if it was one they had used with apparent pleasure before. Were the conditions – sun and temperature – not just right? Was it maybe important just to go through the routine that had produced pleasure for the hen even if it didn't involve the original purpose, the way an excited dog will sometimes race back down a lane after getting out of a vehicle and make the arrival a second time, the way a human will revisit a site that has pleasant memories of an earlier time?

4. Sonya Dakers, *Animal Rights Campaigns: Their Impact in Canada*, Science and Technology Division, Research Branch, Library of Parliament, Ottawa, revised 1990, p.13., warned farmers to prepare for the "anticipated onslaught by animal rights groups."

5. Harrison, *Animal Machines*.

6. Interview at Bruce Weber's farm, June 30, 1999.

7. Rollin, "Ethical Use of Animals: Law and Morality."

8. Bernard E. Rollin, *Farm Animal Welfare* (Ames: Iowa State University Press, 1995), p.138.

9. "Farm Animal Welfare in the 1990s," proceedings of a symposium sponsored by the Alberta Institute of Agrologists, Edmonton Branch, Oct. 19, 1990, in National Library, Ottawa.

10. Interview with John Youngman, Winnipeg, June 10, 1998.

11. Interview with Vicki Burns, Winnipeg, June 8, 1998.

12. The two reports, by M.H. Anil, J.K. McKinstry, M. Field, and R.G. Rodway, appeared in *Animal Welfare* 5 (1996), pp.435-41 and 6 (1996), pp.3-8. This journal is a publication of the Universities Federation for Animal Welfare, England.

13. Interview with Frances Rodenburg, Nepean, Ont., October 1998.

14. Scientists at Lethbridge Research Centre, searching for better ways to figure out how stressful various procedures are for animals, have reported that castration causes "significant distress" in lambs for at least twenty-four hours after the procedure. They measure changes in hormones, a process considered more exact than simply looking at animals to decide if they are upset. Other studies had already documented distress from tail-docking on lambs aged two to six weeks. Isolation is also stressful – according to science.

15. The sheep code is issued by the Canadian Agri-Food Research Council, Ottawa. Other codes are also available from this agency, or from the Canadian Federation of Humane Societies, Nepean, Ont.

16. Jennifer Greenbaum, "What's Wrong with Wool," *Mainstream* 27,4 (Winter 1996).

17. Interview with Mike Cooper, Cambridge, Ont., June 30, 1999.

18. Interview with Dr. Laurie Connor, Winnipeg, June 9, 1998.

19. Interview with Ted Muir, Winnipeg, June 10, 1998.

20. Interview with professors David Fraser and Dan Weary, Vancouver, June 4, 1998. The animal welfare program they head is billed as a way of finding consensus about the use of animals in food, research, entertainment, and companionship. Both professors are cross-appointed to U.B.C.'s Centre for Applied Ethics.

21. Catherine Brown, "Getting Sows out of Stalls," *Ontario Hog Farmer*, February/March 1999, p.40.

22. Bob Hunsberger allowed me to visit his farm near Waterloo, Ont., June 30, 1999.

23. *Rescue* (B.C. SPCA), Winter 1996-97, pp.8-9.

24. *Egg Industry* 102,8 (August 1997).

25. Interview with Temple Grandin, Toronto, Nov. 4, 1998.

26. Brad Evenson, "The Horse Rescuer," *National Post*, April 12, 1999. B.C. doctor Ray Kellosalmi won a permanent spot in the hearts of animal activists across the country for his outspoken opposition to the treatment of the mares and foals, for his promotion of alternative, plant-based drugs to Premarin, and for his purchase of foals at auctions to keep them from slaughter. The North American Equine Ranching Information Council Web site, with its defence of the PMU industry, could be found at <www.naeric.org/faqs.htm> in summer 1999.

27. Interview with Tom Hughes, Aug. 12, 1999.

28. Jim Romahn, "Meat Auditors Watch for Black Market," *Ontario Farmer*, July 13, 1999.

29. Canadian Food Inspection Agency, statement, Ottawa, May 29, 1998, presented as background to *Spent Laying Hen Transportation Survey*.

30. Canadian Food Inspection Agency data, *Selected Species Found Dead at Registered Canadian Establishments*, by year, provided through an access to information request.

31. Interview with Gord Doonan, Humane Transportation Program, Canadian Food Inspection Agency, Ottawa, July 28, 1999.

32. "Chicken Victory – Canadian Style," *Canadians for the Ethical Treatment of Food Animals (CETFA) Newsletter* 26 (Fall 1997); and "Food Animals," *Animal Alliance of Canada Newsletter* 1,2 (July 8, 1998).

33. All of the trucker's comments are from the interview published as *The Last Ride*, a forty-one-page booklet printed by Canadians for the Ethical Treatment of Food Animals, Vancouver. The booklet is a transcript of the anonymous trucker's answers to questions from Vancouver documentary filmmaker Jennifer Abbott of Flying Eye Productions, Vancouver, after Harrison arranged for them to meet in August 1996. The meeting, arranged by the organization, was part of a cross-Canada trip by the filmmaker as she prepared the documentary *A Cow at My Table*.

34. Laura Eggertson, " 'Approved' Meat Went Unchecked," *The Toronto Star*, June 23, 1999; and Laura Eggertson, "Meat Inspectors Supervised," *The Toronto Star*, June 24, 1999.

35. Interview with Dr. Jacques Caron, Hull, Que., June 30, 1999.

36. Memo from G. Roy Kelly, veterinarian in charge of "Est 92C," to Dr. Moosa, Regional Veterinary Supervisor, Food Production and Inspection Branch, New Westminster, B.C., Dec. 19, 1993. No identification of the facility other than the number is given in the document released by the Canadian Food Inspection Agency under an access to information request.

37. Memorandum to Dr. C. Enwani, Manager, Meat Products, B.C. Region, from Dr. C. Boissonneault, Chief, Regulations and Procedures, Meat and Poultry Products Division, Jan. 20, 1994, provided through an access to information request from the Canadian Food Inspection Agency.

38. Temple Grandin, "Handling and Stunning Practices in Canadian Meat Packing Plants," report for Agriculture Canada, CFHS, Canadian Meat Council, and Canadian Poultry and Egg Processors Council, June 30, 1995, p.16. Grandin applauded the method of gathering and loading chickens at one farm she visited, saying it greatly reduced the industry-wide problem with dead and injured birds. Key to this one farm's accomplishment was the use of a new kind of truck that carried fewer birds and used a system of drawers and a forklift so that the birds did not need to be stuffed through small doors into cages or yanked out of them, actions involved during catching the birds on the farm for loading and removing them at the plant so they can be hung upside down. For spent hens, already fragile from non-stop egg-laying and lack of exercise, this would make an important difference.

39. Interview with Temple Grandin, Toronto, Nov. 4, 1998.

40. "Review of Humane Handling and Slaughter in Canadian Registered Establishments," memorandum to the Minister of Agriculture, Dec. 21, 1995, provided by CFIA under access to information legislation. In early January 1996 the procedure was replaced by a more acceptable one after the Alberta Society for the Prevention of Cruelty to Animals raised objections with the province.

41. Poultry Industry Council, Web site at <www.easynet.ca/~pic/factmenu.html>, fact sheet no. 62, February 1995.

42. Information from Jennifer Abbott, Vancouver, June 5, 1998.

43. In one ironic development in southwestern Ontario, where large hog farms had blossomed, two farmers won a reduction in their tax assessment because they lived beside a big hog farm. They argued that their properties had lost value thanks largely to the odours produced next door. While municipalities might lose revenues if these sort of appeals caught on, they have little control over whether large livestock operations can be established. For a report on this issue, see Patrick Gallagher, "Hog Smell Equals Lower Residential Tax Bill for Kent Farmers," *Ontario Farmer*, Sept. 8, 1998.

44. Orville Schell, *Modern Meat* (New York: Random House, 1984), offers a good history and fascinating tour through the U.S. farm world. He provides a shocking reminder of the careless way in which the synthetic hormone DES (diethylstilbestrol) was used and abused as a growth promoter from 1950 to a 1979 U.S. ban, of its harmful impact, and of how casual the industry was with other drugs, on p.107.

45. Garry Fairbairn, *Canada Choice: Economic, Health and Moral Issues in Food from Animals*, a study commissioned and published by the Agricultural Institute of Canada, Ottawa, 1989, p.65.

46. For some of these research reports, see *New England Journal of Medicine*, May 20, 1999, including leading author Kirk Smith, a Minnesota epidemiologist. An earlier study in *New England Journal of Medicine* 337 (1997), p.1158, found similar evidence on Dutch turkey farms. See also related work by Dr. George Khachatourians of the University of Saskatchewan in *Canadian Medical Association Journal*, Nov. 3, 1998.

47. Note to "Dear Stakeholder" from Rebecca Irwin, co-ordinator of the Food Programme Antimicrobial Resistance Project, July 24, 1998; the note went to those who took part in the June 10, 1998, workshop attended by sixty people and "facilitated" by a company called INTERSOL.

48. *New Scientist*, Dec. 6, 1997, p.5; and Christine Middap, "Animal Feed Drugs Breed Super Germs," *Queensland Courier Mail*, Aug. 1, 1999. Avoparcin is not approved for use in Canada.

49. Interview with David Fraser, Vancouver, June 4, 1998.
50. Interview with Tom Hughes, Newmarket, Ont., Jan. 19, 1999.
51. Yanne Boloh, "France's 'Red Label' Chickens," *Broiler Industry* (U.S.), March 1999, pp.34-38.
52. Esther Klein, speech to farmers at Agriculture Day, March 6, 1991, Morrisburg, Ont., sponsored by the South Dundas Economic Development Commission of Morrisburg.

CHAPTER FIVE. EXTREME AGRICULTURE

1. Rob Dunham, speaking to the Ontario Deer and Elk Farmers Association (ODEFA) convention, Guelph, Ont., March 13 1999.
2. Figures from the Alberta, Department of Agriculture, Web site, 1999. They were attributed to the Alberta Venison Council.
3. Figures from the Alberta, Department of Agriculture, Web site on elk, as of summer 1999.
4. Dr. Jeong Sim, Department of Agriculture, Food and Nutritional Science, University of Alberta, Edmonton, speaking to the ODEFA convention, Guelph, Ont., March 13, 1999.
5. Telephone interview with Cathy Lauritsen, Regina Humane Society, Regina, Aug. 25, 1999. The Saskatchewan hunt ranches with Web sites play up the ease of hunting on private property with no licences necessary and all arrangements made.
6. The Boone and Crockett Club was formed in 1887 by Theodore Roosevelt and some of his cronies who loved big game hunting, including Gifford Pichot, the first head of the U.S. Forest Service and the man credited with coining the word "conservation." The club, based in Missoula, Montana, is famous for its Rules of Fair Chase, which are supposed to encourage ethical hunting practices. The Club explains all this on its Web site.
7. Reports from Associated Press, July 1999, plus information from a New Mexico Web site on hunting, at <hunts.net/ek42ha.html>, posted as of March 15, 1999.
8. *Alberta Report*, March 22, 1999, pp.22, 23.
9. Canadian Wildlife Federation, *Game Farming in Canada: A Threat to Native Wildlife and Its Habitat*, booklet, Ottawa, 1992.
10. Bruce Masterman, "Major City Poaching Ring Busted," *Calgary Herald*, Dec. 18, 1998.
11. "We guarantee a successful hunt," Big Shot Hunting Preserve, Wynyard, Sask., told its potential customers. The Preserve, in the central part of the province, offers elk hunting packages that start at $5,000. Elk Horn Ranch in the northwest, at Maidston, offers wild boar hunts at $500, fallow deer at $1,500, elk at $4,900, and buffalo at $2,700 (all in U.S. dollars). There are

added fees, into the thousands, for the biggest trophy animals. The Big Shot Hunting Preserve's Web site is at <www.quill-lakes.com/wynyard/bigshot/> and Elk Horn Ranch at <www.ameri-cana.com/saskelk.htm>. Most of these businesses seem to be aimed at the U.S. market.

12. Tom Blackwell, "Ottawa Orders 500 Elk Killed after Outbreak of Tuberculosis," *National Post*, April 8, 1999.

13. Letter from Agriculture Minister Harry Enns to Vicki Burns, Winnipeg Humane Society, June 27, 1996.

14. Dr. Ian Barker, Pathology Department, Ontario Veterinary College, in a paper presented to the ODEFA convention, Guelph, Ont., March 13, 1999. Chronic wasting disease in deer and elk was also a subject of concern among U.S. experts. About a year after Barker's presentation, Sandra Blakeslee, "Clues to Mad Cow Disease Emerge in Study of Mutant Proteins," *The New York Times*, May 23, 2000, reported that experimental work soon to be published would show that the deer version of the disease could be transmitted to humans.

15. Tim Harper, "Ottawa Dismisses Fears of 'Mad Deer Disease,'" *The Toronto Star*, Jan. 9, 1999.

16. Gloria Galloway, "Emu Farmer Uses Club to Cull Flock after Rifle and Arrows Fail," *National Post*, April 30, 1999.

CHAPTER SIX. WILD LIVES: KEEPING HUMANS HAPPY

1. Nature House, Inc., Sparrow Trap Letter with brochure for Trio Systems Bird Houses. The food-baited trap costs $56.55. Each trap has two units, and "you can even catch starlings and grackles with it." The literature was provided by the company's Canadian distributor.

2. Environment Canada, *The Importance of Nature to Canadians*, a 1996 survey prepared by the Federal-Provincial Territorial Task Force on the Importance of Nature to Canadians, Ottawa, 1999, showed that $11.7 billion was spent by Canadians and U.S. tourists on activities related to nature – ranging from caring for and watching birds and wildlife around home (38 per cent), to viewing wildlife (19 per cent), recreational fishing (18 per cent), and hunting (only 5.1 per cent).

3. Keiko, a killer whale, was captured in fishing gear in 1978 and kept in Iceland until he was bought with five others by Marineland. His stay in the Niagara Falls, Ont., amusement park and animal attraction was short. He was sold to a Mexican amusement park and languished there in a small tank until he was used in the movie *Free Willy* (1993). An international campaign began in 1993, after the movie came out, to send him home to the wilds off Iceland. In September 1998 he was shipped to an ocean holding pen where, in August 1999, he was still being prepared for release.

4. Patrick Tivy, *Calgary Stampede and the Canadian West: The Official Calgary Stampede Book* (Canadian Rockies/Vancouver: Altitude Publishing Canada, 1995), p.28.

5. Listen to the race commentary and you hear: "Burns Meats' got some ground to make up," and "the Calgary Herald is on the rail." Watching it, you see Shoppers Drug Mart, American Express, or Canaccord Capital emblazoned on the canvas covering the wagon. When cowboys rake their spurs from a horse's shoulder to behind the saddle in the saddle bronc competition, you hear references to the gentle euphemism "spur licks." The television closeups you see in calf-roping are not when the calf, only a few months old, is jolted by the neck after running full speed into the end of the rope. The camera prefers the resolute faces of big, satisfied men walking away from a smallish, muddy body, downed with its feet tied. In the wild horse race, you see three men. You can't really see that one of them is biting the horse's ear.

6. Jack MacDonald (guest column), "Rodeo Animals Have Few Worries, *Calgary Herald*, July 11, 1996.

7. Interview with Trudy Sattler, Calgary, Nov. 9, 1998.

8. Jack Tennant, "Cut Loose Calf Roping," *The Calgary Sun*, July 17, 1998.

9. Interview with Michael Alvarez-Toye, Calgary, Nov. 10, 1998.

10. Interview with Cathy Thomas, Calgary Humane Society, Calgary, Nov. 9, 1998.

11. The two men were interviewed by the author on the condition that their identities not be disclosed. Both had years of rodeo experience and were not members of animal groups. Unfortunately, without names and specifics, their allegations cannot be tested.

12. John Down, "Tightening the Reins," *The Calgary Sun*, July 5, 1996. Down reported that one of the 1995 chuckwagon drivers whose horses tested positive for banned substances had positive tests for the same horse for two nights in a row.

13. Letter from Stampede Media and Publicity Manager Denise Guichon, Dec. 8, 1998.

14. "Bucking Bronco Dies in Corel Centre Rodeo," *The Ottawa Citizen*, Aug. 9, 1999. The Calgary Stampede is not alone among animal entertainments in facing rumours of cheating or abuses against animals for gain. *Ontario Farmer*, August 1999, reported that the prestigious Royal Agricultural Winter Fair was warning exhibitors that it might require blood and milk samples from dairy cattle entered in the upcoming show. A win in Toronto at the Royal can be a valuable asset to farmers with breeding cattle heading for sales that draw an international audience. Rumours – never proved – of competitors inserting foreign substances into udders to make them look better or of substances injected under the skin are to be laid to rest by new

testing rules, Royal Assistant General Manager Doug McDonell said in an interview, Aug. 24, 1999.

15. Alexander Norris, "Bullfight Either Thrills or Chills," *The Gazette* (Montreal), Aug 20, 1999.

16. Interview with Dr. Hugh Chisholm, Halifax, Aug. 24, 1999.

17. Interview with Angela Miller, Sackville, N.S., July 31, 1999.

18. Rick Mofina, "Symbols Used to Make Point," *The Calgary Herald*, April 5, 1998.

19. By the time a show arrives in town, complaints are lodged and investigated, and any charges laid, the circus would have left, Bisgould concluded in an assessment of Nova Scotia's Animal Cruelty Prevention Act, which, she said, used language similar to Ontario's OSPCA Act. See Lesli Bisgould, "The Animal Cruelty Prevention Act: Can It Address the Problems Faced by Performing Animals?" unpublished paper, Toronto, March 1997.

20. Ontario SPCA Inspector Debby Hunt allowed me to watch her at work, June 25, 1998, in the Toronto area.

21. Interview with Debra Pobert, Vancouver, June 1998.

22. Interviews with Rob Laidlaw, Toronto, August 1999 and June 1998.

23. Rob Laidlaw, *Captive Animals in Ontario: An Informal Look* (Toronto: Zoocheck Coalition Canada, 1987). This was an earlier name for Zoocheck Canada.

24. Samantha Lindley, *While Rome Burns: A Report into Conditions in the Zoos of Ontario* (Toronto: Zoocheck Canada and World Society for the Protection of Animals Canada, September 1998), p.8.

25. See Dr. John Gripper, *Zoos in Maritime Canada: An Investigative Report*, August 1996.

26. Interview with Gerry Redmond, Fredericton, N.B., June 16, 1999.

27. From reports in *Niagara Falls Review*, including Alison Langley, "Prince of Whales," Aug. 22, 1998; Corey LaRocque, "Holer, City Boycott Zoocheck Meeting," Aug. 24, 1998; and Corey LaRocque, "Zoocheck Bashes Marineland," Aug. 26, 1988.

28. Interview with John Holer, Niagara Falls, Ont., Aug. 18, 1999.

29. Interview with Toby Styles, Toronto, Aug. 19, 1999.

30. Canadian Press report, *Province* (Vancouver), April 15, 1999.

31. About half of the sixty-eight belugas are said to have died since capture. In late August 1999 a five-week-old Beluga calf at the Shedd Aquarium in Chicago, known only as "the little boy," died after a struggle to nurse. His was the fourth death of Belugas in seven years at the Shedd, a facility targeted by activists. The live capture of killer whales – orcas – has not been approved since the 1970s.

32. Brian McAndrews, "The Bear Hunt's Bete Noire, *The Toronto Star*, Feb. 6, 1999.

33. Interviews with Liz White and Ainslie Willock, Toronto, May 1998; and with Willock, Toronto, August 1999.

34. Greg Middleton, "Bear Hunters in Crosshairs," *Province*, April 11, 1999.

35. B.C. Ministry of Environment, Lands and Parks, *Economic Value of Wildlife Activities in British Columbia*, Victoria, 1996.

36. Interview with Rick Smith, IFAW Canada, Ottawa, Aug. 23, 1999.

37. *BBC Online*, Aug. 10, 1999. The report indicated that illegal caches of ivory had been found in Russia, north Kenya, and South Africa and that Kenya was worried that it would lose its game.

38. Barry Kent MacKay, "Snow Geese Aren't Putting Ecosystem in Peril," *The Toronto Star*, Aug. 9, 1998.

39. Finn Lynge, *Arctic Wars: Animal Rights, Endangered Peoples* (Hanover: University Press of New England, 1992).

40. Barry Kent MacKay's regular column, on-line, "Opinionatedly Yours," for the U.S.-based Animal Protection Institute. This particular column, "Mrs. Brown and Other Gods of Nature," is dated Feb. 2, 1999, but remains accessible with others on the API Web site at <www.api4animals.org>.

CHAPTER SEVEN. PETS: KEEPING HUMANS COMPANY

1. Statistics Canada figures, provided June 16, 1999. They show 1996 Canadian household expenditures include, in about 47.6 per cent of those surveyed, an average $239 spent on pets each year. (This includes vet etc., $75; pet foods, $131; pets and goods, $33.) Thus you can assume that 47 per cent of households have pets.

2. Interview with Christine Schramm, Rainforest Reptile Refuge, Surrey, B.C., June 6, 1998.

3. Donald R. Griffin, *Animal Minds* (Chicago: University of Chicago Press, 1992), p.129.

4. Griffin, *Animal Minds*, pp.172-74, 251-52.

5. Eric S. Grace, *Snakes* (Toronto: Key Porter Books, 1994), describes reticulated pythons. John Breen, *Encyclopedia of Reptiles and Amphibians* (Hong Kong and Toronto: T.F.H. Publications, 1974), has many details of the natures and needs of these creatures.

6. Interview with Louis McCann, Pet Industry Joint Advisory Council of Canada, Aug. 12, 1999.

7. Canada, Department of Justice, "Crimes against Animals," consultation paper, 1998.

8. Elizabeth Caldwell, "Legislator Quits Farm Group," *Arkansas Democrat-Gazette*, April 10, 1999. In July 1999 the Associated Press reported that a

court in Sacramento, Cal., had sentenced a man who trained dogs to fight to seven years in jail. The offender had faced multiple charges of cruelty and torture to animals for the dog fights, which earned him some $5,000 a month from gamblers. For other information on U.S. laws, see J.C. Conklin, "Animal Abusers Face Jail Terms as States Crack Down," *The Wall Street Journal*, Oct. 28, 1998.

9. Barnes, "Offences against Animals," pp.2, 88, 14.

10. Ontario SPCA Inspector Debby Hunt, Toronto, June 25, 1998.

11. Jim Rankin, "Dragged Dog Taken for 'Jog,'" *The Toronto Star*, Aug. 10, 1999. For complaints in other provincial jurisdictions, see Martin Mittelstaedt, "Animals Beaten, Starved, Shot and Pitted against One Another," *The Globe and Mail*, Feb. 8, 1999.

12. "Steckle Writes on Bill C-17," *Lucknow Sentinel*, April 19, 2000, pp.4, 5.

13. Thomas Walkom, "Animal Cruelty Bill Attacked by Lobby Groups," *The Toronto Star*, May 23, 2000.

14. Interview with Judy Stone, Vancouver, Nov. 13, 1998.

15. Letters to the editor by Judy Stone and Stephen Huddart, *North Shore News* (North and West Vancouver), May 15, 1998, and June 10, 1998.

16. Claudia Gahlinger, "A Cat Tale with One Wrong Turn," *The Globe and Mail*, Dec. 8, 1998.

17. Katherine Ashenburg, "Papermaking: Eyewitness Accounts from Out There," *The Globe and Mail*, Dec. 12, 1998.

18. Interview with James Pearson, Winnipeg, June 8, 1998.

19. Animal Defence League of Canada, position paper on pet shops, Ottawa.

20. Letter from the Consulate General of the Republic of Korea, Toronto, "To Whom It May Concern" (to reporters inquiring about the protests), July 26, 1999.

21. Visit, Oct. 17, 1998, to Carignan, Que., and the Fauna Foundation chimpanzee sanctuary, where Arryn Ketter, Gloria Grow, and Dr. Richard Allan were interviewed. The chimpanzees were not. Accounts of their lives come from their human friends.

CHAPTER EIGHT. PARALLEL WORLDS

1. G. Davidson (Tim) Smith, "Commentary No. 74," Winter 1998; available on the CSIS Web site <www.csis-scrs.gc.ca/eng/comment/comsume>.

2. Animal Liberation Frontline Information Service archives, at <www.enviroweb.org/alfis>. Newspapers also carried reports.

3. The FBI Web site <www.fbi.gov/> carries speeches and policy statements. This is from Louis J. Freeh, speech to the U.S. Senate Committee on Appropriations, Feb. 4, 1999.

4. Mackenzie Intelligence Advisory, "The Animal Rights Movement in Canada," Mackenzie Institute, Toronto, January 1993.
5. Interview with John Thompson, Mackenzie Institute, Toronto, Dec. 8, 1998.
6. Animal Liberation Frontline Information Service.
7. Mark Nusca, "Stolen Monkey Carries Deadly Virus," *The London Free Press*, Jan. 2, 1985.
8. Paul Dalby, "Animals Used in Experiments 'Freed' in Raid on Hospital," *The Toronto Star*, June 16, 1981.
9. Western Wildlife Unit, *Memories of Freedom*, Animal Liberation Front, no place, undated, distributed by the North American ALF Supporters Group, Toronto. This offers an interesting history and a description of Operation Bite Back.
10. Marcus Gee, "A New Breed of Terrorist Fights for the Animals," *The Globe and Mail*, Dec. 5, 1998.
11. The FBI issue paper "Encryption: Impact on Law Enforcement," June 3, 1999, was posted on the FBI Web site at <www.fbi.gov/>.
12. The Animal Liberation Frontline Information Service offered news flashes and briefings on Barry Horne, December 1998.
13. An Animal Liberation Frontline Information Service fact sheet on the Justice Department.
14. Interview with Darren Thurston, Vancouver, April 16, 1999; interview with David Barbarash, CBC Newsworld, *Big Life*, April 28, 1999.
15. The Americans for Medical Progress Web site is at <www.ampef.org/news/arcter.htm>.
16. The American Center for the Defence of Free Enterprise makes interesting reading, at <www.cdfe.org/menu.html>.
17. Andrew Rowell, *Green Backlash* (London and New York: Routledge, 1996), p.153.
18. *Alberta Report*, July 31, 1995, p.21.
19. Ron Arnold's testimony on June 9, 1998, was posted on the Center's Web site at <www.cdfe.org/menu.html>.
20. "A Guerilla War for Animal Rights," *The Bulletin* (Bend, Ore.), Aug. 3, 1997.
21. Bob Paquin, "E-Guerillas in the Mist," *The Ottawa Citizen Online*, Oct. 26, 1998.
22. Patti Hartigan, "They Call It 'Hactivism,'" *The Boston Globe Online*, Jan. 24, 1999.
23. Karolinska Institutet, "Karolinska Institutet Reports Recent E-mail Harassment to Police," press release, Stockholm, Sweden, Oct. 27, 1998.
24. "CSIS Tracking Animal Rights Organizations, Spy Agency on Alert for 'Terrorism, Sabotage,'" *The Ottawa Citizen*, Dec. 15, 1997.

25. *The fifth estate*, Jan. 26, 1999, program on British animal liberationists. The quotes were checked against a transcript prepared by Bowden's Fulfillment Services.

26. *Underground*, Issue no. 9 (Winter 1997), pp.14 and 15. This is the magazine of the North America Animal Liberation Front Supporters Group. This issue offered a synopsis of the case.

27. For details of the Terrorism Bill, see the British government Web site at <www.parliament.the-stationery-office.co.uk/pa/cm1999900/cmbills/063/00063>.

28. Warren Hoge, "Animal-rights Activists Take Aim at Professor" (New York Times News Service report), *The Globe and Mail*, Jan. 11, 1999.

29. Telephone conversation with Francine Pelletier, Toronto, May 3, 1999.

30. Senator Orrin Hatch of Utah, quoted in an on-line CNET news.com report by Courtney Macavinta. The Senate had passed similar legislation against posting information on bombs several times, but never got the approval of full Congress.

31. Jim Adams, "Animal Activists Suspected in Lab Damages," *Star Tribune* (Minneapolis), April 6, 1999.

32. Interviews with Liz White, Animal Alliance of Canada, Toronto, May 1998.

33. Newkirk, *Free the Animals!*

34. Barry Kent MacKay, "The Violent Side of a Just Cause," essay posted on the Web site of the Animal Protection Institute, p.11.

35. Ibid., p.23.

36. Singer, *Animal Liberation*, 1990 edition, p.xii.

37. Newkirk, *Free the Animals!* outlines the roots and development of the original British ALF and the boot-camp style training provided there for the startup of the U.S. ALF. Newkirk reported that the Band of Mercy returned to the direct action scene again in 1990, but in a gentler form.

38. Animal Liberation Front, *Against All Odds: Animal Liberation, 1972–1986* (London: ARC Print, 1986). Also, the fact sheets of the Animal Liberation Frontline Service describe ALF development.

39. *The Animals' Agenda* 18,4 (July/August 1998).

40. Canadian David Barbarash took over the ALF press office job from Fedor in July 1999, operating out of British Columbia. Fedor was said to need to concentrate on battling the grand jury process underway in the United States in the wake of a lab raid there.

41. Interview with Lesli Bisgould, Toronto, Feb. 18, 1999.

42. Interview with Nicholas Read, Vancouver, June 4, 1998. Two years later, in 2000, Read was on leave and the future of his column remained unclear.

43. Interview with Darren Thurston, Vancouver, April 16, 1999.

44. Telephone interview with Hilma Ruby, Detroit, Feb. 20, 1999.

CHAPTER NINE. BACK TO THE FUTURE

1. Interview with Robyn Weiner, Royal Oak, Mich., March 26, 1999.

2. Fur Institute of Canada, press release, Toronto, April 3, 1997.

3. Posted on the Web site of the Animal Liberation Frontline Information Service, some time after the mink raid, available in the service archives.

4. William McLellan's testimony, provincial court proceedings, Chatham, Ont., April 20, 1999.

5. David Cameron's testimony, provincial court proceedings, Chatham, April 20, 1999.

6. Alan Hoffman's testimony, provincial court proceedings, Chatham, April 20, 1999.

7. Telephone interview with Hilma Ruby, Detroit, Feb. 20, 1999.

8. Chatham Ontario Provincial Police testimony, provincial court proceedings, Chatham, April 20, 1999.

9. Bob Boughner, "Mink Farm Warned of Raid," *Chatham Daily News*, April 21, 1999. Rik Scarce is the author of *Eco-Warriors: Understanding the Radical Environmental Movement* (Chicago: Noble Press, 1990). Scarce, who later became an assistant professor at Montana State University, was a postgraduate student at Washington State University in 1993 when he was called before the grand jury. Rod Coronado, then under suspicion for ALF activity in a number of states, had been house-sitting for Scarce, and the grand jury apparently assumed that the author would have information about Coronado's activities. Scare said in an e-mail to me that he had refused to answer some of the grand jury questions on the grounds that, like journalists, scholars had a right to keep their research private. He was jailed for contempt for 159 days, from May 14, 1993 to Oct. 19, 1993, and then released, although he did not answer the questions. California activist Jonathan Paul also spent 158 days in jail for refusing to testify.

10. Interview with Gary Yourofsky, Detroit, March 25, 1999.

11. Animal Liberation Frontline news bulletin on the Chatham case, March 1997. *Underground* recommended reading articles in *No Compromise*, which maintains an on-line record of illegal actions at <www.enviroweb.org/nocompromise/>.

12. *Underground*, Issue no. 7, spring 1997.

13. This version of events was also from my interview with Robyn Weiner, Royal Oak, Mich., March 26, 1999.

14. Interview with Clayton Ruby, Toronto, May 12, 1999.

15. Weiner's two-year sentence was conditional, meaning she did not go to jail. She forfeited her $10,000 bail, made an apology to the McLellan family, and was awarded four hundred hours of community service.

16. Telephone interview with Hilma Ruby, Detroit, Feb. 20, 1999.

17. Letter from Hilma Ruby, March 28, 1999.

18. Interview with Gary Yourofsky, Detroit, March 25, 1999.

19. Gary Yourofsky, speech at Plymouth-Canton High School, Detroit, March 26, 1999.

20. Letter from Plymouth-Canton teachers, Detroit, to Gary Yourofsky, March 29, 1999.

21. Proceedings in provincial court, Chatham, April 27, 1999, before Mr. Justice Anthony Cuisinato. *The Final Nail*, in its latest updated edition, was available at <www.animal-liberation.net/finalnail/fn2.html>. Since its first edition, the one found in the Americans' van, the activists involved had added updated addresses of fur businesses, telephone numbers, and new listings.

22. A brief interview with William McLellan outside the courthouse, Chatham, April 27, 1999.

23. John Wisely, "Activist Risks Life, Liberty and Lawsuits to Protect Animals," *The Oakland Press*, Aug. 1, 1999.

24. Agriculture Canada, *Recommended Code of Practice for the Care and Handling of Mink*, Ottawa. Codes are being updated by the non-profit agency CARC, with its expert committee and the CFHS. Information is available on the CARC Web site at <www.carc-crac.ca>, which reminds readers that they are "recommended guidelines, not required standards."

Index

AGMV Marquis

MEMBRE DU GROUPE SCABRINI

Québec, Canada
2000